TEXAS MYTHS

TEXAS MYTHS

Edited by

ROBERT F. O'CONNOR

Penny Moran

*Published for the Texas Committee for the Humanities
by Texas A&M University Press, College Station*

Library of Congress Cataloging-in-Publication Data

Texas myths.

Includes bibliographies and index.
1. Texas—History.   2. Texas—Social life and
customs.   3. Ethnology—Texas.   4. Folklore—Texas.
I. O'Connor, Robert F., 1943–   .   II. Texas
Committee for the Humanities.
F386.5.T484   1986   976.4   85-40743
ISBN 0-89096-264-2

Manufactured in the United States of America
FIRST EDITION

Contents

Preface

TEXANS love to tell the story of our state from all sorts of perspectives. Historians, writers, and folklorists among others have enthusiastically engaged in this process. Legendary heroes of the Alamo and of border ballads as well as such generic types as the cowboy and the trickster have figured prominently in their renditions, which at times have blurred, if not collapsed, the distinction between myth and history. Although these mythic stories and heroes are intimately woven into the fabric of Texas history, their nature and function as myth have rarely been examined. The purpose of this collection is to interpret key myths of our state's major ethnic groups, as they illuminate aspects of Texas history. Since myths express the basic beliefs and values of a people, this study can reveal the tension points among cultural groups and the pressures for change within society.

If the analysis of Texas history through its myths constitutes this book's distinctiveness, it also presents the chief stumbling block. *Myth* is an ambiguous term in our society. Its more popular meaning as something false is not the one predominantly used here. Rather, the classical definition of myth underlies this project: myths are "true" stories that explain our reality and present a system of values, thereby giving meaning to our lives. The fundamentally didactic function of myths is found, for example, in the tales of exemplary heroes, who embody particular values for a whole society and hence serve as models for emulation. In varying degrees, our writers have delved into different types of myth: (1) cosmological stories of the Comanches, (2) heroic legends of border bandits and the Alamo defenders, (3) folk tales of Texas cow camps, and (4) Br'er Rabbit fables. For their materials, they have sifted through traditional oral and written stories and songs as well as stories and images in the modern mass media of magazines, film, and advertising.

To conduct this investigation, we invited fourteen writers, academic and nonacademic, to focus on various aspects of the Texas experience. We also sought an interdisciplinary approach with writers drawn from such fields as folklore, history, literature, anthropology, American studies, cultural geography, religious studies, and journalism. Although we assigned the general topics to selected writers, they had a free hand in developing their papers and are ultimately responsible for the content. Our only stipulation was to explore the topics through the lens of myth.

Some of the scholars looked at myths that were specifically Texan, such as the Alamo story or the *corridos* of border conflict; others, Sterling Stuckey and Juan Ortega y Medina, considered the myths of African and Spanish origin that have influenced generations of Texans descended from these ethnic groups. All in all, Texas has provided, and continues to provide, a rich source of mythological material—both imported, borne by the peoples who came here, and homegrown.

One of the nagging, still unresolved, questions as the project unfolded was: Does Texas have a mythology? That is, does it have a coherent and consistent body of myths that together form a unified whole, in the way we speak of Greek mythology or Roman mythology? If we confine ourselves to just one tradition, such as the Anglo-Texan myths, which have tended to dominate the scene, then the answer would probably be yes. But if we take into account other groups, such as American Indians, Afro-Americans, Mexican Americans (to mention only a handful of the thirty ethnic groups in Texas identified at last count by the Institute of Texan Cultures), then it seems unlikely, since each group has its own distinctive myths, which are still operative in varying degrees. In this regard, Texas is a microcosm of the United States, which is also faced with the challenge of defining a single culture within a plurality of cultures.

We have not attempted to resolve this challenge. Nor probably could we have, since its resolution depends, in part, on the intellectual climate of the day. Right now, cultural pluralism with its stress on cultural diversity is in vogue; a generation ago the Melting Pot theory of America and, by extension, Texas would have elicited an unqualified yes to the question of a coherent myth. Similarly, this study has not intended to present an exhaustive account or definitive interpretation of Texas myths. Rather, the intent was merely to open a new discussion and stimulate further exploration, probing the richness of various traditions.

The outline of the book is as follows. Part I provides a theoretical overview of the nature and function of myth, including allusions to American myths, as well as of the transmission of myths. Part II explores the fundamental myths underlying the clash of cultures on the nineteenth-century Texas frontier during the formative period of the state's development. The cultures featured are Native American, Mexican, Anglo-American, and Afro-American. Part III then examines some specific myths of different cultural groups regarding nature, the individual, and aspects of social and political life. At the discretion of the writer, these topics are studied crossculturally during a single period in Texas history or mono-culturally, tracing gradual changes over time within a culture, usually that of Anglo-American tradition, which has typically exerted the most influence in the state for the last 150 years. Finally, James Veninga's epilogue describes the challenges of forging a shared culture from the cultural mosaic that is Texas.

Like myths themselves, this book has a historical matrix. It was part of the 1984 special emphasis of the Texas Committee for the Humanities and was funded by an award from the National Endowment for the Humanities. Other components of the project included a session at the 1984 meeting of the Texas State Historical Association, where three of the writers (William Goetzmann, Sterling Stuckey, and W. W. Newcomb) presented their papers. Some of the essays in this book also appeared in the January–February, 1985, edition of the *Texas Humanist*.

Again like myths, this book is not the product of a single person's efforts. In particular, I would like to express my appreciation to two of my colleagues, whose contributions permeate this final product. The conception and outline of this book came in large part from James Veninga, the executive director of the Texas Committee for the Humanities, who also selected many of the writers. In addition, I am indebted to my assistant, Sherilyn Brandenstein, for her unfailing assistance in helping coordinate these commissioned essays and in perceptively critiquing draft versions of them. Finally, I would like to thank Ann Sitton and Sherilyn Palmer for their patience and perserverence in typing and retyping the manuscript as it underwent manifold changes throughout the past year.

ROBERT F. O'CONNOR
Austin, Texas

Part I
Theory

Louise Cowan

Myth in the Modern World

I

Myth is a term of many turnings, much like the wily Odysseus—or perhaps even more like the Old Man of the Sea, whom one had to seize and hold with veritable superhuman might if one were to catch the god hiding behind his slippery disguises. In the same way, left to its multiple shiftings, myth assumes an indeterminate identity that can be interpreted in a confusing variety of ways. At one extreme, the word has been given an honorific connotation by twentieth-century humanists, who connect myth with truth and value. At an opposite extreme, it persistently retains in the popular mind its Enlightenment sense of falsehood, or something to be regarded as contrary to historical fact or counter to scientific evidence. Somewhere in the middle, myth is customarily viewed in an antiquarian light by academics, who consider it "mythology," or fanciful tales of pagan gods describing events once, unaccountably—in "olden times"—given serious credence.

The general reader ordinarily encounters only these last two meanings—when the word is being used to discredit or patronize. In the public media, for instance, such derogatory expressions as "the myth of American supremacy" or the "myth" of George Washington and the cherry tree imply, in the one instance, a generally held notion entirely without basis and, in the other, a fabricated incident given wide circulation by its appeal to public fancy. In educational institutions, the word likewise suggests an aura of untruth in the context of, for example, Greek or Sumerian myths: stories of Zeus or Aphrodite, Enlil or Inanna are considered "only myths" and hence anthropomorphic projections arising out of fear and childish lack of logic. It is against a rising tide, therefore, that those who would restore to the word a semblance of dignity or veracity must swim. And yet, among a number of scholars in various disciplines, the call to breast that tide has become compellingly clear, since many of them have come to believe that myth does indeed represent a mode of truth, that it codifies and preserves moral and spiritual values, that, in fact, a civilization without myth fosters a way of life not fully human.

What is the case for myth? Those who look on it with favor would say that it is all-important to our civil life, the life we share in society. As a container for the diverse aspects of existence, a pattern or design based not on fact but on value, it has the virtue, they maintain, of enlisting participation in a communal order that transcends—yet includes and dignifies—the lives of individual human beings. Myth, they would argue, enables us to place ourselves within a destiny larger than our own small and relatively insignificant circle of success or failure. It empowers us to face disappointment, defeat, and death without self-pity or bitterness. Paradoxically, however, as they would point out, rather than imposing a rigid uniformity on society and thus stifling individual passion and creativity, such a vision of order—in which people agree about the meaning of life—supports and enhances diversity and endows ordinary acts with purpose and grace. According to its defenders, myth is not necessarily racial, but political, in the ancient sense of the word *polis*, that is, pertaining to a people who are bound together less by bloodlines than by living together in a communal attempt to found and to perpetuate a good society. Myth, they hold, is rooted in the land and its ordering, to which a people give their allegiance and into which they welcome and initiate others. Indeed—and this is myth's most frequently emphasized aspect—social codes of honor, hospitality, courtesy, heroism find their support not in reasoned principles, practicality, or even convention, but in a mythic consciousness of what is fitting and right. When character and sensibility have been shaped by myth, people hold certain values as "self-evident," not to be questioned. Thus, myth's advocates would argue, the modern tendency to "demythologize," to explain away sacred events by attributing to them material causes, has, with disastrous results, deprived countless young men and women of models for emulation.

The case sometimes made in our day against mythic thinking is that it could lead to a dangerous irrationalism, a step backward into superstition and darkness. And certainly, it must be acknowledged, the suprarational authority that myth undoubtedly wields is subject to manipulation by the unscrupulous. The Nazi Aryan mystique held sway such a short time ago that we can no longer call up in our memories the blond, wholesome young men singing their traditional racial songs with the transported look of angels. Further, our generation has witnessed the messianic myth of the Soviet Union exercising its fearfully destructive movement toward world domination. And finally, it must be admitted, even our faith in the innocence of our own American "myth" of Manifest Destiny has been shaken.

Indeed, as Dostoevsky was at pains to demonstrate in the Grand Inquisitor section of *The Brothers Karamazov*, the mystique of totalitarianism is an ever-present danger in modernity. Since his time the situation has incalculably worsened; we find ourselves surrounded by irrational ideologies and cults, by false mysticism and fanatical devotion to strange gods. Not only in the political arena do bizarre and brutal aberrations manifest themselves; society in general glorifies notorious figures such as rock stars, murderers, and cult leaders, elevating them to positions of pseudomythical eminence. It is, as Yeats predicted, a time when

> Things fall apart; the center cannot hold;
> Mere anarchy is loosed upon the world,
> The blood-dimmed tide is loosed, and everywhere
> The ceremony of innocence is drowned;
> The best lack all conviction, while the worst
> Are full of passionate intensity.[1]

But the situation here is clearly not caused by the desertion of reason in favor of the irrationalism of mythic thought. Such widespread chaos as Yeats describes has been brought about by nothing less than the neutralization of myth, its utter failure. For his ominous warning, one that has been reiterated in various forms by countless poets and novelists in our time, is that the "center" of our society is the no-longer-credited myth of Western civilization, which has produced, along with its numerous ills, ceremonies "of innocence" that we have enjoyed. Now, with an increasing number of people committed only to their own interests, what we have is "mere anarchy," the blood-red tide of violence.

"Without his myths," I. A. Richards has said, "man is only a cruel animal without a soul."[2] For mythic consciousness is not only a basic need of the human spirit but a characteristically human mode of thought, like imagination, memory, and reason. To be sure, mythic thinking functions differently from logical reasoning: it takes hold of a thing or a situation intuitively and wholly, so that motive and method are perceived simultaneously with the good to be served. It allows a person to grasp entire forms, discern the coherence of their parts, and apprehend the totality of their purpose. Myth, then, is a power, an enablement, separating people from beasts. It is an ancient way of thought, but a profoundly human way. And the modern person is no less in need of it than his or her ancestors.

If circumstances are as dire as Yeats describes them, is the task, then, either to revive the old myth or, failing that, to forge a new one? The answer, one fears, is hardly so simple. We cannot "make" our myths, nor can we consciously modify them to our desires. What we can do, however, is to enlarge our understanding of the mythic mode of thought. For discernment is an indispensable guide to right action— the ability to recognize not only "these fragments [we] have shored against our ruin" but, as well, the shadowy beginnings of a new variant of the old order that seems already in the making—in America and in Texas in particular, a region that has never prided itself on lack of change.

Theories of Myth

Among the early Greeks *mythos* meant "word," the thing spoken or uttered by the mouth, hence the oral tale.[3] This could be contrasted with *logos*, the "word" concerning the rational structure of things, hence argument. By Aristotle's day mythos referred to the plot of a drama, which, as the philosopher reminds us, is not the action itself but the imitation, the image of the action. Consequently, one might say mythos is truer than fact, or, in Aristotle's words, "more philosophic than history," since as fiction it is capable of being modified and shaped to express the universal laws of being. In later times mythos was replaced by the Latin *fabula*, meaning discourse, narrative, the plot of a play. Some form of the word *fable* was used for the work of poets all during the European medieval and Renaissance epochs and retained, even with the accruing connotations of frivolity and falsehood, some of its earlier implications of a truth superior to factuality. *Mythological* began appearing in English in the seventeenth century, and with the rise of scientific rationalism and the new puritanism, mythological fables were regarded with increasing disdain and even disapproval.

Myth was not used in English until the nineteenth century, as the revival of interest in mythopoesis, or mythmaking, among the romantics accompanied the turn against the domination of empiricism and logical reason. No need had existed in the previous centuries for a word such as *myth* (just as there was no need for *folklore*) until traditional oral narratives began to be regarded as keys to the culture of a people and not simply as fanciful tales. By the end of the nineteenth century, with the scholarly work of such authorities as Max Muller in philology, Andrew Lang in literature, E. B. Tylor and Sir James Frazer in anthropology, and Emile Durkheim in sociology, serious thinkers representing a wide range of fields had given consistent attention to myth as a perennial force within both the human psyche and the social order.

Despite disagreements concerning origins and interpretations and an almost unanimous tendency to reductionist theories, these scholars and their successors, such as Gilbert Murray, Jane Harrison, Sigmund Freud, Carl Jung, Ernst Cassirer, Walter Otto, and Carl Kerenyi, made available to twentieth-century thinkers a conception of myth as an experiential psychic force basic to the formation and continuation of culture. Bronislaw Malinowski, writing in the 1920s and 1930s of his actual experiences among the Trobriand Islanders of Melanesia, where myth still existed as a living force, made his readers aware of its essentially social nature. Seeing the constant relation between belief and practice, he tended to interpret his findings almost entirely in pragmatic terms. "Myth serves principally to establish a sociological charter," he wrote in his best-known work, *Magic, Science, and Religion*; "myth is above all a cultural force."[4] He concluded that the mythmaking activity goes on in a society as its customs and institutions require justification.

In contrast to so secular an outlook, Mircea Eliade has viewed myth as having, above all else, a sacred origin. "Myth narrates a sacred history," he writes; "it relates an event that took place in primordial Time, the fabled time of the 'beginnings.'" It describes, he believes, the "dramatic breakthroughs of the sacred (or the supernatural) into the world." For Mark Schorer, however, the significance of myth is not solely religious: "That myth cannot be so limited is made clear by our own civilization, which seems to be struggling toward a myth that will be explicitly ethical, even political." He goes on to declare, "Myth is fundamental, the dramatic representation of our deepest instinctual life, of a primary awareness of man in the universe, capable of many configurations, upon which all particular opinions and attitudes depend."[5]

Thus, though Nietzsche's characterization of the modern as "mythless man," who "hungers after times past and digs and grubs for roots"[6] seems indisputably true, it nevertheless may be said that in our time as in no other myth has become an object for intellectual analysis. The genius and persuasiveness of the minds devoted to this study have attracted numerous followers in the humanities and cultural disciplines. A resulting examination of the mythic way of thought has made clear that this essentially imaginative mode is still operative in the world about us, even though it may generally be ignored or dismissed as irrelevant in a technological society. In any consideration of Texas and the American Southwest, then, an understanding of myth in this sense and of the mythic dimensions of psyche and culture should shed light on the region's distinctiveness, its true identity, in contrast to that which is attributed to it in the stereotypes of the public media.

If we are to speak of myth in the modern world, however, certain basic questions remain. Is myth a story of creation and of gods, sacred in its very beginnings, or is it a pattern of social order that, because it authenticates experience, comes to be regarded with veneration and gives rise to sacred stories? Does myth enter culture from a divine source, or is it entirely a product of the human mind? Does it shape events, or the other way around? Is myth created by individuals or by communities? What is its relation to the hero? to the archetypal? to history? to legend? to folklore? Does it occur only in primitive societies? Can there be myth in a technological era? in a pluralistic society? Does each community have a single myth, or are there many in each polity? Does a myth grow sui generis in a culture, or can it be the product of cross-cultural influences? Can a myth be transferred to a new land? Can a community in a constant state of expansion perpetuate its founding myth? And finally, can a people irrevocably lose touch with their mythic pattern and purpose?

These and other sober questions arise among various authorities, and most of the issues remain unsettled, if we are looking for any general agreement. The Old Man of the Sea presents his multiple features. But since, like Telemachus, our need is urgent, we should do as he did and, rather than letting the many-faceted phenomenon slip out of our hands or giving up in defeat at its polymorphous appearances, hang on for dear life. We shall be forced, then, to try to get at the thing itself—to discern what myth is, in its essential nature, behind its many aspects.

II

Myth and the Mythological

I have suggested that myth is a moral, organizing force in a society and provides that society's members with security and purpose. It may be regarded, then, as a total outlook that affects the lives of individuals and of society as a whole. If we attempt to see what it is in itself, however, we shall be forced to hazard a few theoretical distinctions. To begin with, it might be helpful to clarify the relation of myth to other phenomena with which it is frequently associated. The first of these is the mythological. Strictly speaking, this is a body of narratives that arise from and define a myth, its inner consistency, its functional efficacy. As Richard Slotkin has written: "Mythology is a complex of narratives that dramatizes the world vision and historical sense of a people or culture, reducing centuries of experience into a constellation of compelling metaphors. The narrative action of the myth-tale recapitulates that people's experience in their land, rehearses their visions of that experience in its relation to their gods and the cosmos, and reduces both experience and vision to a paradigm."[7]

The tales that provide the texts for mythology might be termed "mythologems" or simply mythological fables, sacred narratives of gods and semidivine heroes, a kind of bible for a people. These stories are conscious formulations that use portions of the large governing story of a society—its myth. They reflect salient aspects of it; they dramatize analogues of it; but they are the result of a poetic making and hence are *words*, not the word. The mythopoeic imagination has been at work in their composition, dredging up nuggets of precious ore from the rich mine of the communal unconscious, wherein the mythic resides. Mythological fables seem to emerge, like islands in a sea or individual trees in a forest. When we look at Greek mythology, for instance, we are not viewing the Greek myth directly; we are intuiting something submerged underneath these fragments, something austerely beautiful and demanding, which provides a common substratum for the mythologies as well as the rest of Hellenic culture before its decline into Hellenism.

Myth itself seems to be a given, not a constructed thing. Yet, to be known at all, it must be brought into consciousness by the mythological. We could perhaps say, then, that a myth, whatever its origin, first begins to be known through the mythopoeic imagination, which is like the prophetic imagination in being the property of individual persons, even though the reality that it reveals is for a whole people. The mythmaking imagination, by being subjected to the daily realities of a community, comes to intuit the character of a tribe or a polis and to express that identity in fables and symbols. These fragments gathered together form a mythology, though strictly speaking this mythology is not myth. Myth itself is never ascertainable except in the residue that it leaves in a people's traditions and culture, their fables and stories— the tracks, as it were, left in a cloud chamber by the passage of an invisible fundamental reality.

Myth and Legend

Myth, then, being like a Weltanschauung, a "world picture," is not simply a fable, though the fables of a society are shaped and determined by its myth. In the same way, legend and folktales are outcroppings of the mythical. One discerns a society's vision of the nature and destiny of humanity through its legendary material, its folklore, its fairytales. Such stories are products of tale-tellers who transmit and modify striking events in the telling, preserving notable deeds—sometimes exaggerated to the impossible. The viability of folktales depends on their aptness—their truth to the land, the environment, and the character of the people they celebrate. Legends arise from the stream of history like its spume, but, grounded or not in fact, they come into being when events are given interpretation by myth. As the medieval European civilization was gaining in might, for instance, it created or resurrected the legends of Troy, thus expressing a reluctance to relinquish the mother city, the feminine origins, at the same time that its transformation of the grail legends began expressing the essentially masculine quest of a supernal spiritual goal. In America, the tales of Paul Bunyan's and Daniel Boone's mammoth feats of comradeship with nature became legends because they demonstrated a portion of the outlook, both spiritual and practical, that gave rise to a shared *interpretation* of life on all levels in a particular land. Hence, though farther removed than are mythological fables from the sacred and mysterious—and essentially hidden—mythic substance, legends and folklore express the myth and provide our most direct and at times our only access to it.

Myth and Archetype

The archetypal, like the mythological and the legendary, is frequently spoken of interchangeably with myth and indeed is closely associated with it. Yet just as the mythological and the folkloric lie nearer the surface of awareness than does the realm of myth as I am attempting to describe it, so too is there a region more deeply buried in consciousness. This region is the realm of *archetypes*, the ultrasensory patterns that are preconditions of life itself, that reach down into the secret regions of organic and inorganic matter. This primordial level is not concerned with a culture so much as with the profoundest recesses of the psyche, ultimately with those experiences that are universally human, rather than societal—with *physis* rather than *nomos*, nature rather than culture. This realm precedes consciousness and is available only through archetypal images. The desert, the wilderness, the vast sky, the garden—these are images in the Texas experience that allow the emergence of the archetypal, the primordial. Though they are common to all humanity, they reveal themselves in the depths of each person rather than to entire communities and are thus not, in the strict sense, political or cultural, as is the mythic. When the myth has loosened its hold upon the individual's conscience, when, in Yeats's phrase, "things fall apart," the archetypal is unleashed, and without the restraint of myth, expresses its force in violence. Rape, murder, insanity, horror, the grotesque—these are the manifestations of the titanic, which governed more anciently than the mythic gods. Yet the archetypes animate the myth, provide its vitality, ground it in reality.

A myth, then, as I have been saying, is not so universal as archetype, not so internal, but is rather a cultural phenomenon, bespeaking a particular set of household gods for any one people, encompassing its customs and mores, and coming into being when a community *intends* to found a social order, rather than simply to be an aggregate. As we have been viewing it, myth is social, binding together a particular people, a land, a city, a region. It operates as a compact structure containing in germinal form the design—one might say, the imprinting pattern—of a culture, which will mark all its endeavors. The mythic form that is the seed of this founding is eminently specific, local (for these people alone), and compelling. It is the word containing the secret of their nature and earthly destiny and hence all their moral and social codes, as well as, in inchoate form, their styles and modes of behavior. Yet it remains inarticulable and in large sense unconscious, even though it is expressed in the community's major symbols and lived out in daily experience.

Myth and Poetry

Poetry (imaginative literature) is the vehicle for giving form to the myth, bringing it into consciousness, where it may be contemplated and known. Unlike folktales or legends, a literary work of art produces in mimetic form the wholeness of a people's unconscious sense of themselves, providing an image of humanity in action in a world constituted by value. The epic in particular, in its story of a hero's conquest of disorder and establishment of a cosmos, has a close relationship with the mythic. But rather than *being* myth, epic is the literary genre that gives tangible form to this vital seed of a community's life, that not only portrays a world in the making but, by looking toward final things, brings about a new order and fulfills the implicit mythic promise.

Homer's *Iliad* and *Odyssey*, the earliest documents of the Western world, gave form to the Greek vision of things and, in so doing, in a mysterious way conquered the powers of darkness. These epics gathered up mythological fables, history, saga, and legend, veiling the archetypal and chaotic and allowing it only at times to break in, for primordial forms cannot be denied; rather, they must be restrained, since the epiphany of an archetype is likely to be monstrous, the cinematics of a nightmare, destroying any carefully cultivated patterns of civility. The Cyclops, Scylla and Charybdis, the corpse-choked river rising to fight with the fire of Achilles's fury, the dark Underworld where shades of men must drink blood to speak—these are archetypal images, to which epic heroes must be subjected and over which they must triumph.

The epic, then, gives the myth symbolic form, establishes it in the communal mind, makes it available for contemplation, as indeed Homer's poems first made available to the Greek mind and imagination the splendid vision of the Hellenic outlook. For it is the epic perspective on life, as distinct from tragedy, say, or comedy, that establishes in imagination the cosmos implicit within the myth. In fact, the epic struggle is an attempt to subdue primordial forces and to found an order that, like Achilles's shield, manifests the mythic pattern.

And yet literary transmission of the myth is not limited to epic; three other great "kinds" of which Aristotle speaks in his *Poetics*—tragedy, comedy, and lyric—also reveal aspects of the *praxis*, the mythic action that is the object of mimesis. Lyric has as its norm the harmonious fusion of the archetypal and the mythic (the natural and cultural realms); tragedy portrays the breaking apart of the cultural order to glimpse the archetypal, with its resulting terror; comedy depicts the "diaspora," the dispersion that occurs when a people, having lost connection with the wellsprings of their culture, begin their antic progress toward regaining community "in a strange land." But it is epic that validates the myth in its heroic nobility.

Myth as a Communal Psychic Response

The literary work is not myth, however; literature is a created aesthetic form bearing the stamp of its creator. The situation is rather that, as Allen Tate has said, "the form requires the myth." His implication is that there can be no genuine art without a shared underlying vision of life. Myth, then, as I have been depicting it, is a participatory intuition of reality, a revelation, rather than an invention: "At the beginning stands always the god," as Walter Otto has insisted.[8] Myths do not create or imagine divinity; they respond to it in a vital and dynamic psychic configuration that gives rise to an entire culture, its arts, games, stories, manners and codes, laws and customs, images and ideas, philosophy and religious rituals (as distinct from the *content* of its religious faith, which is a given). Myth is a form existing largely in the spiritual unconscious of a people; parts of it are continually being brought into consciousness as symbols. Sacred narratives, then, are not themselves, as I have said, myths, but are fragments of myth, bits and pieces of it, as are particular beliefs or themes. Thus we might say that when anthropologists catalog and analyze narratives they are concerning themselves, in actuality, with folkways, folktales, works of art, practices and ideas. All of these reflect portions of myth but can never recapture the whole, since they are intelligible only to those who accept and are formed by the large ordering pattern itself.

A shared spiritual response to a revelation given to a people at the time of their becoming a people—this is, finally, the way in which I should like to define myth. In the same manner that a marriage sacrament occurs when a man and woman come together in their intent to form a permanent union, so the myth of a people comes into being with the community's intention of founding an order and fulfilling a particular destiny. It is then that the imprint, like a sacramental mark, occurs in its depths. The founding is usually attended by an occurrence in history that assumes so crucial a position in the memory of an entire people that it cannot be allowed to die. When an event of this distinction enters into the communal mind and heart, seeming to reveal the deepest sense of the character and destiny of a people, then it may be regarded as myth in action. It is not simply legend or saga, not fable or tale, but the very action of the myth incarnating itself in human life. Such an event, for Texans, is the Battle of the Alamo. Whatever Texans are, the story of the Alamo is part of their myth and may be so considered, despite the fact that the Alamo still stands in downtown San Antonio and that the heroic battle actually occurred and is historically documented. It is a story that fulfills the myth. It did not make the myth, but expressed it, just as Easter, 1916, the time when, as Yeats wrote, "a terrible beauty [was] born," did not make the Irish myth but manifested it, as a sort of epiphany, becoming forever sacred in a people's memory.

Myth and the Hero

Cultural heroes, who may or may not have existed but who, like Arthur, are always *believed* to have existed, are those who take upon themselves in the communal imagination the task of incarnating the myth, of bringing it into the world of time and action, embodying it so fully that they advance the community a step nearer to its destiny. It is they on whom the epic hero—a literary figure—is modeled. The hero of myth is committed, as Caroline Gordon has informed us, to "lifelong combat with the monstrous in whatever guise it showed itself."[9] His or her pattern is Herakles, who must undertake the arduous labors of overcoming darkness; other such figures are Gilgamesh, David, Moses, Perseus, Beowulf, Charlemagne, Arthur, Daniel Boone, Davy Crockett—all expressing and extending the myth of their people. These are not legendary or literary but mythic heroes and are akin to the gods of creation in that they bring light out of darkness, order out of chaos. Indeed, many times they are semidivine beings or, like Gilgamesh, two-thirds god and one-third human. They found and govern cities; they perform superhuman deeds; they advance the entire human enterprise nearer to its fulfillment. Around their deeds myths take form, in the recesses of the human spirit in which we all share. Through the apertures that they open, light from another world streams in; their deaths are an immolation through which the very nature of life and death is transfigured.

III

The American Myth

Myth has apparently always been considered transportable: the Mycenaean and Egyptian as well as the ancient Sumerian civilizations give evidence of considerable interchange in ritual, fable, and cult.

When a people migrate with the intention of building a new version of the old order, we may conclude that myth may actually be *transplanted* in a new land, as when Aeneas, taking with him his household gods from his burning city, went in search of the place that was to be the home for the New Troy and that became the mighty Rome. The Western myth has been transplanted many times in foreign soil, in Europe and the "New World," and has proved both durable and flexible in its ability to absorb diverse elements and even take on a different direction without losing its ancient values, its art and wisdom. It is precisely this myth's composite nature, however, that complicates the question of the American—and certainly the Texan—myth. Can a people not indigenous to a land, committed to pluralism in matters of religion, share a myth? That question, of course, sums up the very drama of American history, for the American effort, with its commitment to democratic schooling and civil rights, has essayed to be the distinctive pattern for myth in our time. The American colonists, bringing with them the traditional pieties and lore, brought this heritage to be given a different form, in a new founding of an old myth.

Americans have always known that they are not European. They are aware of being transplanted—"twice-born," so to speak. As Robert Frost has written, "The land was ours before we were the land's." We gained possession of a country, he is saying, before we knew it or loved it, when its very terrain—its soul—was an enigma to us. A poem by John Peale Bishop, "Experience of the West," expresses the American's particular dilemma in being descended from a people who came to a new continent, bringing with them their European heritage and confronting, not other cities and towns, but virtually a pristine land. When they "wading came / From shallow ships and climbed the wooded shores,"

> They saw the west, a sky of falling flame,
> And by the streams savage ambassadors.

Bishop is here picturing the American colonists as Trojans, those who fled a burning city, bringing with them, as Aeneas did, their fathers, borne on their backs as a burden of love and piety:

> Each on his shoulders wore a wise delirium
> Of memory and age: ghostly embrace
> Of fathers slanted toward a western tomb.[10]

They face the dangers of the wilderness and the ambiguity of "savage ambassadors" who, as Lewis Mumford has pointed out, brought the European invaders face to face with an ancient paleolithic and neolithic way of life. As Leslie Fiedler writes in *The Return of the Vanishing American*, "The heart of the Western is not the confrontation with the alien landscape . . . but the encounter with the Indian, that utter stranger for whom our New World is an Old Home, that descendant of neither Shem nor Japheth, nor even, like the Negro imported to subdue the wild land, Ham. No grandchild of Noah, he escapes completely the mythologies we brought with us from Europe, demands a new one of his own." [11]

The situation is complicated because it was not traditional Western man who confronted the American wilderness and the "utter strangers"; it was modern Western man: in a crisis of which he was himself unaware. The century of the colonization of America was to see the cultural shift in England spoken of as the seventeenth-century revolution, wherein a scientific explanation of the universe rejected the traditional metaphysical one, a Puritan morality denied the old bounty and chivalry, and a financial oligarchy took the place of a landed gentry. There he stood, decent, frugal, honest, taciturn, solitary, rational, religious, and incredibly naive—the modern Western hero confronting in the Indian a totally dissimilar culture and a myth that he could not comprehend.

Many authorities would agree with R. W. B. Lewis that the "native American myth" is that of the "authentic American as a figure of heroic innocence and vast potentialities, poised at the start of a new history." This image of the "American Adam," as Lewis calls him, was, as he says, "crowded with illusions, and the moral posture it seemed to endorse was vulnerable in the extreme." [12]

Leo Marx in *The Machine in the Garden* insists that it is the pastoral dream that has defined the meaning of America to Americans ever since the age of discovery and that this romantic pastoralism has not yet lost its hold on the native imagination. "With an unspoiled hemisphere in view it seemed that mankind actually might realize what had been thought a poetic fantasy." The Earthly Paradise, Arcadia, the Golden Age, the New Eden—these were the terms Americans used to describe this new land as a fresh beginning for Western society. "Yet within the lifetime of a single generation," Marx tells us, "a rustic and in large part wild landscape was transformed into the site of the world's most productive industrial machine." In a remarkably short time "this fresh green breast of the new world had been replaced by a man-made landscape."[13]

Lewis Simpson speaks of this event as a "Second Fall" for Americans—after they have been given a second chance and misuse their freedom and power. And Lewis Mumford, speaking of the Americans' failure to live up to their new opportunity in their contact with a virgin land, makes the following statement: "Properly interpreted, the rise and fall of New World Man is a more significant drama than anyone has yet portrayed, though the pioneer was only partly aware of the significance of his actions and the implied goal of his efforts."[14]

This view of the American myth—that it is based on a conception of the possibility of unfallen innocence, that it saw the new continent in an idealized pastoral light while, by its technological development, recklessly destroying natural resources, that it placed wealth in the place of the aristocratic virtues, that it advocated in a wholly unrealistic way equality and justice for all—is implied, in all its ironic ramifications, in Nick Carraway's speech at the end of *The Great Gatsby*:

> Most of the big shore places were closed now and there were hardly any lights except the shadowy, moving glow of a ferry-boat across the Sound. And as the moon rose higher the inessential houses began to melt away until gradually I became aware of the old island here that flowered once for Dutch sailors' eyes—a fresh, green breast of the new world. Its vanished trees, the trees that had made way for Gatsby's house, had once pandered in whispers to the last and greatest of all human dreams: for a transitory enchanted moment man must have held his breath in the presence of this continent, compelled into an aesthetic contemplation he neither understood nor desired, face to face for the last time in history with something commensurate to his capacity for wonder.[15]

It is all there: the innocence, the Paradise, the vanished trees, the implied wealth, the rapacity, and—in the absent Gatsby—the quest for aristocracy for everyone, through money.

Confrontation with the Other

Yet, though all these interpretations of the American experience are no doubt accurate to some degree, what I see as the foundation of the American myth is something quite different. In *Myth and Reality* Eliade has said that the effort "rightly to understand peoples demonstrably 'other' than we ourselves who are the heirs of Greece and Judaeo-Christianity has the effect . . . of enriching the Western consciousness." He reaffirms this statement in another work with a parable of a man who journeys far in search of hidden treasure. The man later finds that it was to be found in a dusty old corner of his house, where it had been buried behind the stove: "The real treasure lies buried in our own house: that is, of our own being. It is behind the stove, the centre of life and warmth that rules our existence, the heart of our heart if only we knew how to unearth it. . . . [We must journey to a new land to find it, and] he who reveals to us the meaning of our mysterious inward pilgrimage must himself be a stranger, of another belief and another race."[16]

All American literature, all American thought shows the impact of this confrontation with "the other." This is to say, in the terms I have been attempting to establish, the Indians have been archetypal images for the American, just as are the images of the West and of the desert. According to Henry Nash Smith, "Until the very end of the eighteenth century the West beyond the Mississippi was so shadowy and removed that it could be pictured in almost any guise." It was conceived of as a passage to India, as the Great American Desert, which mongrel and nomadic tribes could plunder, as the Garden of the World. Walter Prescott Webb has commented that Frederick Jackson Turner's major insight concerning the peculiar character of American development came out of his realization that "when Stephen F. Austin brought his colonists to Texas he brought them to the edge of one environment, the Eastern woodland, and to the border of another environment: the Great Plains." Jay B. Hubbell has written concerning the Western desert, "It was not until about the turn of the century that man began to see the desert country as a thing of beauty and not of horror."[17]

The Texan Myth

The American myth, then, which had itself been transferred from Europe, was carried with the settlers to the West. Texans brought with them when they came to this new terrain a memory of the classical and European civilized order, the Puritan commitment to a sacred text, the particularly American experience of having looked upon and settled in the primordial forest with its possibility of a New Eden, and the Southern agrarian code of courtesy. That the emigres regarded these past achievements as fallen into decay or at least as having failed for them contributed in large measure to the commitment of Texans to progress, to their looking forward rather than backward, as well as to their jaunty iconoclasm. In Texas these pioneers dealt with the frontier as a way of life, not simply as a boundary; they worked beside and adopted the ranching methods of members of another civilized culture, the Hispanic, whom they came to regard as both ally and enemy; they accepted uncritically the social attitude of the South toward the blacks; they looked into the eyes of members of a people that seemed to them savage and autochthonous, the Indian; and they had intuitions of an archetypal reality, the infinite and uninhabitable desert, which stretched before them as prairie or plains. They told tales, created legends; their sensibility was epic. Only the hardy, both men and women, could endure and prevail in such surroundings. Only the strong—or those who pretended or aspired to be—could be the channels for the mythic consciousness that we now call Texan.

Thus Texans from the beginning were confronted with a dual consciousness: were they transplanted Americans or a new breed? Should they look to the aristocratic landed gentry for their ideals or to Rousseau's noble savage? Should their allegiance be with the Anglo-Saxon or the Spanish culture? Should they be cultivated or primitive? Should they hold to the idea of progress or to pastoralism? Were they pious or iconoclastic? barbarian or civilized? isolated or communal? materialistic or ascetic? Was the new territory they settled garden or desert? Caucasian, Christian, Yankee, Southerner, Westerner—Texans found themselves to be all of these. And they defined themselves, as I have indicated, against the two other peoples who have entered ineradicably into their consciousness and into the history of the region: the Latin American and the Indian.

But unlike other Western territories, Texas had a founding and thus a myth—composite yet exceptional enough to produce a definite identity that has been able to survive into the twentieth century and that gives every sign of continuing well beyond. As the following essays indicate, the Texan myth gives no sign of having been forgotten or emasculated. It may appear as the quest for the good life, as a love of power and money, as the attempt to construct the largest buildings in the world, but it gives every evidence in our time of keeping its original nature. As an invisible pattern ordering all aspects of life, it still produces a character that holds to the sacredness of the land and the biblical faith, respects courage and prowess, cherishes freedom and independence, boasts of heroic achievement, is boisterous in rejection of the affected or effete; though it may minimize the need for education and the arts, it is basically unprejudiced and pluralistic, welcomes the stranger, roots for the underdog, mocks itself with an ironic irreverence, and looks to the future with a capacity for hope and wonder.

NOTES

1. William Butler Yeats, "The Second Coming," in *Collected Poems* (New York: Macmillan, 1949), p. 215.

2. I. A. Richards, *Coleridge on Imagination* (Bloomington and London: Indiana University Press, 1969), p. 172.

3. Henry A. Murray, "The Possible Nature of a Mythology to Come," in *Myth and Mythmaking*, ed. Henry A. Murray (Boston: Beacon Press, 1960), p. 350.

4. Bronislaw Malinowski, *Magic, Science, and Religion* (New York: Doubleday, 1954), p. 144.

5. Mircea Eliade, *Myth and Reality*, trans. Willard Trask (New York: Harper Torchbooks, 1968), p. 5; and Mark Schorer, "The Necessity of Myth," in *Myth and Mythmaking*, p. 355.

6. Friedrich Nietzsche, *The Birth of Tragedy and the Genealogy of Morals*, trans. Francis Golffing (New York: Doubleday, 1956), p. 137.

7. Richard Slotkin, *Regeneration through Violence: A Mythology of the American Frontier, 1600–1860* (Middleton, Conn.: Wesleyan University Press, 1973), p. 7.

8. Allen Tate, "Horatian Epode to the Duchess of Malfi," in *Poems, 1922–1947* (New York: Scribner's, 1948), p. 71; and Walter F. Otto, *Dionysus: Myth and Cult*, trans. Robert B. Palmer (Bloomington and London: Indiana University Press, 1965), p. 29.

9. Caroline Gordon, "Cock-Crow," *Southern Review*, n.s. 1 (Summer, 1965): 569.

10. Robert Frost, "The Gift Outright," in *Collected Poems* (Garden City, N.Y.: Halcyon House, 1942), p. 445; and *Collected Poems of John Peale Bishop*, ed. Allen Tate (New York: Scribner's, 1948), pp. 78–79.

11. Lewis Mumford, *The Myth of the Machine: The Pentagon of Power* (New York: Harcourt Brace Jovanovich, 1970), p. 8; and Leslie Fiedler, *The Return of the Vanishing American* (New York: Stein and Day, 1968), p. 21.

12. R. W. B. Lewis, *The American Adam: Innocence, Tragedy and Tradition in the Nineteenth Century* (Chicago: University of Chicago Press, 1955), pp. 4–5.

13. Leo Marx, *The Machine in the Garden: Technology and the Pastoral Ideal in America* (New York: Oxford University Press, 1964), pp. 3, 229.

14. Lewis Simpson, *The Dispossessed Garden: Pastoral and History in Southern*

Literature (Athens: University of Georgia Press, 1975), pp. 2–12; and Lewis Mumford, "Introduction," *The Golden Day: A Study in American Literature and Culture* (Boston: Beacon Hill Press, 1957), p. xx.

15. F. Scott Fitzgerald, *The Great Gatsby* (New York: Scribner's, 1953), p. 182.

16. Eliade, *Myth and Reality*, p. 136; and idem, *Myths, Dreams, and Mysteries*, trans. Philip Mairet (New York and Evanston: Harper and Row, 1957), p. 245.

17. Henry Nash Smith, *Virgin Land* (Cambridge: Harvard University Press, 1950), p. vi; Walter Prescott Webb, *History as High Adventure*, ed. E. C. Barksdale (Austin, Tex: Pemberton Press, 1969), p. 10; and Jay Hubbell, *Literary Essays and Reminiscences* (Durham, N.C.: Duke University Press, 1965), p. 303.

RICHARD BAUMAN

The Transmission of the Texas Myth

IN the usual discourse of folklorists and anthropologists, myself included, myths are usually considered to be oral narratives telling of
sacred beings and semidivine heroes and are laid in a world and a time
supposed to have preceded the present order or to operate outside it.
Myths are characteristically about origins: the creation of features of
the world as we now know it or the transformation from a prior existen-
tial order to this one. Dealing as they do with sacred forces, beings,
and events, myths are intimately connected with the religious beliefs
and practices of a people.

In these terms, strictly speaking, there are no Texas myths. For
the overwhelming majority of Texans, our true myths have been codified, recorded, and canonized by institutional religion; they are recounted in Genesis and in other parts of the Holy Scriptures. In our
contemporary understanding and worldview, Texas is situated in this
world- and time order, and matters of origin are not recounted in sacred narratives, but in historical and secular ones.

This is not to say, though, that we do not tell ourselves stories
about the origins of things Texan, for we do, in plenty. Indeed, Texans
seem to be unusually preoccupied with recognizing and recounting the
formative forces and events that gave shape to Texas as a place, a society, and a culture, and to their own place within it. Moreover, like
true myths, these stories use events outside the present world order as
symbolic means of accounting for the way things are in this one. We
may, then, consider these stories as in some respects the functional
analogues of myths in the narrower sense, and that is what I propose to

do here. I will be concerned in this essay with the forms these stories have taken and the contexts in which they have been recounted, as a means of exploring the transmission of the quasi-mythic information they contain. I will deal first and most fully with the folkloric expressions of these narratives of formative experiences and factors, taking account as well of other folk symbolic expressions of the same themes, namely, celebratory enactments of them. By folklore, I should say, I mean the traditional, vernacular, expressive forms of a culture, unofficial, informal, rooted in community, and passed on orally or by customary example in face-to-face interaction. Finally, I will consider modern transformations of these traditional expressions, both written and performed.

I

One common function of myths the world over is to account for how a people came to be located in place—"how we got here." This function of myth is especially important because of the deep and intimate relationship that people in preindustrial societies feel with their land, their territory. Myth serves to establish and validate in symbolic ways a people's claim to place.

Again, contemporary Texans do not account for their arrival here in terms of divine creation or transformation, but in secular, historical terms. Still, stories of migration to Texas are no less important to us. An especially interesting case is represented by the American Indian groups currently in Texas. Where one might expect true origin myths to be current among native peoples, the fact is that neither the Alabama-Coushatta nor the Tigua Indians are indigenous to Texas, having come here during the relatively recent historical past. Thus the Tigua people, for example, account for their presence in Texas with historical legend, not myth. Here is a telling of the Tigua migration legend, as recorded by Thomas A. Green:

> People say that the Tigua ran away with the Spanish after the fight over there in New Mexico [Pueblo Revolt of 1680], but, you see, that is not true. They [the Tigua] got here long time before. There, uh, was Indians here already. There are old pueblos in the sandhills and level places where they would plant at Hueco [area near modern Ysleta]. That's why

the Spanish people don't stop here. That's why they move down to Juarez
to stay. They are afraid to [of] the Tigua.

The first people came a long time ago. They followed Coronado. They
follow Coronado to kill him.

Coronado came to New Mexico to take the things the Indians had, to
kill the people, even the womens and the little babies, but he wore that
armor, and the people couldn't kill him with their arrows, you see. He
wore the gold he took from the Indians here on his arms and around his
neck, you see, and he wore a crown made out of gold on his head, *una
corona*, and that is how he got his name of Coronado ["the crowned one"],
from that *corona*, you see.

So, these Tigua people got the idea to kill him, and they followed him.
They were like servants and pretend to be afraid of him, and waited all
the time to catch him without that armor on. So one day Coronado decided he would not need to worry about these people any more, and took
off this thing he wore over his chest. *Como se dice* [How do you say it?],
Green?

Green: His breastplate?

Sí. He leave it off, and when they see him, *chinga el cabrón . . .* they
shoot him with a poison arrow.

Then when those people kill Coronado, they don't go back to New Mexico. Maybe they are mad with those people at [Isleta] del Norte because
they will not help to kill Coronado, who can say? But that is how the
oldest people say we got here.[1]

Conventional historical accounts hold that the Tigua arrived in El
Paso in the loyal retinue of Spaniards who fled to Texas after the New
Mexico Pueblo Revolt of 1680, but the efficacy of myths is not measured by the standard of historicity. More important by far is the way
that they establish a charter for the present. The story of the killing of
Coronado, as Green observes, "is told (to both Tiguas and outsiders) as
a reason for pride and as an example to the Tiguas of how they may
overcome superior forces by relying on wit, patience, and courage, a
strategy that remains viable in their contemporary struggles against assimilation."[2] Note also the appeal to traditional authority in this legend; the story gains weight by attribution to "the oldest people" of the
pueblo, the bearers of knowledge and wisdom—they must know how
it was.

The Tigua migration legend accounts collectively for the contemporary presence of the entire group in Ysleta del Sur, but this is the

exception in Texas migration stories. For European settlers, by contrast, the tendency is to tell of the migration to Texas of individual founding ancestors or single families. Here is a classic example of the genre, taken down by Mrs. Stacy M. Labaj from Mrs. Lillie Kaase Maresh Kamas, of Nelsonville, Texas:

> My father, Coblyn Kaase, left out of Germany at age twenty to escape military service, leaving behind his maternal grandparents who were to him as parents from his infancy; never having known his mother who died at childbirth nor his father who soon remarried, his grandparents were his immediate family.
>
> The passage to America was exceedingly rough, the sailing vessel was caught in a storm, buffeted backward time and time again. All on board were violently ill and despaired of survival. When the seas finally calmed down it took fourteen days to regain the lost point. In Papa's mind the memory of that nightmare crossing the Atlantic clung stubbornly, though he found the pioneering life in Texas uncompromisingly difficult, devoid of all but hardship and though longingly he spoke of returning to Germany, that voyage like a specter remained to haunt him. He never quite got around to setting a date; Papa died at age 74, in 1919, the dream unfulfilled.
>
> Upon landing at Galveston Papa immediately made acquaintance with a cotton freighter from Industry who was looking around for possible return freight. To Papa Industry was as good a-sounding a place as any especially after being informed German people were settled within the area and that nearby New Ulm held even more German immigrant families. So in 1865 by oxen and handmade wagon freighter, he arrived and put down roots in Industry—and America.[3]

The family migration story typically consists of three parts: a reason for departure from the former home, the journey (often fraught with difficulties), and the struggle for survival in the new home.[4] Although there may be a dramatic narrative about only one of the episodes, all three are often touched on by the family narrator. Mrs. Kamas's story exhibits the full pattern. Like many other young men, her father left his home in Europe to escape military service. So nightmarish was his sea journey, marked by storms and illness, that the hardships of the pioneering life in Texas were overshadowed by it ever after in his mind.

Mrs. Kamas's story relates the epic journey of her father from the Old World to the New. For those whose ancestors were already established in the more settled parts of the United States, however, the migration stories might take on the familiar lineaments of the "G.T.T."—Gone to Texas—story in which the reason for departure often involved a brush with the law back East and a journey to Texas to start afresh in a new society. Nor was this solely a phenomenon of the early frontier period; the following account was recorded by Mrs. Labaj from Edward H. Canada, who came to Texas from West Virginia in 1916:

> I came to Texas to get away from the law. Moonshine whiskey got me in trouble. The officers caught the man who was making the whiskey for me red-handed and he tol' 'em it's my whiskey, so I had to high tail it, being alerted by my man. That was, I believe, in 1916. I was married . . . . So I came to Texas.[5]

If they survived the rigors of the journey that brought them here, migrants to Texas were faced, as all new settlers must be, with the struggle for survival. For an agrarian society under frontier conditions, the natural environment must loom large in this struggle, but in Texas it seems to have loomed larger than in other places. The formative effect of the environment on Texans' sense of themselves has been noted by many observers—the sheer size of the place, its extremes of fecundity and barrenness, heat and cold, flood and "drouth"—and these factors still rank among our principal expressive resources, the subject matter of legends, jokes, songs, and tall tales. From the earliest days of American colonization, newcomers were amazed by the scale and bounty of the American landscape. Exaggeration came easily, and the great American tradition of the tall tale was not long in establishing itself. Texas is thus far from unique in providing a home for the tall tale, but where bigness was brought down to size fairly soon in other parts of the country, it remained a salient component of Texans' sense of their environment. A fine example of this verbal art form is "The Bee Tree," told by Ed Bell, of Luling, Texas, and recorded by Patrick Mullen. He learned the story from a hunting companion as a youth in Caldwell County:

> No, that happened, oh, up near Luling. We had pretty good woods up in there, and some of the trees was big, but I started up on a tree one day that I didn't believe. I couldn't believe my eyes. I couldn't . . . it just

looked like the tree took up nearly the whole country. And I heard a terrific roarin' and I looked up and about forty feet high there was a big ol' knothole 'bout a foot across, and there was a solid roll o' bees just workin' out and in there—honey bees. Oh, man, I just knew that I could get a big bunch o' honey outa that.

So I went off and rounded up a bunch of my friends; we got about ten of us with axes. We loaded up the wagon with all the tubs and ol' barrels and dishpans, everything we could find, 'cause we didn't know how much honey we might get out of it. We went down there with our camp outfit too. We was gonna camp there while we chopped it down.

So it took us . . . we chopped on it three days, and an ol' boy says, "You know, I can hear somethin' that sounds like the echo of us choppin' on this tree."

I says, "You know, I've never been on the other side o' that tree. I'm gonna walk around there and see what it is."

Well, it took quite a while to walk around it. Got over there and there was ten other fellows choppin' on the other side. They'd found the bee tree too.

So we all lit in together, decided to pool our choppin' and get it down. So we all got busy, and we chopped the tree down.

There was a big branch there about twenty-five foot deep, 'round a hundred feet across, pretty steep sides on it, and this tree fell across that, and it just busted open, and big limb broke open at the same time, and there's squirrels in that limb, and a roll o' gray squirrels big as a flour barrel rolled outa that hollow limb for three days and nights. Don't know where they all went to after that, but there sure was a lotta squirrels in there.

So we looked, and this tree had split open and turned over into halves, and there was small knotholes on the sides of it—in different places, but they's there. So there's just streams o' honey comin' outa there, and we told one o' them other . . . that other bunch they could catch out of one stream, and we'd catch out of the other'n.

We filled everything we had: all the barrels, dishpans, tubs, and everything we could find we filled with honey. It was still runnin' out of there. And these other guys didn't have near as much as we did to catch honey with.

So we took off. They went one direction, and the way we went we had to cross this branch about five miles further down. We got there and it hadn't rained in six months, and that thing was bank full. We wondered what in the world had happened, and we got there and looked at it, and it was pure honey runnin' down that branch. It done filled that branch plum full. We had to wait two days for it to run down so we could cross and get home.[6]

This story has it all: a tree of awesome size that yields to those who labor to fell it an endless bounty of game and honey, that most symbolically resonant of natural substances. The mythic link with Judaeo-Christian tradition is, I believe, no accident. What more appropriate indication could we ask that Texas was a Promised Land than a super-abundance of honey?

But, unfortunately, it wasn't all rivers of honey in Texas. Although nature could be bountiful, it could also be harsh—in fact, harsher than one might believe. Often enough, the rivers flowed with nothing at all, and it was wind and drought that people had to deal with. In his *Tall Tales from Texas Cow Camps*, Mody Boatright re-creates a tall tale session featuring windies like this one:

> Why, there was a feller come in here one time and filed on a section of land in Colonel Slaughter's pasture, and a big sandstorm come along, and he never did find that section. He advertised in all the papers for it, offerin' a reward for its return, and he got lots of answers from people down in the brush country that had stray sections on their hands that they wanted to get rid of, but he looked 'em over and said none of 'em had his brand on 'em. And so he had to go back East.[7]

There are several classic Texas elements in this tall tale. It demonstrates, first of all, the Texas penchant for what J. Frank Dobie calls "braggin' on the worst"—taking the worst that the place has to offer and exaggerating it still further.[8] There is a fine reflexive element in these stories: they help to generate an image of Texas people so toughened by the rigors of their environment that they can treat a sandstorm that blows away whole sections both matter-of-factly and humorously. Note that the cowboys have stuck it out; they are still here, whereas those who couldn't take it gave up and went back East, the homeland of the effete. Texans are tough, and the environment has made them so.

The tall tale, of course, is a comic form. It represents a humorous and reflexive commentary by Texans on their own preoccupation with the scale and power of their natural environment. But there is a tragic potential in the environment as well, and this too may be memorialized in folklore. Perhaps the worst natural disaster ever experienced in Texas was the Galveston storm of 1900, in which six thousand persons on the island were killed by the hurricane and two thousand more by the tidal wave that swept over the Texas Gulf Coast. Here is one of a number of songs that commemorate that terrible Texas story, as sung by the Reverend Sin-Killer Griffin and recorded by John Lomax:

The Galveston Flood

Now Galveston built a sea wall
To keep the water down,
But the high tide from the ocean
Pushed water over the town.

chorus
Wasn't that a mighty storm?
Oh, wasn't that a mighty storm with the water?
Wasn't that a mighty storm,
That blew the people all away?

The trumpets give them warning:
You'd better leave this place.
They never thought of leaving
Till death looked them in the face.
chorus

The trains they were loaded
With people leaving town,
The track give way on the ocean,
The trains they went on down.
chorus

Just like a cruel master,
The wind began to blow,
Rode out on a train of horses,
Said, "death, let me go."
chorus

Now death in 1900,
That was 15 years ago,
You throwed a stone at my mother,
With you she had to go.
chorus

Now, death your hands are clammy,
You've got them on my knees,
You done carried away my mother,
Now come back after me.
chorus

The trees fell on the island,
The houses give a-way,
Some people crushed and drownded,
Some died most every way.
chorus

The lightnin' blazed like kindling,
The thunder began to roll,
The wind it began to blowing,
The rains began to fall.
chorus

The sea it began roaring,
The ships they could not stand;
I heard the captain crying,
"Please save a drowning man."
chorus[9]

The storm remains a vivid memory on the coast. As Francis Aber-nethy has written, "Those who lived then haven't forgotten it yet. It was also very real to those who knew its story and have sat out other Texas Gulf Coast hurricanes."[10] In fact, Galveston itself bore the devastating brunt of Hurricane Alicia in 1983, better prepared than in 1900, but still vulnerable to the natural forces that continue to shape our lives in Texas.

II

If the physical environment exerted a strong influence on Texans' emergent sense of themselves, the social environment was no less important. Every social group defines itself in part by reference to others—"we" are like or unlike "them"—and this is as true of ethnic and regional groups in Texas as elsewhere. But if one were to seek to identify the intergroup confrontation that has most dominated the formation of Texan society and culture, the most symbolically potent confluence of cultures in Texas, one would have to turn to the contact of Anglo and Mexican Texans. The Texas repertoire abounds with folklore of every kind—legends, songs, proverbs, jokes, riddles—rooted in the contact of Anglo and Hispanic cultures. When we seek oral narrative forms that record the formative events and experiences that shaped relations between the groups, though, we find that this is predominantly a folklore of conflict.

For Anglo Texans, as they pushed south of the Nueces River after 1836, the Mexicans of Nuevo Santander were an obstacle to the realization of Manifest Destiny. One of the earliest events memorialized in our extant corpus of folksong is Zachary Taylor's invasion of Mexico during the Mexican War, a cheerful call to "take the greasers now in hand / And drive 'em in the Rio Grande." The song was apparently still current more than a half-century later among cowboys when John Lomax collected the materials for his pioneering compilation of *Cowboy Songs*, first published in 1910.[11]

Way Down in Mexico

O boys, we're goin' far to-night,
Yeo-ho, yeo-ho!
We'll take the greasers now in hand
And drive 'em in the Rio Grande,
Way down in Mexico.

We'll hang old Santa Anna soon,
Yeo-ho, yeo-ho!
And all the greaser soldiers, too,
To the chune of Yankee Doodle Doo,
Way down in Mexico.

We'll scatter 'em like flocks of sheep,
Yeo-ho, yeo-ho!
We'll mow 'em down with rifle ball
And plant our flag right on their wall,
Way down in Mexico.

Old Rough and Ready, he's a trump,
Yeo-ho, yeo-ho!
He'll wipe old Santa Anna out
And put the greasers all to rout,
Way down in Mexico.

Then we'll march back by and by,
Yeo-ho, yeo-ho!
And kiss the gals we left to home
And never more we'll go and roam,
Way down in Mexico.

From the Mexican side, as we might expect, the confrontation had a very different cast. In the face of Anglo encroachment and the institutions and agents of oppression, the Mexicans of South Texas extolled defiant resistance. There grew up in South Texas and Northern Mexico a rich corpus of border balladry, giving voice to the Mexican side of the border conflict. These *corridos*, again as we might expect, do more than simply reverse the moral valances attached to players in the social drama of border encounters; rather, they articulate the character of the Texas Mexican border hero, the peaceful man goaded into violence and defending his right with his pistol in his hand, as in this *corrido* of "Jacinto Treviño." [12]

Jacinto Treviño

Ya con esta van tres veces
que se ha visto lo bonito,
la primera fue en Macalen
en Bronsvil y en San Benito.

Y en la cantina de Bekar
se agarraron a balazos,
por dondequiera saltaban
botellas hechas pedazos.

Esa cantina de Bekar
al momento quedó sola,
nomás Jacinto Treviño
de carabina y pistola.

—Éntrenle, rinches cobardes,
que el pleito no es con un niño,
querían conocer su padre,
yo soy Jacinto Treviño!

—Éntrenle, rinches cobardes,
válidos de la ocasión,
no van a comer pan blanco
con tajadas de jámon.—

Decia el Rinche Mayor,
como era un americano:
—Ah, que Jacinto tan hombre,
no niega el ser mexicano!—

Decía Jacinto Treviño
que se moría de la risa:

With this it will be three times
that remarkable things have
happened;
the first time was in McAllen,
then in Brownsville and San Benito.

They had a shoot-out
at Baker's saloon;
broken bottles were popping
all over the place.

Baker's saloon was
immediately deserted;
only Jacinto Treviño remained,
with his rifle and pistol.

"Come on, you cowardly *rinches*,
you're not playing games with a
child.
You wanted to meet your father?
I am Jacinto Treviño!"
"Come on, you cowardly *rinches*,
you always like to take the
advantage;
this is not like eating white bread
with slices of ham."
The chief of the *rinches* said,
even though he was an American,
"Ah, what a brave man is Jacinto;
you can see he is a Mexican."

Then said Jacinto Treviño,
who was dying of laughter,

—A mi me hacen los ojales,
los punos de la camisa.—

Decía Jacinto Treviño,
abrochándose un zapato:
—Aquí traigo más cartuchos
pa' divertirnos un rato.—

Decía Jacinto Treviño,
con su pistola en la mano:
—No corran, rinches cobardes,
con un solo mexicano.—

Decía Jacinto Treviño:
—Yo ya me vo' a retirar,
me voy para Río Grande
y allá los voy a esperar.—

Decía Jacinto Treviño,
al bajar una bajada:
—Ay, qué rinches tan cobardes,
que no me haigan hecho nada!—

Decía Jacinto Treviño,
andando en Nuevo Laredo:
—Yo soy Jacinto Treviño,
nacido en Montemorelos.—

Ya con esta me despido
aquí a presencia de todos,
yo soy Jacinto Treviño,
vecino de Matamoros.

"All you're good for is to make
the buttonholes and the cuffs on my
shirt."
Then said Jacinto Treviño,
as he was tying his shoe,
"I have more cartridges here,
so we can amuse ourselves a while."

Then said Jacinto Treviño,
with his pistol in his hand,
"Don't run, you cowardly *rinches*,
from a single Mexican."

Then said Jacinto Treviño,
"I am going to retire.
I'm going to Rio Grande City,
and I will wait for you there."

Then said Jacinto Treviño,
as he came down an incline,
"Ah, what a cowardly bunch of
rinches;
they didn't do anything to me!"
Then said Jacinto Treviño,
when he was in Nuevo Laredo,
"I am Jacinto Treviño,
born in Montemorelos."

Now with this I say farewell,
here in everybody's presence;
I am Jacinto Treviño,
a citizen of Matamoros.

The Jacinto Treviño of the *corrido* is actually a figure born of the merging in oral tradition of an earlier *corrido*, now lost, about one Jacinto Treviño, who killed an Anglo who had beaten his brother to death and then stood off and defeated a Ranger ambush, and a second song about Ignacio Treviño, "who did battle with the *rinches* [Texas Rangers] in a Brownsville saloon."[13] Historicity is of far less moment here, though, than symbolic image: Jacinto Treviño takes his place in popular tradition beside Gregorio Cortez and Ignacio Treviño and the other Mexican heroes of the lower border who stand up bravely and against long odds for their rights. One can hardly find stronger evidence for the mythic functioning of these narrative songs than the way they have been taken up by the contemporary generation of Mexicano activists as a charter for their own campaign for social justice.

In the foregoing discussion, guided by the conception of myth and its functions set out at the beginning of this essay, I have concentrated my attention on a range of folk narratives—songs and stories—that have memorialized in verbal form the formative experiences of Texan cultures. As mentioned earlier, however, there are other symbolic forms that operate in conjunction with mythic narratives by which people give expression to these same formative themes. The symbols, themes, and meanings of sacred myths, for example, are embodied in religious ritual as well, where they are enacted as well as told. As with myths, though, our own sacred rituals have been codified, institutionalized, and rendered official, as part of organized religion. But again, as with myths, we can identify analogues of religious ritual in the secular festivals and celebrations that commemorate and present our formative experiences for performance to ourselves and others.

One of the best known of such folk events in Texas is Juneteenth, celebrated in black communities to commemorate the delivery to Texas of news of emancipation from slavery: on June 19, 1865, General Gordon Granger landed at Galveston and read a governmental order freeing all of the slaves in East Texas. For black people in Texas, emancipation represents par excellence a formative event marking the transition from an old to a new order. Although Juneteenth celebrations use the building blocks of festivity that are worldwide in their distribution—food, drink, music, contest, dance, noise, costume, and so on—"the theme of freedom is ever-present" in parade floats depicting the struggle of black people,[14] in the election of a parade queen called the Goddess of Liberty, in symbols, slogans, and oratory. Juneteenth is preeminently a celebration of black Texans, but, significantly, it has not been simply a means by which they have enacted mythic themes for themselves alone. Like most such cultural performances, Juneteenth has also been an occasion for blacks to present themselves symbolically to others; indeed, it has provided certain participatory opportunities to Anglos as well, as spectators at the parades and pageants, as participants in Juneteenth baseball games, as sharers in the festive feasting, and so on.[15] The festival thus enacts both the formative experience of blacks and their role in the later multiethnic society of Texas.

III

To this point, I have considered forms of mythic expression that are authentically part of Texas folklore. The migration stories, tall tales, cowboy songs, *corridos* of border conflict, Juneteenth celebrations, and the like are traditional, part of vernacular culture, rooted in community, and passed on orally or by customary example. But folklore, like all forms of communication, grows out of social structure and the structure of social relations. Whereas folk expression retains its vitality in the intimate, face-to-face social relations of family, friendship, and community, the more complex and ramified social structures of our modern institutions generate other forms, modes, and organizations of expression. Thus, although modernity does not eliminate our interest in the experiences that we consider to have had a formative influence on our social and cultural identity, the symbolic forms through which we relate and enact those experiences are framed and organized in new ways that supplement—and sometimes supersede—our folklore. Some of the important changes of the kind I mean to identify may be revealed by consideration of the very place of folklore itself in Texas culture.

In my preceding discussion, I have dealt with folklore in its primary manifestations: stories told, songs sung, festivals enacted in traditional settings. In traditional folk communities, though, the concept of "folklore" does not exist. "Folklore" is a notion that operates outside of such contexts, labeled, reflected on, and analyzed chiefly by outsiders. The term was coined by cultivated scholars as a way of objectifying traditional forms most fully current in social settings not their own. Although it has achieved wide currency among the lay public, that has been the consequence of the kind of scholarly objectification just mentioned. Thus, to be a folklorist, or someone interested in "folklore," is to confront folklore as something transformed, lifted from its traditional context and objectified in a special way. A cultural awareness of "folklore," then, is a relatively recent, modern phenomenon, and it is almost invariably accompanied by a perception that the traditional, agrarian ways of life that characterize classic "folk" society are declining under the impact of technological and economic change.

In Texas, public awareness of folklore has been to a considerable degree a consequence of the activities of the Texas Folklore Society.

Founded in 1909, at a time of rising consciousness that the formative era of our history was drawing to a close, the society is the oldest continuously functioning state organization of its kind in the country. But here, as elsewhere, the activity of folklorists keeps folklore current in a growing sector of our society only in a mediated form, as an objectified phenomenon that belongs to a way of life no longer our own. It may be valuable and attractive, but it is not seen to be fully consonant with modern life.

Indeed, J. Frank Dobie, who did more than anyone to cast the die in which public conceptions of folklore have been molded in Texas, was quite explicit that his own tastes and purposes required that folklore be "improved." He valued folklore as "the essence of a cultural inheritance,"[16] but seemed to feel that it was most effective when rendered by cultivated writers into literature. A patronizing tone sometimes creeps into his writing about the expressive quality of oral folklore: "After I have heard a tale, I do all I can to improve it," he wrote in 1960. "If the characters in an orally told tale do not talk effectively the business of any writer who adopts this tale is to make them talk better—with more savor, more expressively of both themselves and the land to which they belong."[17] And elsewhere, "My custom is to try to tell a tale as the original teller should have told it."[18]

Now this view of folklore as both the necessary basis for an authentic literature and yet as inadequate for the purpose without the intervention of cultivated writers is not original or peculiar to Dobie—it is the essence of the Herderian romantic nationalist program and lives on in every national *folklórico* dance ensemble and folklore commission in the world. My point is that Dobie was more than anyone else responsible for the strong dominance of this retell-it-and-improve-it approach to folklore in Texas and that the result is not folklore, but a form of regional literature. I say nothing about the quality of this folksy literature, for that is for individual taste to decide. For present purposes, I merely want to make clear that such writings give us not folklore, but fundamental transformations of it rendered for a different audience in a different medium. I dwell on the point at such length because most people in Texas confuse these literary adaptations of folklore with the real thing. Nevertheless, I hasten to add, the mythic function persists through the transformation. The adaptations of folklore that we get in most publications of Texas folklore are still stories we tell ourselves about our formative experiences, but after we have distanced ourselves from them in time and social space. This is once again clear in Dobie's writing: "And what, some people are asking, is to be done with all this collected folklore? For one thing, a number of intelligent people read it and enjoy it and are instructed by it as they read and enjoy and are instructed by history."[19] Thus, what Dobie gives us is rooted in folklore, but "improved" by cultivated "writers" for "intelligent people."

This, then, is one transformation that the Texas myth has undergone: from folklore to folksy literature. But it remains an ambiguous one, because the nature and mode of expression by which the myth is transmitted are hedged; the work of Dobie, Bill Brett, Ben Green, and others passes (and is passed off) now as folklore, now as literature, though always as rooted in "our heritage."

There are clear signs in recent assessments of Texas writing, however, that such "folklorized" literary productions are themselves coming to be viewed as having outlived their day.[20] There is another set of cultural productions that seems to be in the ascendant, representing a further transformation of the Texas myth. I refer to the burgeoning phenomenon of "folklife festivals," staged for the most part in urban areas for the public display of folklife to the general public. What the regional literature of Dobie and others is to traditional oral folklore, these festivals are to traditional folk celebrations; they give us folklore lifted out of context, objectified, and put on exhibit for an audience already distanced from its traditional past.

The biggest and best-established of these productions is the Texas Folklife Festival, staged since 1972 in San Antonio by the Institute of Texan Cultures. This festival has set the pattern for the others, in Austin, Houston, Fort Worth, Dallas, and elsewhere. Two related elements are characteristically put on display at folklife festivals: our traditional past and our ethnicity. To a certain extent, the original Folklife Festival and its descendants use traditional building blocks of festivity in the organization of the event: special holiday foods, from boudin to bagels; music, dance, and song, from *conjunto* to country and western; fancy costumes, from lederhosen to leggings; and, of course, plenty of beer to wash it all down. These are all traditional markers of the set-aside time of festival in folk communities.

Interestingly, however, there is a significant new element in the mix, namely, traditional work skills: "Whether the pioneer was Anglo or Danish, clothes were needed, fields had to be tilled, and plates put on the table. A whole area . . . is set aside to salute the practitioners of the basics of life. Visitors can learn how to throw a pot or mold a ceramic plate, discover how cotton is carded and spun into thread, or hear a farm hand coax work out of a field mule."[21] Labor becomes in these enactments a new kind of commodity—not a means of production, but a performance, "presented for your enjoyment." This, more than anything, highlights the essential difference between these new cultural productions and traditional festivals that operate in contrast to workaday existence. But, of course, the spectators at folklife festivals *are* on holiday, and the work skills on display do not figure in their workaday world. In folklife festivals, we are tourists in our own cultural past, spectators at performances of staged authenticity.

I do not mean to appear completely critical of folklife festivals, for they do serve some positive functions. We have not come so far from the days of race hatred and ethnic prejudice that the public and positive reaffirmation of ethnicity and the celebration of cultural diversity cannot be seen as real progress. Moreover, the positive valence attached to traditional ways in these festival settings does help to offset the negative views of the traditional, the rural, and the ethnic that have been fostered so strongly by our American ideologies of progress through technology and homogenization in the melting pot. And ultimately, I continue to believe, an awareness of our cultural past enriches our sense of the present.

What is important, however, is to realize that these folklife festivals *are* the constructions of the present, though made up of performances of the past. Clearly understood, they stand as truly *modern* versions of the myth. Dean MacCannell is exactly right in suggesting that

> the best indication of the final victory of modernity over other sociocultural arrangements is not the disappearance of the nonmodern world, but its artificial preservation and reconstruction in modern society. The separation of nonmodern culture traits from their original contexts and their distribution as modern playthings are evident in the various social movements toward naturalism, so much a feature of modern societies. . . .

These displaced forms, embedded in modern society, are the spoils of the victory of the modern over the nonmodern world. They establish in consciousness the definition and boundary of modernity by rendering concrete and immediate that which modernity is not.[22]

Thus, it is not folklore that is featured in folklife festivals, but staged, framed reconstructions and reenactments of it. The festivals are nonetheless vehicles of mythic expression for all that—our modern way of presenting ourselves to ourselves in light of the formative forces and experiences that made us what we are. We have been transformed by history and our myths must follow suit, for myth is of the present though it draws its sanction from the past.

NOTES

1. Thomas A. Green, "Folklore and Ethnic Identity in Tigua Nativism," in "*And Other Neighborly Names": Social Process and Cultural Image in Texas Folklore*, ed. Richard Bauman and Roger D. Abrahams (Austin: University of Texas Press, 1981), pp. 233–34.

2. Ibid., p. 234.

3. From the Stacy M. Labaj Collection of Oral History in the Folklore Archives, Center for Intercultural Studies in Folklore and Ethnomusicology, University of Texas, Austin.

4. Stephen J. Zeitlin, Amy J. Kotkin, and Holly Cutting Baker, *A Celebration of American Family Folklore* (New York: Pantheon, 1982), p. 62.

5. Stacy M. Labaj Collection of Oral History.

6. Transcribed from field recording of Ed Bell, made by Patrick Mullen, 1971, Folklore Archives, Center for Intercultural Studies in Folklore and Ethnomusicology, University of Texas, Austin. For a previously published transcription of this tall tale, see Mullen, *I Heard the Old Fisherman Say* (Austin: University of Texas Press, 1978), pp. 145–46.

7. Mody Boatright, *Tall Tales from Texas Cow Camps* (1946; reprint, Dallas: Southern Methodist University Press, 1982), p. 41.

8. J. Frank Dobie, foreward to *Sam Slick in Texas*, by W. Stanley Hoole (San Antonio: Naylor, 1945), pp. ix–x.

9. Transcribed from *Folk Music of the United States: Negro Religious Songs and Services from the Archive of American Folk Song*, ed. B. A. Botkin, AAFS 10. Washington, D.C.: Library of Congress Division of Music, 1952.

10. Francis Abernethy, *Singin' Texas* (Dallas: E-Heart Press, 1983), p. 170.

11. John A. Lomax, *Cowboy Songs and Other Frontier Ballads* (New York: Macmillan, 1930), p. 314.

12. Américo Paredes, *A Texas-Mexican Cancionero: Folksongs of the Lower Border* (Urbana: University of Illinois Press, 1976), pp. 69–71.

13. Ibid., p. 31.

14. William H. Wiggins, "'They Closed the Town Up, Man!': Reflections on the Civic and Political Dimensions of Juneteenth," in *Celebrations: Studies in Festivity and Ritual*, ed. Victor Turner (Washington, D.C.: Smithsonian Institution Press, 1982), p. 284.

15. Ibid., p. 289.

16. William Wittliff, "J. Frank Dobie in Folklore," in *The Sunny Slopes of Long Ago*, ed. Wilson M. Hudson and Allen Maxwell, Publications of the Texas Folklore Society, no. 33 (Dallas: Southern Methodist University Press, 1966), p. 93.

17. Ibid., pp. 92–93.

18. Ibid., p. 93.

19. Ibid., p. 97.

20. Larry McMurtry, "Ever a Bridegroom: Reflections on the Failure of Texas Literature," *Texas Monthly*, October 23, 1981.

21. Program of the 1980 Texas Folklife Festival (San Antonio: Institute of Texan Cultures).

22. Dean MacCannell, *The Tourist: A New Theory of the Leisure Class* (New York: Schocken Books, 1976), pp. 8–9.

Part II
The Clash of Cultures on the Texas Frontier

William W. Newcomb, Jr.

Harmony with Nature, People, and the Supernatural

Se-ket-tu-ma-qua, or Black Beaver, a Delaware Indian, was born in the early years of the nineteenth century. As a young man he and a large fragment of his tribe were forced to move westward across the Mississippi. Like a number of other young Delawares, Beaver was not content to settle down on the land the government designated for them, becoming instead a footloose wanderer. He trapped beaver with the mountain men in the Rockies, gained a reputation as a warrior while fighting the Blackfoot in Montana, contemplated the Pacific Ocean on the beaches of Southern California, and for a time was a trader to the Comanches. He learned English and a number of Indian languages, became adept in using the Indian sign language, and was a noted tracker and hunter. Because of his experience and skills, Beaver became much sought after as a guide and interpreter for exploring parties probing the little-known American West.

One of the men who employed Black Beaver was Randolph B. Marcy, an army officer who spent most of his active career in Texas and on the western frontier. It was customary for soldiers and other whites to eat, sleep, and warm themselves at one campfire and for the various Indians who accompanied them to bed down nearby around another fire. On one of Marcy's expeditions, he employed a Comanche guide in addition to Beaver, and one evening the soldier was drawn to their fire for an earnest and not very friendly discussion taking place between them. Marcy asked the Delaware the reason for the heated exchange and he replied,

"I tell him 'bout the steam-boats, and the rail-roads, and the heap o' houses I seen in St. Louis."

"Well, sir, what does he think of that?"

"He say I'ze d——d fool."

"What else did you tell him about?"

"I tell him the world is round, but he keep all e'time say, 'Hush, you fool! Do you s'pose I'se child. Haven't I got eyes? Can't I see the prairie? You call him round?' He say, too, 'Maybe so I tell you something you not know before. One time my grandfather he make long journey that way (pointing to the west). When he get on big mountain, he seen heap water on t'other side, just so flat he can be, and he seen the sun go straight down on t'other side.'"

Beaver responded to the Comanche: "I then tell him all the rivers I seen, all e'time the water he run; s'pose the world flat, the water he stand still. Maybe so he not b'lieve me?"

Marcy agreed with Beaver that he probably could not persuade the Comanche that the world was round (and he did not criticize the accuracy of Beaver's rebuttal). Marcy then asked him to tell the Comanche about the magnetic telegraph, saying,

"You have heard of New York and New Orleans?"

"Oh yes," he replied.

"Very well; we have a wire connecting these two cities, which are about a thousand miles apart, and it would take a man thirty days to ride it upon a good horse. Now a man stands at one end of this wire in New York, and by touching it a few times he inquires of his friend in New Orleans what he had for breakfast. His friend in New Orleans touches the other end of the wire, and in ten minutes the answer comes back—ham and eggs. Tell him that, Beaver."

His countenance assumed a most comical expression, but he made no remark until I again requested him to repeat what I had said to the Comanche, when he observed,

"No, captain, I not tell him that, for I don't b'lieve that myself."

Marcy assured Beaver that it was a fact and that he had seen it himself. But Beaver countered: "Injun not very smart; sometimes he's big fool, but he holler pretty loud you hear him maybe half a mile; you say 'Merican man he talk thousand miles. I 'spect you try to fool me now, captain; *maybe so you lie*."[1]

This conversation is cited because it indicates the theme of this essay: an exploration of some shared values, traits, and outlook that characterized nineteenth-century Texas Indians and differentiated them from Texans. It also attempts to illuminate the reasons why Indians failed to comprehend and were often bewildered by Texans, and it suggests why Texans acquired at best a shallow understanding of Indians.

The argument between Black Beaver and the Comanche also bears on the persistent and widespread notion that all Indian tribes and nations were (and are) as similar to one another as the leaves of a mesquite tree. Actually, there were thousands of distinct Indian groups in North America and dozens in Texas, although by the nineteenth century their number had shrunk dramatically. The natives of Texas spoke many different languages and dialects, made their living in a variety of ways, were organized economically, socially, and politically in an assortment of ways, and viewed their human, natural, and more-than-natural universes in equally diverse ways. Some, like the immigrant Delawares, long had been exposed to and much influenced by Western civilization; others, like Comanches, had had little direct contact with Anglo-Americans. In short, there was no single native cultural flower; instead it was a cultural landscape of many hues. There was no single "Indian mind."

Despite the considerable cultural differences among Indian peoples, they shared some fundamental characteristics that created a tremendous chasm between themselves and Anglo-Americans, lending credence to the stereotype of Native American homogeneity. Such similarities did not necessarily or even usually arise out of a common past, but rather out of broadly similar ways and conditions of making a living. In contrast to Western nations, for example, they were technologically underdeveloped and socially less complex in that their relationships with one another were predominantly ordered by bonds of kinship rather than by differing occupations, classes, and wealth. Communication with their variously conceived supernatural universes was generally more direct, personal, and intimate than Western people's. Living close to the physical world, their primary problems and philosophical concerns were associated with its fecundity and dangers as well as with the relationship of humanity to its creatures and forces.

I

Perhaps the most dramatic differences between Anglo-Americans and Indians are found in attitudes about the earth. No Indian people in

Texas regarded the varied lands they hunted over or raised corn on as commodities to be bought and sold, or to be held or owned by individuals. The majority, at least implicitly, regarded themselves as belonging to or as part of the natural world. Often the earth was regarded explicitly as Mother. Many consciously sought to live in harmony with the earth, with the animals it nurtured, and the forces that created it all. None regarded themselves as its conquerors or exploiters.

The various Caddoan-speaking Southern Plains peoples who emerged in the nineteenth century as the Wichita tribe clearly exemplify such concepts about the earth. They were a semisedentary people, and during the growing season related groups of women raised corn, beans, squash, and other crops in extensive gardens near their grass-house villages. After the harvest the villages were abandoned for a fall and winter bison hunt, the people returning in spring to their villages for the new planting season. One might expect that the Wichitas would have had strong proprietary landholding interests, but this was not the case, at least in an Anglo-American sense. They believed that Earth Mother, one of a vaguely graded hierarchy of deities, had given birth to everything, that she had taught women how to grow corn and other crops, and that she nourished and preserved humanity. People lived on her and flourished under her guidance; it was unimaginable that individuals might possess her, inconceivable that they could sell her.[2]

Similarly, among the bison-hunting Comanches, "Mother Earth was implored to make everything grow which they ate; that they might live; to make the water flow, that they might drink; to keep the ground firm, that they might walk upon it; to make certain herbs and plants grow, that they might be able to heal the sick; and to cause the grass to grow on which the animals fed. The Great Spirit put the Earth here and put them upon it. Without the Earth nothing could live; there could be no animals or plants."[3]

In a sense the Indian perception of the earth as a noncommodity is similar to our view concerning the atmosphere above us. Most of our citizens, one might suspect, would be quite willing to part with the space over their heads, particularly over public parks and their neighbors' yards, for a few dollars' worth of junk jewelry, the price that was allegedly paid the Indians for Manhattan Island. If someone is foolish enough to offer you something of value for what is free or available to all, why not accept it?

The Indian attitude about the earth undoubtedly contributed to the relative ease with which many of them were dispossessed, and it also probably contributed to the American rationalization that, since natives did not utilize large portions of their land "properly," leaving it for foraging or hunting, it was right and just for land-hungry farmers and ranchers to appropriate it for a higher purpose. It is ironic that the higher purpose often has led to overgrazed, eroded lands, to the stark desolation of clear-cut forests, and to the pollution of rivers and lakes. It is not that the Indian, as Noble Savage, was imbued with a mystical ecological wisdom his successors lacked; he simply did not possess the technological means, the economic greed, and the ethical and philosophical mandate to seize, subdue, and ultimately desecrate the landscape.

Today, those Indians who have managed to survive and to maintain something of their cultural identity still possess about 3 percent of their ancient patrimony. The American public is largely unaware and perhaps uncaring that mining, agricultural, timber, and fishing interests, with the active collaboration of governmental agencies, seem dedicated to exploiting or appropriating that pitiful remnant for their own benefit. The point here, however, is not the terrible injustices that have been and are being perpetrated against Indians, but that through centuries of incredible struggle and defeat their spiritual attachment to the land has not been extinguished. Probably the fire burns brighter today than for many generations, and sometimes Indian efforts have met with modest success. The sacred Blue Lake of Taos Pueblo has been restored to its rightful owners, natives of Maine have regained thousands of acres of forest illegally seized from their ancestors, and Indians of Puget Sound have successfully asserted old treaty rights to fish in those waters.[4] Even in Texas, although its natives were dispossessed by the stroke of a pen in 1846 and later physically removed from their homelands, some of their descendants—Kiowas, Comanches, and Apaches—have been compensated monetarily for that loss. But that millions of dollar bills could be fairly exchanged for that earth is a white notion, not one characteristic of Indian minds.

Another deep-running characteristic that distinguished Texas Indians from other Texans was their feeling that people were part of nature and not morally or spiritually removed from its animals or from its other various manifestations. Over and over this is reflected in native mythologies and folktales. Among Comanches, for example, a human could become a buffalo, a buffalo a human, and buffaloes could talk to people, fall in love with them, bear their children, and become a person's guardian spirit. Thus, according to one of their tales, a handsome Comanche boy while on a hunt picked out a beautiful calf to kill. Although his two arrows found their mark, the calf through its supernatural powers refused to die. The wounded animal made its way to the middle of a stream, and though the boy wanted to reclaim his arrows he did not do so because the water would ruin his clothes. In time the buffalo, who had fallen in love with the boy and been impregnated by his arrows, gave birth to a calf. Other buffalo calves would have nothing to do with him, and although other calves had fathers, his was not evident. After he questioned his mother and learned who his father was, he insisted on going to visit him, despite his mother's warning that his father's people would kill them. They embarked on the journey and when they neared the Comanche camp the buffalo mother turned them both into humans. She sent her handsome son into the camp, and there he was united with his father. The boy related the story of his origins, and his father, remembering the hunting incident, asked about the boy's mother. Father and son sought out the mother and brought her back to live with the Comanches. The buffalo woman returned the arrows to the boy's father with the admonition that he should not drink from any stream without her approval.

With the buffalo woman's expert help in locating bison herds, the Comanches soon were well fed. But one day, as the boy's father was traveling across the prairie, he became thirsty. He remembered the buffalo woman's warning, but thirst drove him to wet his mouth from a stream. As soon as he did, the buffalo woman and her son were transformed back into bison. They stampeded out of the Comanche camp and disappeared. The father and the other Comanches were sad, for they had come to love the buffalo woman and her son, particularly as they had made them prosperous.[5]

Natural forces were also merged or associated with humans. In a Kiowa-Apache tale, for example, Nistcre, a supernatural, humanlike stone monster or monsters, fattened a family and ate them all except a girl. While fleeing from Nistcre the girl encountered Thunderman, who hid her, destroyed Nistcre, and then married her. But Sun, apparently already married to Thunderman, was jealous and attempted unsuccessfully to kill her and the twin boys she had conceived. The boys subsequently had a number of encounters with animals, various humans, and finally with Cyclone before they vanished.[6] Other Kiowa-Apache heroes, like Thunderman, were normally portrayed as animals or natural forces, although they also sometimes adopted human disguises. This characteristic was shared by other Texas Indians, suggesting a deeply embedded theme that people were weak, perhaps inferior creatures, who had to seek help from or through the more powerful and superior forces and creatures of nature.

II

The socioeconomic condition of nineteenth-century Texas Indian tribes, although individually varied, was basically similar and also contrasted markedly with that of other Texans. Such tribes as Tonkawas, Lipan Apaches, and Wichitas may be described as having production-for-use economies in which everybody shared equally in the game hunters killed or in the produce raised in gardens. The eminent Indian agent Robert S. Neighbors, impressed with the sharing propensity of Comanches, remarked, "He who kills the game retains the skin, and the meat is divided according to the necessity of the party, always without contention, as each individual shares his food with every member of the tribe, or with strangers who visit them."[7]

The value attached to generosity and sharing also extended to personal property—tools, weapons, ornaments, and the like. Comanches, for example, had relatively little personal property, since as nomadic bison hunters they could possess only as much as they could haul around with them. But the accumulation of property and its conspicuous consumption did not signify or confer high social status; on the contrary, generosity and sharing were characteristic of successful and highly regarded individuals. There was virtually no theft, since a person who fancied what another possessed had only to ask for the object to receive it. Most tools and material equipment were produced by the users or their families; there were no specialists who devoted themselves full-time to bow making, skin tanning, or the like. When an individual died, his or her personal property was destroyed or buried with the body, and ordinarily there were no problems of who would inherit. In fact, Comanche customs following death of prominent men signaled a giveaway of even their relatives' property. Neighbors remarked, for example, that

> the death of a chief causes great tribulation to the tribe—on such occasions they assemble without distinction, and bewail his death with extreme lamentation, until they receive from the relatives of the deceased, sufficient presents to cause them to stop; for instance, if a man wants a favorite horse belonging to the brother of the deceased, he continues crying till he obtains it. When they are killed in battle, it is a cause of much greater lamentation than from a natural death, and a much greater number of mourners bewail the loss. The presents given by relatives are also much more valuable. . . . From the liberality with which they dispose of their effects on all occasions of the kind, *it would induce the belief that they acquire property merely for the purpose of giving it to others* (emphasis added).[8]

It should be added that the adoption of horses by the Comanches created problems of inheritance that were never fully resolved. Horses were regarded as the personal property of men and women, and some people built up herds of several hundred animals. If tradition was honored they would be slaughtered at their owner's death, but the economic importance of horses was such that a number of devices were adopted to avoid their destruction. Besides distributing them to mourners, sometimes the tails and manes only were deposited on the grave or buried with the person, or only a favorite horse was killed, or bequeathed to a best friend.[9]

It is not surprising that such economic and ethical systems contributed to misunderstanding and conflict with grasping, profit-minded nineteenth-century Texans. Comanches, for example, freely asked for articles that appealed to them, and their women, in particular, simply appropriated items that took their fancy. In part, of course, Texans were probably looked on as fair game by women who would never dream of taking another Comanche's property. Texas Indians naturally

assumed that the hospitality they extended to visitors would be recip-
rocated. The problem for Texans was that a hungry Indian could eat a
prodigious amount, and travelers, exploring parties, and treaty com-
missioners were ever hard-pressed to fill the bellies of their guests.
The origin of the stereotype of Indian as thief, beggar, and freeloader
can thus be readily understood.

As surprising as it may seem, given the egalitarian nature of most
Texas Indian societies, individuals placed considerable emphasis on
"getting ahead." Their ultimate goals were not so different from those
of Anglo-Americans, but the avenues they took to achieve their aspirations were. Among Wichitas and Kiowa-Apaches there were even folktales that were rough equivalents to the Horatio Alger theme. In the
Indian versions, however, the poverty of the "poor" boy is a dearth of
relatives, not of material things. The tales often involve orphans or
near-orphans who escape their plight by some imaginative ruse or by a
heroic act. Consequently, they marry well, often the daughters of
prominent men, and so gain the richness of a circle of kinfolk.

In a typical Kiowa-Apache tale, for example, a young orphan boy is
being reared by his grandmother and, like other orphans, has sores on
his body, lice, and is generally unattractive to girls. Like the other
young men of the camp, he would like to marry a very pretty young
woman, but she has announced publicly that she will not marry until
her younger brother has killed an enemy and counted coup (touched
the dead enemy's body with a special stick). The clever and fearless orphan makes friends with the girl's young brother, gains his trust, and
after careful preparations takes the boy with him on the warpath. After
a long journey into mountainous country, they discover a Ute about to
skin a deer he has just killed. While the Ute is sharpening his skinning
knife, the orphan seizes his gun and kills him. He then gives the young
boy the coup stick and tells him to strike the body, having already instructed him to say, "I counted coup before my brother-in-law." He has
the boy scalp the Ute and take his gun and powder horn; then they ride
home on the Ute's pony. The young boy's parents, who have thought
him dead, are delighted to see him alive and in possession of a scalp.
He tells them that he has been on the warpath with his brother-in-law,
and at a feast given by the boy's father, the brother-in-law is identified

as the orphan boy. Since the boy has now counted coup and since boys have the right to give away their sisters in marriage, the orphan succeeds in marrying the beautiful girl.[10]

Another attitude many Indians possessed and persisted in maintaining long after their initial contact with the white world was disdain for much of the material wealth and know-how of their conquerors. As soon as Europeans reached North American shores, natives realistically recognized that a steel axe was superior to a stone one, that a metal pot was more convenient and durable than one of crockery, and that firearms were more lethal weapons than bows and arrows and clubs. They attempted to acquire these and many other items, with the result that they soon became dependent on Europeans for such goods; this dependence initiated changes that ultimately reverberated throughout native cultural systems. But many of the material things Americans possessed or came to possess had no parallels in Indian life, and nineteenth-century Americans were sometimes puzzled by the lack of appreciation Indians had for their technological wizardry.

A good illustration of this and other attitudes is provided by a delegation of Texas Indians that was escorted to Washington, D.C., in the summer of 1846, immediately following Texas' gaining statehood. When Texas became a state, it became encumbent on the federal government to deal with the new state's Indians, who had suddenly become its responsibility. As many Indians as possible were collected, and a treaty was duly signed with X's by chiefs and leading men on blank paper. After the treaty making was concluded, a miscellaneous group of more than forty Indian leaders of eleven tribes and subtribes, including at least some of their wives and children, was recruited to make the then-long journey to the nation's capital. The purposes of the undertaking were to impress on the Indians how populous and powerful the United States was and, secondarily, to have their leaders under control during the Mexican War. It was assumed that on their return home, the Indians would spread the word about the might of the United States and that they would submit to whatever demands were made on them. The government was only partially right.

The journey to Washington via steamboat and train was initially terrifying, since many of the Indians had never seen a vehicle more complicated than a buggy, if that. The number of people seen in crowded cities and towns was far higher than they had ever imagined or thought possible. Yet after their stay of more than a month in the capital, save for Catlin's gallery of Indian paintings, which visibly excited them, they did not seem tremendously moved by their experiences. And in a final audience with President Polk, one of the Wacos (a Wichita subtribe) named Acoquash gave a speech recounting his reactions to the visit. He concluded with the observation that "the greatest wonder to him was how the white man ever thought that he wanted a steamboat, a railroad, a ship and all the machinery that he had seen. *It did not seem, he said, so wonderful to make all those things as it did to conceive the idea that man should stand in need of them*" (emphasis added).[11]

When the Indian delegation returned to Texas, its members did not, or could not, effectively communicate to their tribes what they had seen and learned. They had what might be called the "Black Beaver problem." Tales of what they had seen were so marvelous, so alien to what their kin had ever experienced, that they simply could not be believed. Moreover, if such sophisticated travelers had persisted in expressing what their peers regarded as fantasies, whatever credibility they retained would have been quickly dissipated. Ultimately, they would suffer the fates that were variously imposed by their societies on misfits, crazies, and cranks.

Many of the domestic arrangements and customs of white society could not be appreciated by Indians, and when some particular aspect of white society was revealed, their ignorance was apt to be replaced by perplexity. An appropriate illustration is again provided by Randolph Marcy. In this instance, Marcy was escorting a wagon train of emigrants westward when they encountered Ketumsee's band of Southern (or Peneteka) Comanches. After Marcy and Ketumsee had concluded the customary formalities, Marcy realized that Black Beaver and the chief continued in animated conversation. He asked the interpreter what it was about:

> At this time there were probably five hundred emigrants and soldiers collected directly around our circle, all manifesting the utmost curiosity to hear everything that was said. Beaver, in reply to my question, then said, "He say, captain, he bring two wife for you," pointing to two girls who were sitting near by. I was a good deal embarrassed at such a proposition,

made in presence of so large an assembly, but told Beaver to inform the chief that this was not in accordance with the customs of white people; that they only had one wife at home, and were not at all disposed to marry others when abroad. This was interpreted to the Comanche and, after a brief consultation, Beaver interpreted the chief's response: "He say, captain, you the strangest man he never see; every man he seen before, when he been travlin' long time, the fust thing he want, *wife*.[12]

Beaver probably was unable to help improve the Comanche's understanding, since the shabby fringes of white society the Delawares had experienced could hardly have enlightened him either. It had long been the custom of white traders, for example, to settle in Delaware communities with Indian women, often the daughters of prominent men. When economic opportunity called such so-called squaw men elsewhere, they usually abandoned—or divorced, depending on your point of view—their wives and Indian families.[13] Since Delaware men with children rarely divorced their wives, one suspects that Black Beaver did not have a high regard for Anglo-American morality. As far as Comanches were concerned, premarital chastity was not valued, and male adultery was not regarded as immoral or sinful. It is unlikely that whatever experiences they had had with traders and frontiersmen had persuaded them that Americans were different from themselves in these regards, Marcy's protestations to the contrary.

III

As with other aspects of their cultures, nineteenth-century Texas Indians were tremendously varied in their beliefs about the more than natural world of mysterious forces, demons and witches, spirits and gods. And they were equally varied in the means they employed to affect or control their supernatural worlds. Texans generally displayed little interest in what to them were the superstitions and idolatrous ways of Indians, and even those who were curious and had an opportunity to learn something about native religious matters often were able to discover little or nothing they could equate with their own religious traditions. David G. Burnet, for example, the first (provisional) president of the Republic, "spent a considerable time with, or in the vicinity of," Comanches soon after he came to Texas in 1818, in an attempt to cure his "pulmonary consumption." Many years later, he was asked to respond to inquiries Henry R. Schoolcraft was circulating about Indians. Burnet's response indicated he was quite well acquainted with at least the externals of Comanche culture, but he utterly failed to comprehend their religious beliefs:

> The Comanche notions of religion are as crude, imperfect, and limited, as of geography or astronomy. They believe in, or have some indefinite traditional idea of, the Great Spirit; but I never discovered any distinct mode or semblance of worship among them. . . . I perceived no order of priesthood, or anything analogous to it, among them; if they recognise any ecclesiastical authority whatever, it resides in their chiefs; but I think their religious sentiments are entirely too loose, vague, and inoperative, to have produced any such institution. The elevation of the shield [on a spear early in the morning, facing the sun] is the only act I ever noticed among them, that afforded the slightest indication of religious concernment; and I doubt if they have any opinions relative to future rewards and punishments that exercise any moral influence upon them. . . . I doubt if they have any common plan of religious belief, or of a supernatural agency operating on the affairs of this life, beyond the mystic vagaries of witchcraft; and of these, they do not distinctly believe in anything beyond the potentiality of human means. It may be assumed of them, as to all the practical results of religious sentiment, that "the fool hath said in his heart, there is no God."[14]

What eluded Burnet was that the Comanche relationship with the supernatural world was almost wholly a personal one. Each person communicated individually with supernatural beings and forces that had been revealed in visions or hallucinations. There were virtually no public gatherings during which Comanches collectively appealed to supernatural powers for assistance or thanked them for benefits bestowed. Nor, of course, could Comanches afford the luxury of a priestly class of specialists. Instead, young men in isolated and lonely vigils sought spiritual guardians, and when successful they had mystical experiences during which a buffalo, wolf, or other creature gave them "power" and with it the songs, taboos, and procedures by which it could be utilized. Power varied; some was greater or better as pragmatically demonstrated by the successes or failures of its users. Power or medicine was also specific in that it was variously useful for healing, divination, hunting, and the like.

The Comanches, then, may be fairly judged as an intensely religious people, intimately and continuously involved with the mysterious powers of their belief. Apparently no other Indian tribe or nation in Texas was as individualistic in relationships with the supernatural as the Comanches. The Kiowas and allied Kiowa-Apaches convened annually to celebrate the Sun Dance, the Wichitas had semisecret dance societies that periodically propitiated their varied hierarchy of earth and sky, male and female deities, and the Caddoes were heir to a priest-king theocracy and a structured annual round of ceremonies conducted by priests, some in temples on the earthen mounds their ancestors had raised. But all of these Texas natives received, and many of them actively sought, the guidance and support of personal guardian spirits.

Some of the ancestors of nineteenth-century Caddoes, Tonkawas, and Lipans had experienced the missionary efforts of Spanish padres, but apparently few or none had adopted any of the tenets of Christianity. Surprisingly, perhaps, nineteenth-century Anglo-Americans made no efforts to persuade the state's natives to become Christians. But when the Indian survivors were safely incarcerated on reservations, and particularly in the years following the Civil War, a concerted effort, official and unofficial, was made to force their conversion. It continued well into the twentieth century, until the Indian Reorganization Act of 1934 (Wheeler-Howard Act) granted them at least nominal religious freedom. Many erstwhile Texan Indians became nominal or active Christians during those years, although large numbers enthusiastically embraced the Ghost Dance religion of 1890, a nativistic and messianic movement. Even though the millennium did not arrive, a declining number of Indians continued to dance until 1917.

By that time a new, intertribal religious cult, Peyotism, was attracting many Indians. Peyote is a small, spineless cactus that, when ingested either green, dried, or as an infusion, induces vivid visual and auditory hallucinations.[15] Like the Ghost Dance, the modern peyote cult is an intertribal phenomenon involving a broad spectrum of Indian tribes, including those originally from Texas. Part of its attraction is spiritual and emotional independence from the white world, based in part on the ancient and widespread belief that spiritual knowledge is, or can be, acquired directly and personally through revelations. Peyote provides a convenient avenue to those spiritual experiences and is testimony to the vitality and persistence of ancient belief in spite of, or perhaps because of, sustained efforts to obliterate it.

IV

Only some of the recurring themes that were shared by the natives of Texas and that distinguished them from Texans have been explored here. But even from this partial survey it should be clear that the differences were not confined to how one parted the hair (if it was parted at all), or greeted strangers, or took meals. They went to, or were derived from, the basics of human life—how and by what means people wrested a living from an often niggardly land, how they customarily behaved toward their fellows, how they perceived of themselves, their land, their cosmos, and how they interacted with it all. To Indian minds, people, like other creatures, were of the earth; they partook of its blessings and by sharing with their fellows flourished. Their material needs satisfied, they had no desire to complicate their lives with unnecessary contrivances. Their individual and collective destinies were controlled and assured by ever-present supernatural forces that were accessible to each individual.

That gulf of myth and perception that separated Indian from Texan was so wide and deep that mutual comprehension was never attained. On one hand, natives had but slight opportunity to grasp the magnitude and complexity of what was overwhelming them. On the other, the conquerors—gripped by racist pretensions, a mystical Manifest Destiny, and driven by land-hungry greed—brushed aside and dismissed the Indians as inferior or worse, seldom attempting to recognize, much less appreciate, their common humanity.

Indians have all but vanished from the Texas scene and from Texan consciousness. Although they are occasionally called to mind by a beautifully crafted arrowhead eroding from a storm-washed bank or by the scant evasions that hastily dispose of the subject in officially mandated textbooks, the curious person may sometimes wonder whether anything was ever learned from the collision of Indian and Texan. Perhaps not. We seem to bask secure in our ethnocentrism, oblivious to the ethnic diversity of a shrunken world, unmindful of the need to understand it rather than to transmute it into our own image. We failed to understand the Indians and we failed to assimilate them; pursuing such precedent, we likely will fail on a wider stage.

NOTES

1. Randolph B. Marcy, *Thirty Years of Army Life on the Border* (New York: Harper and Brothers, 1866), pp. 84–85.

2. George A. Dorsey, *The Mythology of the Wichita* (Washington, D.C.: Carnegie Institute, 1904), pp. 19–20; W. W. Newcomb, Jr., *The Indians of Texas: From Prehistoric to Modern Times* (Austin: University of Texas Press, 1961), pp. 270–71.

3. Ernest Wallace and E. Adamson Hoebel, *The Comanches: Lords of the South Plains* (Norman: University of Oklahoma Press, 1952), p. 196.

4. For a recent summation of Indian struggles to hold on to their land base and resources, see Alvin M. Josephy, *Now That the Buffalo's Gone* (New York: Knopf, 1982).

5. Wallace and Hoebel, *The Comanches*, pp. 200–202, quoting from Gene Weltfish, "The Man Who Married a Buffalo Wife, A Comanche Story," in *Caddoan Texts*, Publication of the American Ethnological Society, vol. 17 (New York: G. E. Stechert, 1937), pp. 218–23.

6. J. Gilbert McAllister, "Fire Boy and Water Boy," in *The Sky Is My Tipi*, ed. Mody C. Boatright, Publication of the Texas Folklore Society, no. 22 (Dallas: Southern Methodist University Press, 1949), pp. 30–44.

7. Robert S. Neighbors, "The Na-U-ni, or Comanches of Texas; Their Traits and Beliefs, and Their Divisions and Intertribal Relations," in *Information Respecting the History, Condition and Prospects of the Indian Tribes of the United States*, 6 vols., ed. Henry R. Schoolcraft (Philadelphia: Lippincott, Grambo and Co., 1852–57), 1:133–34.

8. Ibid., 1:131.

9. Wallace and Hoebel, *The Comanches*, pp. 152–53, 240–41.

10. McAllister, "Fire Boy," pp. 85–89.

11. *New Orleans Daily Picayune*, July 18, 1846, quoting from the *New York Journal of Commerce*.

12. Marcy, *Thirty Years*, p. 51.

13. John Conner, perhaps the best-known Delaware to serve the Republic and State of Texas, was the son of such a union. See W. W. Newcomb, Jr., *German Artist on the Texas Frontier, Friedrich Richard Petri* (Austin: University of Texas Press, 1978), pp. 118–19; and Charles N. Thompson, *Sons of the Wilderness* (Indianapolis: Indiana Historical Society, 1937), pp. 123–25.

14. David G. Burnet, "The Comanches and Other Tribes of Texas; and The Policy to be Pursued Respecting Them," in Schoolcraft, *Information*, 2:237–38.

15. Weston La Barre, *The Peyote Cult* (New York: Schocken Books, 1969).

JUAN A. ORTEGA Y MEDINA

Race and Democracy

EVERY nation is caught in the finely woven net of its historical prejudices, its legends, and, therefore, its myths. However, when referring to the now-latent but nevertheless ancient physical and cultural conflict between the Anglo-Saxon (British and U.S.) and Hispanic (Spanish and Ibero-American) worlds, the jealousies, misunderstandings, and mutual resentments still possess a stereotypical force, which thwarts an open dialogue between Anglo-America and Hispanic America. The tenacious and bitter conflicts, started during the sixteenth century between Spanish traditionalism and its opponent, English modernity, came to an end, as everyone knows, with the complete triumph of the modern Nordic European and Anglo-American world. To express this point in better terms, as the American theologian Paul Tillich wrote, it ended with the definitive enthroning of "the Protestant era," or the decisive conquest of the material world.

In the nineteenth century these two worlds, these two "mythologies," clashed in Texas in the conflict between the heirs of the two traditions: first, in 1836, between Mexicans and Texans—the latter consisting chiefly of immigrant Anglo-Americans who poured across the Texas borders imbued with the religious and political beliefs of the North American Protestant tradition; subsequently, from 1846 to 1848, between Mexico and the United States itself. In this chapter, I shall explore the religious dimensions of these beliefs and focus on both traditions' myths, or beliefs, regarding race and democracy. From this analysis the clash of these two cultures on the Texas frontier becomes not only clearer, but seemingly inevitable.

I

The religious reformation of the sixteenth century, initiated by Martin Luther in 1517, caused the splintering of Christendom and hastened the acceleration of the nationalistic tendencies that had been building up since the late fifteenth century. The European Renaissance, the great geographic discoveries, the new markets, and the new inventions and techniques would also hasten the appearance of a new intellectually critical climate and of a Christian Europe fragmented spiritually and politically by the Reformation and Counter-Reformation. Another Europe, which among painful conflicts sought renewal through the propagation of free, unorthodox thought, was an important source of the liberal doctrine against the militant traditionalism of the great reformers, especially Luther. History marched irreversibly on a new road, toward rupture with Rome, the creation of great powers, the absolutism of the state, a different morality, and the secularization of life.

Of the two Protestant creeds, Lutheranism and Calvinism, it was the latter that adapted itself better to the new times and innovations, due not so much to Calvin as to his followers and interpreters. The new creed also helped the emerging historical class, the bourgeoisie, to become conscious of its growing economic and political power and to use it without medieval Catholicism's traditional and anti-utilitarian ethical restraints, such as the prohibition against usury.

The Calvinist doctrine, expressed in the famous *Institutes of the Christian Religion* (1536), gave Anglicanism, established by Henry VIII, a solid theological foundation and also contributed to the rigid dogmatism of the English and Scottish Puritans. Anglo-Saxon Protestantism awakened the latent energies of the incipient bourgeois class, which became wealthy from the Catholic church's rich lands, forfeited under the Act of Supremacy (1534). This class engaged in an inexorable commercial battle against the Spanish Empire, gained possession of the sea in less than half a century, and established colonies (Virginia, New England, and the Caribbean islands) in an American continent previously monopolized commercially and spiritually by Spain. This new class, made up of the freshly minted Tudor nobility and of merchants and landowners who had grown rich as a result of the turmoil of the Restitution, transformed England. Its members were people hardened at commercialism and situated on the margin of the antiquated feudal sense of responsibility.[1] They were, in short, modern.

The conquering campaign of Anglo-Saxon Protestantism in the sixteenth and seventeenth centuries was justified, of course, by spiritual, economic, and political arguments. It was necessary to expel the Spaniards from the wrongfully acquired continent, to supplant them, and to conquer the New World by means of the goodness of Reformed Evangelism. This evangelism would also permit the liberation of the Indians, who had been indoctrinated into Catholicism, from the infernal claws of the papists and, therefore, from exploitation and horrible cruelties denounced by the unquestionable testimony of Bishop Las Casas, no less. In the American Promised Land, in the Puritans' New Canaan, one had to combat the new philistines boldly, whether Indians or papists. Spaniards, French, and Indians—aided by the devil—contributed to the corruption, the weakening, and the adulteration of the primordial goodness of the American paradise. America, in spite of its natural resources, was demonic: a satanic continent populated by the servants of Lucifer and the Anti-Christ. Battle without quarter against such enemies was urgent, indeed necessary; victory was at hand, with the help of Jehovah, who would permit the eradication of evil. In the nineteenth century, North Americans dedicated themselves with similar rebellious enthusiasm, inherited from religion, to cleansing America of such undesired guests.

The religion of the Puritans hindered the acculturation of the American Indians and the mixture of whites and Indians, or miscegenation, the term North Americans prefer to *mestizaje*. Miscegenation could not be accomplished because of the division Calvin's theology established from the beginning between the conformers (the minority) and the wicked (the majority). It forbade the joining of the "chosen ones" and the wicked. Contrary to what took place in the Catholic Hispanic world, the fertile process of miscegenation was not able to get started in Anglo colonies.

With regard to the Hispanic world, the acceptance of *mestizaje*, or racial mixture, among the peoples who through many centuries invaded and settled in the Iberian peninsula, together with the spirit of Hispanic Catholicism, which neither encouraged nor impeded the mixture of Spaniards, Indians, and blacks, allowed for the presence of a new race, the *mestizo*. Queen Isabella was agreeable to it, and the conquerors and colonists did not find it inconvenient to marry Indian women, especially those who, as *cacicas*, or daughters or granddaughters of prominent lords, could bring riches and inherited possessions to the union. Baptism eliminated the Spanish Catholic fear of marrying succubi.

To date, with notable exceptions, North Americans consider themselves the privileged inheritors of the ominous social Congregationalist theology and they feel proud and Darwinianly predestined, as the modern elect, to carry on their shoulders the progressive weight of civilization, "the white man's burden."

II

A sharp distinction between Anglo-America and Hispanic America with regard to their origins has been drawn by Edmundo O'Gorman. The former adapts the European Anglo-Saxon model to its own circumstances and thus opens the way to the practice of religious, political, and economic freedom; the latter imitates the model, but makes the values of the Catholic Hispanic European world its own. Anglo-America will free western Americans from feeling subordinate to Europocentrism; Hispanic America will free them from a closed conception of the world.[2] From here discrepancies, interpretations, and different and even opposing historical experiences would appear. But at least Ibero-Americans were eager to imitate the American Anglo-Saxon model, by virtue of the progressive success it brought when compared with the retrogression and freezing of the Hispanic world. The U.S. Constitution (1787) was imitated and copied and converted into a panacea for the future political success of Mexico. It was believed that the proper application of Mexico's 1824 Constitution would inherently bring the country progress and spiritual and material happiness. No one paid attention to Montesquieu's warning about the difficulty of applying foreign political formulas to the general spirit of a nation.

Mexico's public figures at the beginning of the nineteenth century did not understand that the U.S. Constitution brought together liberties and spiritual and political principles shared by all the British colonies in America. When Jefferson wrote the Declaration of Independence, the ideas contained in it were not original; they were derived from convictions, ideas, beliefs, and practices that not only were widespread and cultivated in the thirteen colonies, but had originated in the religious minorities derived from Puritan Calvinism: Congregationalist, Anabaptist, Presbyterian, Quaker, Moravian, and so forth. In the long run, these denominations opened the door to political democracy.

At times we Hispanics have asked ourselves if, when we invoke political terms such as "liberty," "liberalism," "conservatism," "democracy," "opposition," "federalism," and "republicanism," we allude to the same things as North American historians and political scientists do when they use them. To illustrate this point, let us analyze the word *liberalism*. The term acquired its Hispanic meaning in the Courts of Cadiz in 1812. But with regard to the spiritual, economic, and political values it contained, it simply included and modernized an entire series of diverse elements. It is evident that when Hispanics use this word in a specific historical context, we are expressing the same, or nearly the same, meaning that a scholar from the United States would use when including the term *liberalism*. But without doubt, for an Anglo-Saxon writer the word would possess a resonance, a traditional historical echo, that would not correspond in any way to the evocative resonance for a Mexican writer.

In its Anglo-Saxon usage, liberalism refers, in the first place, to the atmosphere of religious doctrine that made possible the exaltation and development of individual liberty after the Protestant Reformation. In the second place, it refers to political, social, and economic values. Mexicans, although not unaware of its primary spiritual meaning, consider the concept of liberalism not so much a description of spiritual tolerance and freedom as a determined, victorious opposition against the grain of our intimacy, of our historical and spiritual tradition. Anglo-Saxon liberalism develops and follows from the dominant Protestant religious tradition; Mexican liberalism unfolds and prospers as it uproots itself from the dominant Catholic tradition.

This means that our Hispanic liberalism historically turns out much more contradictory than that of the Anglo-Saxon. The latter, appearing prior to the process of social and political seclarization, was initiated with the religious dissidence of the sixteenth century, which proclaimed the spiritual freedom of the new Christian. The spiritual freedom of the reformers slowly guided the ecclesiastical-political democracy promoted by the leaders of the most combative and revolutionary Protestant sects. The famous sermon by clergyman Thomas Hooker in Hartford (May 31, 1683), the "Fundamental Orders" of Connecticut ("the first written Constitution of modern democracy," according to V. L. Parrington), and the religious-political principles advocated by Roger Williams in Providence and William Penn in Pennsylvania all exemplify the process of religious tolerance and, therefore, of democracy—essential contributions to the future configuration of the United States. Likewise, the intensive and emotional religious movement at the beginning of the eighteenth century known as "the Great Awakening" (a new and popular religion of the heart, which extended to all North Americans the sanctity of choice) as well as the opposition of the ecclesiastic John Wise in Massachusetts (1680–1725) to the despotic pretensions of the English colonial governor of New England, Sir Edward Andros, would establish the foundations of the future Jeffersonian democracy. Furthermore, the proliferation of religious denominations—all of them characterized by democratic tendencies— influenced the philanthropic, missionary, educational, prohibitionist, pacifist, and antislavery movements of later years. The original democracy of the United States reveals in its institutions not only the influence of the new English (expressed by Locke) and French (by Montesquieu) philosophy of human rationality, but above all the presence of the old religious roots.

Among the North American patriots, creators of the nation, it was not customary to boast of religious skepticism, much less of atheism. Not even the Quakers, so liberal on the subject of beliefs, tolerated atheism. The famous and defiant "God does not exist" of the Mexican radical Ignacio Ramírez had no counterpart among the North American representative leaders. Abraham Lincoln, who was not actually a member of any church but who during his whole life attended the Presbyterian church, appealed to his countrymen in the "Gettysburg Address" to be always resolved to demonstrate "that this nation, under God, shall have a new birth of freedom." Lincoln knew well that he spoke to a religiously democratic, or democratically religious, people. One could find everywhere—in engravings, shields, coins, and hymns—inciting if not fervid invocations of God, protector of the nation, God who had helped the country in its undertakings from the very beginning: "Annuit coeptis," as the Great Seal of the United States reads.

Mexico's pure liberals of the past century, like the liberals of our time, had to free themselves from the Spanish tradition, in contrast to the politicians of the United States, who were rooted in their English tradition. J. V. Lastarria defined North American republicanism as a natural development issuing from a common bosom; Francisco Bilbao saw in Catholicism the obstacle that prohibited the guarantee of liberty in Ibero-America, and saw in it likewise the root of all Mexico's political evils. Doctor of theology José María Luis Mora, whose liberal ideology has converted more than one researcher to Protestantism, would not have been able to call his own the spiritually heterodox base of liberalism without an intensely dramatic effrontery. For Mora, as for the majority of Mexican liberals of the past, the unrestricted conception of freedom of conscience for himself and for others was beyond all his psychic and historical capabilities. This implies that the liberalism they professed lacked the religious base that made possible the secularization of beliefs and ideas without violent social disorders, without serious and dangerous ruptures among people in the United States during the first stages of national consolidation.

The exclusive and individualistic interest of the Mexican liberal doctrine of the second half of the nineteenth century has an antecedent, which has been called austere North American individualism, the frequent violator of traditional Christian ideals through brutal exploitation of the weak, the poor, and the Indians. But although Mexican liberalism was also cruel to the rural people, the laborers, and above all the Indians, it paternalized and humanized socioeconomic relations and did not totally forget Christian charity; it thereby rejected North American social Darwinism, also of Protestant derivation, with all its demoralizing effects.

In sum, if North Americans were able to proclaim freedom of thought in the Philadelphia Charter, it is because they already had it historically and religiously as descendants of spiritually free ancestors. Step by step the people of the United States proceeded to the political secularization of the sustaining religious ideals. It was customary to express themselves in a characteristic language, politically and religiously liberal, a language that itself revealed a way of living together without stridency and rupture, except with regard to the Indian world. We in Mexico, on the other hand, had to learn how to be liberal because we never had been. We had to break away courageously and painfully from a past that continued to live in each moment of our historical present. This meant, and still means, a life full of anxiety, a constant uneasiness, a permanent revolution of the spirit.

Through painful trials and efforts we have almost managed to adapt the democratic mother and her liberal son to our historical breadth, but past and present difficulties are brought out in the open when we see the crises that yesterday shook and even today shake our Ibero-American republics and, of course, Spain. We adopted certain political principles without having "Protestantized" ourselves enough to make them viable. Our paternalistic backslides are clearly pointing out to us the shaky ground on which our precarious and oscillating democracies sit. Mexico spent the entire past century (and is spending a good part of the present one) bitterly arguing and fighting; our political battles are proof of our psychic imbalance and, therefore, of our political, economic, and social imbalance. The price that has been paid, and continues to be paid, is very high, but it was and is the necessary price to pay for a liberal outfit made to our exact size; to our sartorial political elegance!

The result of this almost illogical constitutional imitation is the fact that in Mexico, even today, our Magna Carta of 1917 and the laws that emanate from it do not present the unquestionable congruence that exists between North American political and juridical life and the written law and its practical application. Lorenzo Meyer puts it this way:

> In Mexico . . . we have lived with two Constitutions for a while: a written one to which homage is paid but which is not obeyed, and an unwritten one, which is criticized in the name of the first but which is difficult and dangerous to ignore. Both are in a constant state of war. The first one is inspired by the liberal, democratic, and republican constitutions of the United States and France, among others. The other originates from our ancient paternalistic and authoritarian practice. When the principles of the two enter into conflict—which is frequently—it is the written Constitution that loses. Almost all of us know this, and thus the high degree

of obedience to the unwritten principles, whose roots are possibly pre-Hispanic but undoubtedly colonial. There are, unfortunately, many examples. Who among us does not know that the Constitution of 1917 establishes the division of powers a la Montesquieu? But who ignores the fact that the real Constitution orders the concentration of all powers in the hands of the president?[3]

It is, therefore, not at all strange that in light of so many failures and disillusionments Mexicans have acquired an inferiority complex before the sweeping success in all areas of the North American model, whereas North Americans have acquired for the same reason an arrogant superiority complex concerning the Mexicans.

NOTES

This article was translated by Raquel Elizondo and Robert O'Connor.

1. Christopher Morris, *The Tudors* (London: Fontana Library, 1967), p. 86.

2. Edmund O'Gorman, *La invención de America* (Mexico City: Fondo de Cultura Economica, 1958), pp. 70–99.

3. Lorenzo Meyer, "Las dos constituciones," *Excelsior*, December 27, 1984.

WILLIAM H. GOETZMANN

Keep the White Lights Shining

"TEXIANS" they called themselves. On the sixth day of creation God
spoke of them clearly: "Let us make mankind in our image and like-
ness; and let them have dominion over the fish of the sea, the birds of
the air, the cattle, over all the wild animals and every creature that
crawls on the earth. . . . Be fruitful and multiply; fill the earth and
subdue it" (Genesis 1:26, 28).

White-skinned, suntanned, rednecked Texans have been following this injunction ever since they became aware that to be Texan was
to be a member of that special tribe of humanity mentioned so prominently just at the very beginning of the Holy Book. The Good Book,
which figured so importantly in the reading of nineteenth-century
Americans, enjoined them to "*have dominion*," to "be fruitful and multiply," to "fill the earth *and subdue it*" (emphasis added). It placed no
limits on them, though in a later chapter of Genesis the Lord did add,
"Cursed be the ground because of you; in toil shall you eat of it all the
days of your life. . . . In the sweat of your brow you shall eat bread, till
you return to the ground, since out of it you were taken; for dust you
are and unto dust you shall return."

As a tribe, the Texians came stark and strong and self-righteously
straight out of a history that to them reached back unambiguously to
humanity's beginnings. They followed the Lord's way as they came into
a land so vast that it might as well have been the whole creation, a land
so hard that even Adam might have been discouraged, and yet a land so
rich that it brought forth the mark of Cain on all who beheld their conspicuous successes with envy. The Texians saw themselves as the heroes of their own special saga; the "Lord could take them, but he could
not take them lightly."[1]

They emerged out of Moses Austin's dream—the vanguard of Manifest Destiny—and they reached the apotheosis of their saga early, at the Alamo and Goliad and San Jacinto. This made the Texian myth, or tale of the tribe, seem distinctive, though it actually conformed to the classic patterns of myth everywhere in the world.[2] Their story, too, began with epic heroes. It also incorporated actual historical events out of which all myths are created so that the bards, the saga writers, and even the historians could make the tales of their adventures as a people plausible enough to engender continuous belief in each chapter of what became a fabulous and sometimes inspiring story.

The overarching theme of the Texian story, however, goes back to those biblical injunctions. Texians, or Anglo-Texans, as we now call them, have always felt it was not only their right but their duty to subdue the land and all God's creatures, including the Indian, whom they often regarded as another species, and the Mexican, who had read the wrong book and hence taken the wrong path into the darkness of idolatry and hedonism so characteristic of Abel's brother, Cain. Thus that familiar cry, "Remember the Alamo," carries a grievous weight of mixed meanings—of deeds to be proud of and deeds to be not so proud of.

Nonetheless, there it stands in the middle of bustling downtown San Antonio—the Alamo—a shrine to heroes' martyrdom with a stained-glass window and plaques on its walls dedicated to those who shall remain immortal. Visitors file through, hushed, silent, reverent. Westminster Abbey and Napoleon's Tomb yield nothing to the Alamo in the way of reverential atmosphere. It should best be viewed by moonlight with a single distant star clearly visible in the sky overhead. The beginning of the Texian saga clearly constitutes in the minds of Anglo-Texans a religious event. Any talk of the deserter Moses Rose and the "back door," of Travis trying to buy his life from sympathetic Mexican privates, or Davy Crockett captured alive, spoils the holiness.[3] And if the holiness is spoiled then so too is the heroic quality of the Texian saga—the myth that constitutes the tale of our tribe.

I use the words "*our* tribe" here on purpose because there is no way to describe the Anglo-Texas myth from the outside. Beyond the tribe it becomes diffuse, absurd, preposterous, as Don Graham makes evident in his recent survey of Hollywood's Texas.[4] Gene Autry and the Lone Ranger and the "William Tell Overture" do not get it. Similarly, what outsider could grasp the true significance, the infinitely refined nuances for Texans, of the Light Crust Doughboys' memorable refrain, "Pass the Biscuits, Pappy"? The Texian saga is encapsulated in a different language of meaning from that of the world outside. We may never know its true dimensions or subtle depths, but as Mark Twain might say, "Keep a firm hold on the Good Book." It remains the key.

But again there stands the Alamo (an abandoned Spanish mission appropriated by the Texians), a Hispanic building in the middle of a Hispanic town. And so the Anglo-Texas myth necessarily involves, begins with, a relationship to the Hispanic culture. The presence of a Spanish culture in Texas, in fact, made it easier for the Texians to define themselves by contrast. Despite the signing of legal documents and protestations of allegiance to Mexico, the Texians knew what they were not—Mexicans. Notice some of the outstanding contrasts in the minds of Anglo-Texans. Texians were not Catholic; they were Christians (that is, Protestants). Texians were not autocratic; they were republican and democratic—never mind their slaves. Texians were not lazy or shiftless; they subscribed to the Protestant work ethic as set forth in the Good Book, Genesis 3:17. Texians were not racially "mongrelized" half-Indian, half-blackamoor Spanish "breeds"; they were simon-pure bred, maybe even of good English *Mayflower* stock (or at least in a line from the D.A.R. to the D.R.T.). In the way of bloodlines, they were certainly dubious about the "Dutchmen" and the "Frenchies" (the remnants of Jean Laffite's "rabble") and the Irish, but not about the Scotch-Irish, which of course a good many of them were. This last stock was all right because of course that made them relatives of Daniel Boone. But to check myth against reality, pause and read the plaques around the Alamo. Hispanics were there, too.

In fact, a good many aspects of Hispanic culture actually appealed to the Texians. Thus endemic to the Texian myth is a love-hate relationship with the Spanish people. To cite a few examples, the Texian admired the life on "the big hacienda," with thousands of cattle and hard-riding *vaqueros* to round them up. Jim Bowie married into one of these "big hacienda" families and resigned himself to being a "big hidalgo"—a success in spite of himself. It was one of the better laidback ways to have "dominion" and "subdue the earth." Basically, the Texian just didn't like *poor* Mexicans because they reminded him of his own precarious economic status. Anglo-Texans adopted the Spanish longhorn as their own—in fact, wished to "adopt" as many as possible. They also thrived on the food, the fandangos, three-card monte, guitars in the moonlight, *vaquero*-cowboying, the violent macho lifestyle, and especially the Spanish sense of pride. Love and hate made the Texian myth complex from the beginning.

It was especially paradoxical because, despite the cultural symbiosis described above, the Anglo-Texans ignored the Spaniards and the Indians and saw themselves as pioneers in a whole new land. They were the descendants of Daniel Boone and, if they could read, true sons of Leatherstocking coming into a big new country. Even the Germans under Prince Solms von Braunfels and Hermann Meusebach, dazzled by Cooper's novels, saw themselves as Leatherstockings. But they read a bit more carefully and, like Leatherstocking, tried to consider the Central Texas Indians as "*der Freund.*"[5] To them, the rapacious and wily Scotch-Irish land brokers were the enemy. But despite their true Anglo-Saxon origins, it was sometimes difficult for the "Dutchmen" to get themselves remembered as Anglo-Texans. Even Captain Seth Eastman, a leading army ethnographer of the day, saw no irony in labeling a drawing in his sketchbook, "Dutch House in Fredericksburg."[6] The Anglo-Texan myth was not all-inclusive even when it came to Anglos. A Texian was something else.

All could agree, however, that Texas, whatever else it was, was a big country. It seemed infinite, even to the Spaniards, who never could chart it and thus get a whole picture of it. To President Mirabeau B. Lamar, Texas was so infinite that it included New Mexico, Arizona, and parts of California. The Pacific Ocean was its only limit. A visionary romantic, President Lamar was perhaps the first to conceptualize the idea of "the Sun Belt," which he called Texas.[7]

But the point is "bigness." Texas was the Big Country, and this sense of bigness has always figured prominently in Texian attitudes as well as in the tale of the tribe. A big country required big men, heroic men, mobile men, men on horseback to conquer and subdue it—to bring it to pasture. Texas in its infinity was a larger-than-human-scale landscape. It was, indeed, a land fit for giants. And every horseman that passed by, say on the six-hundred-mile journey from the state capital at Austin to far away El Paso del Norte, became a giant in Texas mythology. Space—the space that made possible immense cattle ranches—distance—the incredible distances that made the long cattle drive an epic second only to that of the Oregon Trail—these factors were still another very real foundation of the Texian saga. Clearly, it did take vision, courage, strength of will, and incredible organizational skills simply to deal with, let alone conquer, these immense distances and that almost infinite, but also desolate space that constitutes West Texas. Thus it should come as no surprise that "bigger is better" figures very largely in the mythology of Texas.

But consider the proposition even more closely. Big Country Texas also equated with Big Country America in contrast to Europe. Thus the Texians in their feats as conqueror of infinite spaces and distances were more American than, say, the agoraphobic stereotyped New Englander (ignoring, of course, the latter's adventures on the world's oceans). In this respect Texians must be, had to be, the most American of all. They didn't tend some little garden in a backyard in France, as Voltaire had advised; they tended a wilderness as big as all outdoors. And when they turned the wilderness into a garden of ten million bawling longhorns, and then into a virtual forest of oil derricks that made them immensely wealthy, the Texians, at least in their own eyes, became true, archetypal, all-American giants. "Bigger is better" is loaded with meaning for all Americans. It bespeaks a continental vision and the successful conquest of a whole continent, which ties directly into the Saga Americana as proclaimed by the historian Frederick Jackson Turner in his famous essay, "The Significance of the Frontier in American History." He, too, must have been reading the Good Book.

Let us not think that Texians in their wildest dreams thought of their immense land as a garden over which they could wax lyrical. Only latter-day folklorists and poets do that. Texians cursed and swore at the land and the frightful, unpredictable, but relentless weather. A quarter of a million square miles of unrelenting heat in the summer with only scrub oaks and mesquite and dry washes for shade described a West Texas "spread" as well as anything. And then it was the wind and the dust and the wintry freeze brought by winds blown down from Canada, almost a whole continent away. Texas was a hard land and every Texian with any sense knew it. This only made the conquest seem more heroic and heightened the legend of the land of giants. And we well remember those giants: Captain Richard King, Jesse Chisholm, Charles Goodnight, even the wily Shanghai Pierce. But the lesser-known Texian pioneers figure in the saga as well. It includes the story of hard times, of poverty, loneliness, natural disasters, crop failures, cruelties beyond belief, bigotry, class conflict, desperation that led to banditry, and a struggle for civil order if not simple decency.

Listen to Benjamin Peck writing from Gonzales, Texas, to his mother in Bristol, Rhode Island, in November of 1841: "We had no rain for more than three months so you can judge by that how hard times are. . . . This is the hardest country in the world for a young man to get along in."[8] N. B. Gordon writes to General William B. Morton in Tennessee, February 3, 1842: "Mobocracy has the say over most of the country . . . murders are as common as natural death in Tennessee. You must not think this is an exaggeration, for there have been more than sixty murders within my hearing since the first day of last October."[9]

Bird Holland in San Augustine confirmed this impression of lawless violence: "This Red-land is the dambest [sic], meanest area that any White Man ever lived in, though it corroborates with the people—they are fighting, stealing, scrigling and every other kind of a thing that is mean . . . last week a man was shot dead in his own yard by *Mr. Nobody.*"[10]

By 1868 things hadn't changed much. The Honorable C. Coldwell received this anxious note: "It seems to me . . . that we will all have either to join the Ku Klux Democracy or leave the country—to be a loyal conservative man is simply to be an object of scorn and contempt and liable at any moment to be assassinated."[11]

Reconstruction Texas was rife with political chicanery and violence, as the anxious note indicates. But political chicanery came to be a characteristic of the Texian saga—as did the violence, from John Wesley Hardin to Bonnie and Clyde and J. Frank Norris, the Fort Worth preacher who, while standing in his own parsonage, shot his mistress's husband in cold blood when the cuckold blundered in to protest the affair at an inopportune moment.

Maggie Bookman offered a series of sad explanations for the causes of crime in the Lone Star State. She wrote in 1880, "We are the 'hardest run' folks you ever saw and live in a little one room log house. . . . It looks as if I am to be buried alive, don't it?" In 1883 she managed to survive an epidemic of typhoid fever, and in 1886 a hurricane wiped out her sister's farm and destroyed her crops. By that time her brother and brother-in-law had become fugitives from the law.[12]

And Miss Kitty King of Fort Worth put her finger on one of the chief anxieties of the Texian woman: "I am not married yet and no prospects for it for I should be afraid to select a man in Texas to marry unless I had known all about him before he came here, for I should be sure that he had done something and been run off."[13] G.T.T. (Gone to Texas) in time became part of Texas folk humor, but it had a meaning as real in mid-nineteenth-century Texas as Joseph Glover Baldwin's Simon Suggs's slogan, "It's good to be shifty in a new country," had for the flush times in Alabama and Mississippi of an earlier era.[14]

With good historical cause the outlaw-desperado and his nemesis, the Texas Ranger, became integral parts of the Texian saga. Though the Texas Rangers—led by legendary figures like "Bigfoot" Wallace, John Coffee Hays, John Salmon, and "Rip" Ford—maintained whatever order there was on the far-flung Texas frontier, to the Comanches and the Mexicans they represented bloodthirsty terrorists. And yet the Rangers' self-proclaimed image combined the broadest elements of Texas culture in an unabashed salute to their enemies. The Ranger, they declared, could "ride like a Mexican, track like a Comanche, shoot like a Kentuckian and fight like the devil." As self-made legends, they placed themselves at the very center of Texian mythology.[15]

Real law and order came hard to Texas because of its size and because life was so hard in the hard land. Both Ranger and outlaw became folk heroes blown up into cosmic proportions by Hollywood. Only recently have the tribulations and quiet desperation of the common folk become interesting to moviemakers, but the quiet struggle of the common folk runs like an underground river beneath the surface of the Texas mystique. It is a chief source of pride to Texans whether Anglo or not. In William Faulkner's terms, they have "endured and prevailed"—with dignity intact. They have outlasted and outfought the Big Country.

Still another element in the Texian saga is the prominence of the political arena. Sam Houston himself was involved in fights over the location of the state capital that included the theft of the state records in the "Archives War"; there were mudslinging campaigns between Anson Jones and Sam Houston, the likes of which never happened to George Washington, the father of *his* country; there was the perceived duplicity of post–Civil War carpetbag government; and there was the onset of the big interests, led by railroad magnates like Jay Gould. These dramas continually thrust the Texas politician into the limelight. For many Texans, politics became the biggest "game" in the Big Country. An almost unique admiration for bombast, rodomontade, and outright trickery among political leaders became a major part of Texas mythology. The wheeler-dealer, the Bet-A-Million Gates figure, had stepped prominently into the ongoing myth. In Texas, whether honest or dishonest, the Texas myth demanded that politicians be colorful and, above all, entertaining.

Perhaps this in part explains the sudden success of "the Farmer's Alliance," or Populists, who in 1877 in a cabin in Pleasant Valley, Lampasas County, formed a successful third-party movement. Among the first things the farmers of the alliance did was to appoint a first-class rouser—a professional stump speaker, one S. O. Daws, whom they called a "Traveling Lecturer."[16] Armed with platform eloquence, which grew as the rank and file increased, the alliance made Texas politics into a morality play that reached the minds and hearts of the rural, white, Anglo-Saxon Protestant who had endured and continued to endure the hard times described in the letters quoted above. Furthermore, Populism touched that basic chord of biblical fundamentalism that had generated the Texas myth in the first place. It also solidified a sense of Texan regional identity as railroad monopolies, distant grain and livestock markets, and banking trusts—all of which threatened to wrest control from those who had made Texas what it was—began to impinge upon Texas. Thus emerged in the Texas saga a new figure, in his time heroic, but now fallen into disrepute in some circles—the redneck. This yeoman hero, often projected as bigoted and narrow-minded, has never really faded from Texas mythology. Though the Populist party itself folded, the yeomen followed William Jennings Bryan into the Democratic party and still remain its backbone and strength in Texas.

And through the years the Texas yeomanry has not been without colorful figures who have added greatly to the larger-than-life Texas saga. Consider, for example, Ma and Pa Ferguson. Governor Pa, ever the friend of the people, opposed the Ku Klux Klan, the prohibitionists, and the University of Texas. He preferred the comradery of the inmates of Huntsville State Prison, where he often dined and swapped tall tales. All he got for his democratic yearnings, however, was impeachment. But then he ran Ma for governor and with the support of "the boys at the forks of the creeks," that is, the yeomen, Miriam "Ma" Ferguson became the first elected woman governor in the United States. A stylish lady who admired Will Rogers and was interested in Hollywood, she added female glamour to the Texas saga in a more substantial way than the celebrated New York speakeasy hostess Texas Guinan and the notorious outlaw Bonnie Parker ever could, though in a strange way they all reinforced a self-image of strong Texas womanhood—mythologically speaking. If the Texas saga had begun with Adam and was largely based on a male mythology, Eve had definitely arrived—to stay and round out the picture.

Actually she had never been far from the center of Texas mythology, for it was she, as the rugged, enduring pioneer woman, who symbolized the Anglo-Texan's conquest of the Big Country. As her hard-times letters indicate, however, she did not necessarily end the struggle for law and order in Texas. That is still going on.

But the struggle for law and order, comparatively speaking, has always been for Texans at base a minor inconvenience and at most a kind of chivalric game that took one back to the border ballads of Walter Scott. The real strength of the Texas myth can be found in two fundamental and related emotions. The first is optimism. Texas was always a wide-open land of opportunity, according to the true believers and the mythmakers. Listen again to "hard times" Benjamin Peck in 1841: "But I tell you it's a great country for a man who has a family and a little money . . . ," and, he adds wistfully, "girls are prettier here than in any part of Texas." [17] Likewise Miss Kitty King writes in the 1860s, "Don't think that I am running the country down for I do think when this country gets cleared out that it will be *one of the greatest countrys* [sic] *in the world*." [18]

Even more important to the Texan than this ongoing historical optimism has been a belief in the "unfinished saga." The story of Texas is not finished, never has had a stopping place. It was and is a saga still in progress. The official governmental frontier may have ended in 1890, but by then Texas had only just begun. Spindletop was just a decade's conversation away. Today, more than ever, as large parts of the country pass into "postindustrial" maturity, if not senility, and as large numbers of its leaders contract a fashionable "postmodern," "burnout" malaise, Texas retains the vision of infinite possibilities. Never mind the naysayers who nag about the lack of water, the depletion of oil reserves, the rising problems of urban life as it invades the rural bliss of the Lone Star State, or even the increasing clashes of races, cultures, and values. Anglo-Texans firmly believe that these, too, are only temporary inconveniences mainly exploited by politicians as their part of "the Big Game." These temporary problems will be overcome just like everything else that was hard in the past. The real secret is that Anglo-Texans—Texians, if you will—still believe in Manifest Destiny.

If in Genesis 3 they, along with Adam and Eve, had been cast out of Eden to a hard fate in a hard land, still, in the words of John Milton's *Paradise Lost*, for the Anglo-Texans, "the world was [is] all before them." And all is right and bright and mythologically on track in that world as long as "Billy Bob's Texas, the World's Largest Honky Tonk" keeps the bright lights shining, the cowboys are still riding real Brahma bulls, and Willie is out there somewhere "On the Road Again." These are things—fantastic dreams—that Texans, still caught up in the megalomaniacal myth of Manifest Destiny, do not take lightly.

NOTES

1. This is a variant of the preacher's funeral sermon in Sam Peckinpah's *The Ballad of Cable Hogue*.

2. Conventionally, the term "Texian" has been used to denote a citizen of the Texas Republic. In this essay, I have broadened the meaning to signify those Anglo-Texans who considered themselves members of a special tribe that self-consciously shared a common myth throughout Texas history.

3. Kilgore, *How Did Davy Die?* (College Station: Texas A&M University Press, 1978).

4. Don Graham, *Cowboys and Cadillacs: How Hollywood Looks at Texas* (Austin: Texas Monthly Press, 1983).

5. For German attitudes toward the Indian, see Ray Allen Billington, *Land of Savagery, Land of Promise: The European Image of the American Frontier in the Nineteenth Century* (New York: W. W. Norton Co., 1981); and Terry Jordan, *German Seed in Texas Soil* (Austin: University of Texas Press, 1966).

6. Lois Burkhalter, ed., *A Seth Eastman Sketchbook, 1848–1849* (Austin: University of Texas Press, 1971).

7. Walter Prescott Webb, ed., *The Handbook of Texas*, 3 vols. (Austin: Texas State Historical Association, 1952, 1956), 2:14.

8. David Holman, ed., *Letters of Hard Times in Texas, 1840–1890* (Austin: Roger Beachum Publisher, 1974), p. 7.

9. Ibid., p. 9.

10. Ibid., p. 13.

11. Ibid., pp. 37–38.

12. Ibid., pp. 44–52.

13. Ibid., pp. 55–56.

14. Joseph Glover Baldwin, *Flush Times of Alabama and Mississippi* (New York: Sagamore Press, 1957).

15. David Nevin, *The Texans* (Alexandria, Va.: Time Life Books, 1975), pp. 212–13.

16. Lawrence Goodwyn, *The Democratic Promise: The Populist Moment in America* (New York: Oxford University Press, 1976), p. 36.

17. Holman, *Letters*, pp. 8–9.

18. Ibid., p. 56.

STERLING STUCKEY

Afro-American Formative Myths

A pervasive myth in the sections of Africa from which blacks were taken to North America is that a proper burial is essential if the spirit of the deceased is to be at rest and bad luck is not to befall surviving relatives. Ceremonies designed to put the spirit at rest and to establish a creative relationship with it form the most vital body of art to come out of American slavery, an art that is the foundation of black sacred and secular art today. Indeed, a proper study of slave art reveals the degree to which myth has inspired slaves to create a variety of art forms that are inextricably tied to religion and essential to understanding slave reality. In great measure, myth as employed by slaves has been the principal mirror of their reality.

Both the Atlantic and domestic slave trades were responsible for the renewal and spread in America of cultural forms that were sovereign in Congo-Angola, the Gold Coast, and in the area of the old Mali empire in West Africa—all centers of reverence for the ancestors and regions from which blacks were captured for purposes of enslavement in North America. Congo-Angola and Gold Coast blacks, who made up nearly 60 percent of Africans arriving in North America, often expressed reverence for the ancestors in a ring ceremony that may well have been the principal means by which Africans in America discovered oneness as a people. It should be noted that Texas was a depot where Africans from those regions were found, one from which some were shipped to markets in Florida, Louisiana, and elsewhere in the Old South. The domestic trade, of course, worked mainly the other way, with slaves being moved from the Southeast to areas west, including Texas. In any case, African cultural reinforcement—unsuspected by the masters—occurred as a result of that movement of slaves.

Texas masters, like those across the South, had at best a surface understanding of blacks, which is understandable, given their prejudices regarding African inferiority and "savagery." It was a measure, therefore, of the Africans' political and artistic genius that they were able to express deeply held African values without those values, in any real sense, being understood or even recognized by the master class. The clash of opposing values between whites and blacks, therefore, was much greater than imagined by the master class, and far greater than historians of slavery have heretofore imagined.

I

Among the oldest and most important tales of the middle passage is "The King Buzzard." It consists of two parts, the first symbolic, the second an artistic working out of its meaning. Told by Thaddeus Goodson (Tad in the collections of E. C. L. Adams), "The King Buzzard," like scores of tales Adams collected, contains the interplay of storytellers whose voices, impossible to capture adequately on paper, add dramatic tension to the tale. "The dialect is of course English shot through and influenced by the traditions and sentiments of the African slaves." In that dialect, "there is a marked influence of the African sense of melody and rhythm. . . . Sometimes a word that is pronounced correctly has several dialect meanings, and several sounds of the same word may be found in a single sentence."[1]

This language is heard at night around a campfire as storytellers await Tad's return from a swamp in which eerie noises are made and animals roam. Flames command shadows to dance as Tad approaches the fire, "wet and covered with yellow mud." He then enacts an encounter he has just had with a huge buzzard: "An' he spread he whing out an' say, 'Uuh!' He eye been red an' he de nastiest lookin' thing I ever see. He stink in my nostrils. He so stink, he stink to my eye an' my year." In terror, he dodged as the buzzard flew around him in the moonlight and "spewed he vomick every which er way, an' I see de leaf an' de grass wuh it fall on an' dry up. All de air seem like it were pizen." As the buzzard got nearer to him, Tad somehow crawled in a canebrake and was there "for God knows how long, an' when I find myself," he notes with irony, "I been lost."[2]

The buzzard represented something more dreadful than he realized. It was not a buzzard that had been encountered; rather, it was the spirit of a traitor, which had taken the form of a buzzard. Tom joined in the telling of the tale and said he "hear 'bout dat ole thing 'fore 'dis," that his "pa" told him "dat way back in slavery time—'way back in Africa"—there was "a nigger," "a big nigger" who as chief of his tribe tricked his people into slavery, betraying thousands. The chief had to entice them onto the boat "into trap" so that "dem White folks could ketch 'em an' chain 'em." On their last trip—they were not to return to that location—"dey knocked dat nigger down an' put chain on him an' bring him to dis country."

> An' when he dead, dere were no place in heaven for him an' he were not desired in hell. An' de Great Master decide dat he were lower dan all other mens or beasts; he punishment were to wander for eternal time over de face er de earth. Dat as he had kilt de sperrits of mens an' womens as well as dere bodies, he must wander on an' on. Dat his sperrit should always travel in de form of a great buzzard, an' dat carrion must be he food. . . . An' dey say he are known to all de sperrit world as de King Buzzard, an' dat forever he must travel alone.

Those who transmuted the horror of the trade into myth knew a life superior to anything encountered in slavery. This superiority is suggested by the repudiation of the traitor, who enters upon an endless journey of spiritual unrest, a punishment markedly African. Moreover, the tale is replete with suggestions of the Africans' resistance to enslavement. They must be tricked into manacles; even the chief who betrayed his own into bondage resisted being enslaved and had to be knocked down and subdued. In that resistance is the self-generative nature of the Africans' impulse toward freedom.

The importance of spirituality to the African—"Dat as he had kilt the sperrits of mens an' womens as well as dere bodies"—should not be undervalued. The notion of the spirit's being killed, of no life of any kind, suggests the heinous nature of the chief's crime against his people. Thus, spiritual unrest through time and a form of hell, after his enslavement and sharing in the common lot, is his punishment.

But the categories of heaven and hell do not suggest, as it first appears, the distance of the storyteller from the original African chroniclers of the event, do not reflect New World influence on any deep level, but African influence instead. Indeed, endless wandering and restlessness are at the heart of a tale told in almost every particular from an African point of view, yet a tale that stands as a metaphor for treachery wherever performed at any time in history. So universal is concern for the fate of the spirit in Africa that the restlessness of "The King Buzzard" would have been understood by Africans on the plantations of the South, in the North, and elsewhere in the Americas.[3] All the more in the case of a chief who turns on his own, for the socially prominent in West Africa receive, except in special cases, a lavish funeral to ensure harmony between them and those to whom they were responsible on earth. The chief's betrayal of his people by the chief removed the obligation of any funeral observance whatever. Consequently, his spirit is restless for that reason and more.

Features of "The King Buzzard" appear to be especially of Ibo influence, which suggests the experience recounted occurred in Eastern Nigeria during the slave trade:

> All Ibo place great faith in the due and proper observance of the funeral ceremony, for they are of opinion that it enables the soul to go to God, and to its final destination, and without this sacred rite the soul is prevented by other spirits from eating, or in any way associating with them, and, in this manner, from entering into the Creator's presence. So in this way it becomes an outcast and a wanderer on the face of the earth.[4]

According to the Ibos, the spirit of the deceased returns to this world in the form of an animal if, before death, the deceased murdered one or more human beings. If the return of the spirit in the form of an animal is widespread in West African religions, its return as a buzzard as a consequence of crimes committed, specifically referred to by Ibos, does not appear to be. Moreover, the Ibo principle of some spirits not being able to enter the presence of the Creator is the Ibo equivalent of the Christian hell. When one adds the denial of food to the spirit (the King Buzzard ate carrion) and the Ibo reference to God as "the great Spirit" (or the "Great Master"), this strongly suggests that "The King Buzzard" is an Ibo tale in which other Africans in America, especially the Yoruba, found sufficient features of their own faith to embrace it as theirs as well. Many West Africans also understood that the wandering of the soul "forever" meant it would not return to the town in Africa native to the deceased and there relate to the souls of those, including relatives, known during life—a possible source of discouragement for potential collaborators in the slave community.[5] The purgatory in "The King Buzzard" called to mind sovereign precepts of West African religious life and fostered unity of blacks along spiritual and political lines in communities in which the tale was told.

"The King Buzzard" experience occurred prior to the nineteenth century, for one of the storytellers says his father referred to "dat ole thing" occurring "'way back in slavery time—'way back in Africa." Since the tale was alive over generations in South Carolina, and in those regions to which South Carolina slaves were taken via the domestic slave trade, the character of black life there with its movement away from ethnic allegiance was perhaps responsible for no explicit mention of a specific tribe in the tale, the condemnation of the traitor relating concretely to all Africans suffering the humiliation and degradation of the slave trade and slavery. The application of Ibo mythology, largely shared by Yorubas, to the experience of captivity and enslavement was of itself an act of transcendence, since that experience was given the shape of art. The most powerful tool of enlightenment in the slave community, "The King Buzzard" not surprisingly contains only esoteric indications of ethnicity. Though African ethnic groups constituted a powerful presence in America at the time of the creation of the tale, African ethnicity as such was losing much of its relevance beyond revealing what was commonly understood across ethnic lines, all else serving to divide rather than unite Africans in the slave community.[6]

When old men sat around the fire and recalled the past, they called to mind the most meaningful values of their fathers and related them to the new reality as they faced each other in ensemble. Such an ensemble provided grounds for the assumption of a particular role by others in the dialogue on the illness, infirmity, or death of a participant. All the while reinforcing the community's sense of Africanism, Tad had heard Joe's response, and Joe Tad's question, on innumerable occasions over a period of decades. Following the same pattern, he asked him in the twentieth century,

> Tad: Joe 'fore you come here wey did you originate—wey was you' home?

and was answered,

> Joe: I come from Af'ca.

An old man, Joe was tricked into slavery as a youth and brought to America from an area that was to exert a powerful influence on the culture of the slave:

> When I been a boy, a big vessel come nigh to my home. An' it had white folks on it an' dey hab all kind er bead an' calico an' red flannel, an' all kind er fancy thing. An' dem white folks gee a heap er thing to de people er my tribe an' entice 'em on de boat. An' dey treat 'em so good for two or three days, till atter while de people ain't been scared. . . . An' one day dey hab de boat crowd wid mens an' womens an' chillun, an' when dey find dey self, de boat was 'way out to sea.[7]

The Africans understood, in a flash, that they were being carried out of the land of their birth to an unknown destination. Even though they were, from what Joe tells us, in this instance ethnically homogeneous, the conditions described help explain why more heterogeneous African populations made less rigid drawings of lines of ethnicity during forced movement from one world to another.

"Gullah Joe" covers the trade from capture on the Coast to enslavement in the New World and contains insights into conditions in America and in the ancestral home. It provides additional evidence that Africans had a way of life they preferred to slavery on North American plantations. Joe betrays, through the group designation he assigns to blacks, a considerable degree of acculturation or adaptation to his environment in the United States, for the old African refers to "some er dem niggers" jumping off the boat and drowning. Then follows the section that even more effectively symbolizes the Africans' desire to maintain freedom from captivity: the European "overpowered dem what was on de boat, an' th'owed 'em down in de bottom er de ship. An' dey put chain on 'em."

Almost from the start, Joe notes, among others, the new (for him) factor of color:

> Dey been pack in dere wuss dan hog in a car when dey shippin' 'em. An' every day dem white folks would come in dere an' ef a nigger jest twist his self or move, dey's cut de hide off him wid a rawhide whip. An' niggers died in de bottom er dat ship wuss dan hogs wid cholera. Dem white folks ain' hab no mercy. Look like dey ain' know wha' mercy mean. Dey drag dem dead niggers out an' throw 'em overboard. An' dat ain' all. Dey th'owed a heap er live ones wha' dey thought ain' guh live into de sea.

The tension of loyalty to tribe and loyalty to the community of blacks in South Carolina evokes a question:

Tad: Is you satisfy?

Joe: It seems to me I would be satisfied if I jes could see my tribe one more time. Den I would be willin' to come back here. . . . I is a old man now but I has a longin' to walk in de feenda. I wants to see it one more time, I has a wife an' children here, but when I thinks er my tribe an' my friend an' my daddy an' my mammy an' de great feenda, a feelin' rises up in my th'oat an' my eye well up wid tear.

A conception of freedom, reflected in the recoil from enslavement and the longing to see his tribe "one more time," is evident in "Gullah Joe." The spiritual pain of enslavement is polarized longing for one's tribe and attachment to new relations in the American environment. The word *feenda*, Bakongo for "forest," suggests the place of origin of the old man and is one of the few instances, linguistically, in which the folktale contains an African word that reveals origins—the presence of Africans from Congo-Angola on that slave ship. Africans from Congo-Angola, perhaps more than any others, determined the extent to which regard for the ancestors would be expressed in ring ceremonies, for more of their religious vision is expressed in Afro-American ceremonies than that of any other African ethnic group in America.[8]

Though "The Slave Barn" contains no apparent trace of ethnicity, African ethnicity is an influence in it. And though it is possible the Africans described in the poem—recited by a storyteller—were recent arrivals in America, it is not likely. The evidence suggests that the poem is based on experiences long observed, that it is deeply ethnic yet universal in African meaning—almost of necessity that way, owing to the special nature of American slavery and to the requirements of collective survival and eventual liberation. All who experienced or might experience the barn, irrespective of ethnicity, would find meaning in it. The opening stanza, through stark imagery, conveys the cold harshness of life in the New World:

> See dis barn here
> Wid its iron window,
> Its walls er brick?

The second expresses a sense of nationhood in slavery and life in Africa at its worst superior to domination by the white man:

> Here wey de wail an' moan
> Of Af'ica sound
> Wuss dan de cry

Of Af'ica chillun
When dey bone been crack
By de lion' jaw.

The pain of "niggers" was the pain of Africans, their religion utterly disregarded at the end of the process of slave trading:

Here wey de last
Er de slave-trader
Sing a song of misery
To a nigger in pain.

Here wey man an' he woman
Is parted forever,
An' a prayer was answered
Wid de song of a whip.[9]

At times resistance was fierce and roused feelings of oneness, especially when the fight was to keep one's child. That act was not lost on slave or master when separation occurred. The effort to prevent separation helped to preserve the humanity of Africans who witnessed or heard of it, even as they were entering familial relations in important ways different from what they had known and for reasons beyond their control. Resistance in that context could mean death:

Here wey de brains
Of a baby wid fever
Stain de walls,
Kaze a ooman for sale
Shed tears an' fought
For de chile dat she love.

The indictment of slavery in the poem is so severe that one can conclude that this work was not for the ear of the master. Not only is there rejection of slavery out of a continuing impulse toward freedom, but there is consideration of the means by which slavery was perpetuated, a questioning of the society in which it was flourishing:

An' de trader live
To die in honor
Forgiven by de church,
Prayed for, held up,
He sins forgotten,
He name guin to a school—

To de young as a sample
Of virtue an' trute.

A dollar to a school
An' a dollar to a church
Would hang de poor nigger
Dat told dat tale.

But God's my witness,
An' de tale's no tale
But de trute.

The poem, which appears to be more recent than "The King Buz-zard," is probably of nineteenth-century vintage but is regulated spiritually by African values perhaps thousands of years old. There is an Ibo ethnic component in it, the clue to which is found in "Ole Man Rogan," in which judgment is pronounced for crimes of precisely the sort committed in "The Slave Barn." But the application of the tale to slaves regardless of ethnicity is confirmed by the language of the storyteller, who encompasses all Africans made to enter the domestic slave trade. A slaver, who "brings 'em here in drove . . . have 'em chained together," Ole Man Rogan "always buy ooman wid chillun, and ooman wid husband, and ain't nobody can buy from Ole Man Rogan mother and chile or man and ooman." Rogan's deeds leave men with their heads "bowed down in 'stress" and "chillun holdin' out dey arms cryin' for dey mother" and "tear runnin' down de face of er ooman when she weepin' for her chile." Tears evoke laughter in Rogan and so does distress: "You see him look at de womens and mens and chillun, and you see him laugh—laugh at de 'stress and de tears on Boggy Gut."[10]

The tale was also told after slavery, the storyteller returning to scenes of slavery like a Blues singer to a tragic song: "And you kin set on de edge of Boggy Gut and you'll see mens in chains bent over wid dey head in dey hands—de signs of 'stress." After dark, a baby can be heard crying "every which er way" and one can hear "a mother callin' for her chile in de dark night on Boggy Gut." At Boggy Gut, the scene of Ole Man Rogan's death, "he sperrit wander and wander from Boggy Gut to de river and wander 'cross de big swamps to Congaree. Whether it be God or whether it be devil, de sperrit of Ole Man Rogan ain't got no res'." The rejection of Ole Man Rogan by God and by the Devil recalls the King Buzzard, Rogan's purgatory being that of the Buzzard wandering restlessly through time.

II

The same storytellers told tales in which the ancestral circle was the dominant spiritual and artistic motif, the means by which Africans, whatever their ethnic differences, found values proper to them when divorced from their homeland by the slave trade and slavery. Consequently, listeners in the slave community previously unexposed to the ancestral circle, once exposed, knew its spiritual significance was profoundly related to values projected in "The King Buzzard," "Ole Man Rogan," and "The Slave Barn"—values pervasive in Central and West Africa. In short, those who told or listened to one set of tales also listened to and told others, all the common property of the community. Not one but a number of storytellers, therefore, held in their heads (as did those who listened with rapt attention) African cultural patterns that were dominant not simply in North America but in all of the Americas. When one bears in mind that slave folklore, of its very nature, was not created to be transcribed or even heard by whites, it seems clear that what was eventually transcribed compares unfavorably in quantity to that which died on the night air or continues to live, undetected by scholars, in the folk memory.[11]

What has survived of tales involving ring ceremonies, however, is of great and lasting value. The Herskovitses note the persistence of the ring ceremony among the descendants of Africans in Suriname, centuries removed from their ancestral home in the Gold Coast. Indeed, Suriname Bush Negroes retained some features of their heritage, including priestly functions, in almost pristine form. With drums speaking to and interpreting the messages of the dead, they dramatized spiritual attitudes through the language of dance, all the while moving in a counterclockwise direction.

Associated with the ring ceremony in Suriname is the Anansi trickster tale told to amuse the deceased during burial ceremonies. The Herskovitses report that in honoring the dead the Bush Negroes of Suriname appreciated the role of humor, not uncommonly turning to the dead to share amusing stories of tricksters: "Some Trickster proverbs were spoken to bear upon the shortcoming of the white man." One or two of the Bush Negroes then turned "to repeat to the dead what had been said, and there was great laughter."[12]

The father of the dead man assured the anthropologists that "the dead man liked it very much. For the dead, it appears, were especially susceptible to humor and to exceptional occasions." This susceptibility explains the prominence of trickster tales of Anansi, the spider, being used "to amuse the spirit" of the dead in Suriname.[13] But since tricksters, most notably the hare, pervade much of Black Africa, as does the ring ceremony honoring the ancestors, and since the trickster and the circle are associated not only in South America, where Africans were enslaved, but in North America as well, this evidence indicates wide association of the two in Black Africa and, consequently, among numerous African ethnic groups in North America. Such may have been the case, for what is more ironic than the continuing interplay of the living and the dead, and where a more appropriate setting for the trickster than in that spiritual context? Besides, the trickster's character, certainly that of Anansi and Br'er Rabbit, is not known to be significantly different from one region to another.

The most stunning illustration of the trickster's involvement in ancestral ceremonies is contained in "Bur Rabbit in Red Hill Churchyard," collected by Adams. In this tale Rabbit is trickster in ways never before associated with him except for the work of the great collector and storyteller William John Faulkner. He is keeper of the faith of the ancestors, mediator of their claims on the living, and supreme master of the forms of creativity. As presented in "Red Hill Churchyard," Br'er Rabbit gives new resonance to Faulkner's masterful presentations of him through Simon Brown, the former slave, as a man of God and opens new possibilities for understanding a figure in Afro-American folklore heretofore unappreciated for his religious functions.[14] In the Adams tale, ancient qualities of African culture, some of the most arcane kind, appear to yield new and original artistic forms within the circle of culture and are directly related to Anansi and Akan priests in the Suriname Bush. In "Bur Rabbit in Red Hill Churchyard," one finds African tradition and the future flowing from it, the ground of spiritual being and the product of its flowering.

The Red Hill ceremony seems, on its face, one of the many in which Br'er Rabbit uses his fiddle as a kind of magic wand—for example, to realize his will against the predators or in competition for the hand of a maiden. But what seems equally obvious, though inexplicable, is the degree of convergence of the world of the living and that of the dead as a function somehow, it seems, of nothing more than Br'er Rabbit's genius with his instrument. That a deeper meaning lies beneath the surface of the tale is suggested, even without a command of the African background, by slave folklore, which holds that all sorts of things, under the right conditions, are possible in the graveyard: headless horsemen race about, a rabbit is seen walking "on he hind legs wid a fiddle in he hands," and the sacred and the secular are one in moments of masterly iconography as the "buck and wing" is danced "on a tombstone." "It look lik' in de Christmas ef de moon is shinin' an' dere's snow on de ground, dat is de time when you sees all kind er sights." At such times, day appears to light up the night but the glow is from the moon and "every star in de element . . . geein light." The "diff'ence been it ain' look as natu'al." The real seems unreal, the unreal real as the story unfolds in the depths of winter in the South: "De ground was kiver all over wid snow, an' de palin's on de graveyard fence was cracklin; it been so cold. . . . An' I look an' listen . . . an' I seen a rabbit settin' on top of a grave playin' a fiddle, for God's sake."

The dance of the community of animals occurred: "All kind 'er little beasts been runnin' round, dancin'. . . . An' dere was wood rats an' squirels cuttin' capers wid dey fancy self, and diff'ent kind er birds an' owl. Even den ole Owl was sachayin' 'round look like dey was enjoyin' dey self."

Br'er Rabbit got up from his seat on the tombstone, stopped playing, and "put the fiddle under he arm an' step off de grave." Then he gave "some sort er sign to de little birds and beasts, an' dey form dey self into a circle 'round de grave." Within that setting, several forms of music were heard: "Well, I watch an' I see Bur Rabbit take he fiddle from under he arm an' start to fiddlin' some more, and he were doin' some fiddlin' out dere in dat snow. An' Bur Mockin' Bird jine him an' whistle a chune dat would er made de angels weep."

Probably a spiritual, the song whistled by Br'er Mockingbird is made sadder as Br'er Rabbit accompanies him on the violin, the ultimate instrument for conveying pathos. But sadness gives way to a certain joy as Br'er Rabbit, with all the subtlety of his imagination, leads Br'er Mockingbird as they prefigure a new form of music: "Dat mockin' bird an' dat rabbit—Lord, dey had chunes floatin' all 'round on de night air. Dey could stand a chune on end, grab it up an' throw it away an' ketch it an' bring it back an' hold it; an' make dem chunes sound like dey was strugglin' to get away one minute, an' de next dey sound like sump'n gittin' up close an' whisperin'." [15]

The music of Br'er Rabbit and Br'er Mockingbird resembles the improvisational, ironic flights of sound that characterize jazz, especially on 52nd Street in New York in the mid-twentieth century. The close relationship between the music in Red Hill churchyard and jazz finds further support in the behavior of Br'er Rabbit, whose style calls to mind Louis Armstrong's: "An' as I watch, I see Bur Rabbit lower he fiddle, wipe he face an' stick he han'k'ch'ef in he pocket, an' tak off he hat an' bow mighty nigh to de ground." That scene and the others recall the broader context of Louis Armstrong's musical environment in New Orleans, where the melding of jazz and sacred music in funeral ceremonies and African secret societies was important to the sustenance and definition of jazz. Further consideration of the tale reveals its irreducible foundation in Africa.

The Herskovitses' discussion in *Suriname Folklore* of the drum harks back to the Akans of the Gold Coast and enables us, by transferring the power of the drum to the fiddle, to understand the central mystery of the ritual, which at first glance seems inexplicable. The drums have a threefold power in the religious view of the Bush Negro. Of the first power, the Herskovitses write, "Tradition assigns to them the . . . power of summoning the gods and the spirits of the ancestors to appear." The storyteller tells us that after Br'er Rabbit stopped fiddling, wiped his face, and with the other animals bowed in a circle before the grave, "de snow on de grave crack an' rise up, an' de grave open an' I see Simon rise up out er dat grave. I see him an' he look jest as natu'al as he don 'fore dey bury him."

The second power of the drums of the Akans is that of "articulating the message of these supernatural beings when they arrive." A flesh and blood character capable of speech, rather than a disembodied spirit, appears as the ancestor in the tale. Consequently, the other characters are able to communicate directly with him, and he is greatly interested in them: "An' he [Simon] look satisfy, an' he look like he taken a great interest in Bur Rabbit an' de little beasts an' birds. An' he set down on de top of he own grave and carry on a long compersation wid all dem animals."

The third power of the drum is to send the spirits of the gods or ancestors "back to their habitats at the end of each ceremony": "But dat ain't all. Atter dey wored dey self out wid compersation, I see Bur Rabbit take he fiddle an' put it under he chin an' start to playin'. An' while I watch, I see Bur Rabbit step back on de grave an' Simon were gone."

The intensity of the dancing in the circle, to the music of Br'er Rabbit and Br'er Mockingbird, is great, as indicated by the perspiration of the performers, despite snow on the ground. From internal evidence alone, though there is a large body of external data to draw on as well, it is certain the dancers fairly whirled in counterclockwise movement and that to them dance was sacred, as in Suriname, where "one of the most important expressions of worship is dancing" and the dancers "face the drums and dance toward them, in recognition of the voice of the god within the instruments."[16] Only the facing of the drums and dancing toward them seems to have been absent from the ceremony in Red Hill churchyard and elsewhere in North America, for none of the descriptions of the ring shout (the name of the ceremony in North America) mentions dancers facing percussionists as a necessary aspect of ritual, especially since drums were normally not available to slaves.

Since the function of the drum in Suriname and the violin in South Carolina slavery is the same, on the evidence of the tale and the work of the Herskovitses, the temptation is great to conclude that South Carolina slaves, not having access to the drum, simply switched to the violin to express the threefold power. But a case can be made for another explanation of why slaves in South Carolina—and almost certainly elsewhere, as evidence indicates—used the violin on so sacred an occasion. The one-string violin was used in the Mali empire, and is used today among the Songhai of Upper Volta, which is within the boundaries of the old empire, to summon the ancestral spirits. Thus, new light is cast on "Bur Rabbit in Red Hill Churchyard," quite possibly revealing a vital Songhai component in the tale and among South Carolina slaves.[17]

The violin was widespread among the ethnic groups of the Mali empire in contrast to the banjo and guitar, which were used to accompany the griot's declamation or recitation of stories. Although in Upper Volta—and possibly elsewhere in West Africa—one had to be apprenticed to griots to learn the banjo or guitar, a nonprofessional could pick up and, after long practice, achieve mastery of the violin without being apprenticed. The violin was a democratic, as opposed to an aristocratic, instrument for the Songhai, which, together with its use elsewhere in West Africa before and through the centuries of the slave trade, helps explain its widespread use by American slaves. In fact, the violin was the most important instrument of slave musicians North and South. It is small wonder that in "Bur Jonah's Goat," the storyteller says, "Ef you was to take dat fiddle 'way from him [Br'er Rabbit], he would perish 'way and die." [18]

Missionaries in Georgia attempted to take away the fiddle on the Hopeton plantation. Sir Charles Lyell, who visited the plantation in the 1840s, wrote of Methodists' efforts to rid slave culture of that instrument even though nothing raucous was associated with ceremonies in which it was played: "Of dancing and music negroes are passionately fond. On the Hopeton plantation above twenty violins have been silenced by the Methodist missionaries, yet it is notorious that the slaves were not given to drink or intemperance in their merry-makings." [19] Even with large numbers of children and the very old included, Hopeton had an astonishing average of more than one fiddler for every twenty slaves, in a population of five hundred. When the young and old are eliminated from the calculation, about one in every ten slaves played the fiddle, which makes it difficult to conceive of any ceremony, especially burial rites, in which at least one fiddle was not present. And since slaves from Upper Volta were represented on so large a plantation, there was probably a Songhai presence, with ancestral spirits and gods being called forth with the fiddle, as in Red Hill churchyard.

III

In Virginia and elsewhere, slaves helped each other in illness as in death. If a woman fell ill, Simon Brown tells us, "other women came over to help her with the chillen, or to cook the meals, wash the clothes or to do other necessary chores." Simon recalled medical and other practices that were African:

> It wasn't like it is today, when ever'body seem like they tryin' only to git the dollar. Women would come over jus to sit a spell an' sing an' pray 'roun' the sickbed. Nobody was lef' to suffer alone. Sometimes a man or woman with a healin' touch would brew a herb tea, mix a poultice, or apply peach tree leaves to the fevered brow, to help the sick git well. All of this lovin' care cheer' up the trouble' soul, whether he got well or died.[20]

When Sister Dicey died, the women washed and dressed her and laid her out in a homemade coffin resting on chairs. Slaves from all over came to sit, sing, and pray. "The singin' was mostly sad songs with happy endin's, 'cause the folks felt that now Aunt Dicey was freed from all the trials an' tribulations of slavery an' was safe in Heaben, at res' an' in peace forever more. She wouldn't be a bare-foot slave dress' in rags anymore." And so they sang,

> I got shoes
> You got shoes
> All God's chillen got shoes
> When I git to Heaben
> I'm a-goin' to put on my shoes an'
> Walk all over God's Heaben.
>
> I got a robe
> You got a robe
> All God's chillen got a robe
> When I git to Heaben
> I'm a-goin' to put on my robe an'
> Shout all over God's Heaben.

Some of the people "git so happy with this picture of Heaben that they burs' out cryin' an' shoutin' for joy. An' so the 'sittin' up' went on all night—some folks comin' an' goin' all the time." The African custom of "sittin' up" was accompanied by the singing of spirituals, the sadness-joy of the songs in Virginia similar to what was felt at the burial ceremony conducted by Br'er Rabbit in Red Hill churchyard in South Carolina, and by New Orleans' blacks in the nineteenth and twentieth centuries.[21]

The next morning, at the grave, the preacher offered words of comfort that finally led, as the tension mounted, to dance-growing-out-ofrejoicing and to resolution. According to Simon Brown, the preacher's voice carried softly, then with rising emphasis, as he sang the sermon:

> "Sister Dicey, since god in His mercy has taken your soul from earth to Heaben, an' out of your misery, I commit your body to the groun', earth to earth, ashes to ashes, dus' to dus', where it will res' in peace. But on that Great Gettin' Up Mornin', when the trumpet of God shall soun' to wake up all the dead, we will meet you in the sky an' join the host' of saints who will go marchin' in. Yes, we'll be in that number, Sister Dicey, when the saints go marchin' in." Before the preacher could finish his benediction, some of the women git so happy that they jus' drown' him out with they singin' an' han' clappin' an' shoutin'.

The variety and depth of African customs in the Virginia slave community of Simon Brown provide the background against which "they singin' an' han' clappin' an' shoutin'" should be viewed: the "sittin' up," African medical practices, the Kongo cross at the baptismal ceremony, the rhythms of song, sermon, and dance, these elements marked the Virginia slave community as African in important ways. Although the sermon was Christian in message, its mode of delivery and the response it evoked were African. The shouting and hand clapping, in context, then, were almost certainly the ring shout. What followed was a ceremony practiced by millions in Africa:

> Then the men an' boys begin to fill up the grave. When it was full they roun' it up real purty-like, an' put a wood shingle at the head an' another at the foot of the grave. The women-folk lay some flowers an' "ribbon-grass" on the top, an' put different color' bottles, broken glass an' sea-shells all 'roun' the grave of Aunt Dicey. In that way they show' they love for her. It was the bes' that slaves could do in them days, when ever'body was poor an' own' by they massas. But no man could own they souls or keep them from lovin' one another. Them gifts come only from God.

The "sittin' up" and the burial mound are bridges to the hereafter, making communication with God and the ancestors less abstract, for being in proper relation to Sister Dicey eased passage in one's own turn. Although the preacher spoke of meeting her on that great getting up morning, the preparation of the burial mound by relatives meant awareness that continuing contact with Sister Dicey's spirit was unavoidable. Hence, by being certain that her spirit was at rest, contact with her thereafter was more likely to be of a harmonious kind. The two visions of religion in the tale, the African and the European, are complementary and explainable in relation to the African view of religious experience, which does not function from a single set of principles but deals with life at different levels of being. The Africans' spiritual vision of the universe is synthetic. In absorbing aspects of Christianity—such as a belief in Christ—they do not necessarily abandon regard for the ancestors.

Just as slave music reflects the unity of West African culture through syncopation, antiphony, group singing, improvisation, particular instruments, and through its organic tie to dance, so too the essential unity of large sections of Central and West African religion was reflected in the burial mound of slaves in antebellum America and later. The African character of the slave burial ceremony was unmistakable: "Them dishes and bottles what put on the grave is for the spirit and ain't for nobody to touch them. That's for the spirit to feel at home." And, "You put dishes and bottles and all the pretty pieces what they like on the grave. You always break these things before you put 'em down. You break [them] so that the chain will be broken. You see, the one person is dead and if you don't break the things, then the others in the family will die, too." Moreover, actual burial mounds contain evidence of this ceremony:

> The deposit of chinaware and other objects on the Afro-American grave is in contrast with the stark plots of grass which cover the graves of Americans of European descent. Two early twentieth-century graves in Mississippi . . . glitter with surface china, suggesting the rumpled vitality of a vanished life. The use of the fragments seems deliberate: pieces are aligned to show the length of the grave in a simple axial statement. . . . An intimate act characteristic of the deceased is [sometimes] recalled forever on the surface of the grave by means of a particular object selected. What appears to be a random accumulation is in fact the distillation of a life.[22]

The preacher overseeing the ritual assumes major responsibility for the fate of the spirit of the deceased. The obligation of the occasion suggests a power beyond the grave for him, leading him to assume the role of the African priest over the burial mound. Thus the divine-kingship function of mediating with the ancestors was reborn on the plantations of the South as Africa was recalled on a level of precise symbolism. Slaves found objects in North America similar to the shells and close enough to the earthenware of West Africa to decorate the grave in an African manner, and likewise to celebrate the lives of those who, like Sister Dicey, lived long and won the admiration of their fellows. Africans from different points of the continent shared this vision, which could have strengthened an African trait under the conditions of North American slavery: "The fusion of slaves from the Gold Coast, the Congo-Angola area, and other parts of the Guinea Coast in Southern slavery could mean the reinforcement of the African notion that the funeral is the climax of life and that the dead should be honored by having their possessions placed upon the top of their graves." [23]

There is more than an echo in Texas of the formative values through which the spiritual life of the African was mainly organized in American slavery. In Texas in the first quarter of the twentieth century, as in Pennsylvania decades following emancipation, African sacred dance continued to accompany, much like percussive drums, the singing of Negro spirituals—the latter created in the ancestral circle as dancers moved in the immemorial clockwise direction in which the sun orbits in the regions of Africa from which their ancestors came, marking the path taken by the souls of the deceased. Efforts to drive dance from the church because Christians considered it profane heathenism did not entirely succeed, as can be seen in the findings of William A. Owens while a student at Southern Methodist University. By then he knew what to listen for, since in his boyhood he had "chopped cotton in the spring and picked cotton in the fall on small sandyland farms or on the Womack plantation in the Red River bottoms, sharing the work with an occasional ex-slave, or with their sons and daughters, grandsons and granddaughters." [24]

Later, as a college student, he found himself at times lonesome for the sounds of "moanin' low, the humming that came toward the end of work, when the sun was no more than a hand high." By then he understood that black culture was "a mingling of borrowings from European cultures with rememberings from African cultures." He could tell, by timbre and sound, a black voice from one that was white and could make other crucial distinctions as well. While at Southern Methodist

University, he "often went to a church at the corner of Thomas and Hall." Much like Frederick Law Olmsted in a Louisiana black church in the 1850s, Owens was

> given a seat of honor, sometimes near the altar, sometimes in the front row of the balcony. I could watch and listen and let the black religious experience sink deep into my mind. Toward the end of a long meeting they turned from preaching and praying to singing and shouting in a way that paralleled white revivals but with a faster, drumlike, foot-shaking rhythm. Such emotional risings from black souls seemed genuine and natural—in sharp contrast to the preacher's previsions of gates of pearl and streets of gold, borrowings from white men.[25]

Of course, the blacks Owens encountered were essentially the same people among whom J. Mason Brewer spent so much time as one of their own and as a collector of their folklore. In this regard, it is especially important to recall that Brewer collected ghost stories and tales of Br'er Rabbit, that the two, as we see in "Red Hill Churchyard," can be related. An examination of his ghost stories may well yield new findings, or at least a new perspective, regarding their meaning, especially when relating them to the Africans' regard for the ancestors. Although European ghost stories abound, the Herskovitses and others, especially Newbell Puckett, believe that most ghost stories by blacks are rooted in the African past. Of particular relevance is this passage from Puckett: "it is considered bad luck to . . . sass the old folks. This latter idea may have at one time had a real meaning, since the old folks were almost ghosts, and hence worthy of good treatment lest their spirits avenge the disrespect and actually cause bad luck to the offender."[26] The fear expressed here was precisely that which led blacks to elaborate means of showing respect for the dead by constructing the burial mound and by encircling the dead while shouting. Study of Brewer in this light should help us determine the relationship and extent of European and African elements in the ghost stories.

It has been argued that "it is this . . . feeling of identity with the dead which characterizes and explains the Southerner." The statement can stand as an emblem for the African in Texas and the South generally in antebellum times and since. What better illustration, however, of possible analogues—born of some measure of cultural interaction?— between black and white Southerners than Texas novelist William

Humphrey's observation regarding the need for the Southerner to be aware of his ancestry because "in his time he is priest of the tribal scripture, to forget any part would be sacrilege. He treasures the sayings of his kin. . . . If he forgets them, he will be forgotten. If he remembers, he will be remembered, will take the place reserved and predestined for him in the company of his kin, in the realm of myth, outside of time." [27] No doubt cultural cross-play occurred, but the Afro-American attitude toward death has been, overall, far too distinctive—and too inaccessible in slavery and since—to argue sweeping analogues.

The elaboration of art forms in accordance with their vision of death marks off black Americans from Anglo-Americans in relating to the ancestors. Their culture was vastly more African in slavery than we have assumed, and there is a need to explore its offshoots in the twentieth century in light of changing perceptions of the content and meaning of that culture. Certainly Texas, with its substantial body of Afro-American folklore, is an excellent laboratory in which to examine that folklore systematically to further our understanding of Afro-American myth. Such an examination should lead to a reconsideration of the formative values of blacks in slavery and in Africa and help usher in what promises, over the next quarter-century, to be the most exciting period yet in scholarship on blacks in North America.

NOTES

1. E. C. L. Adams, *Nigger to Nigger* (New York: Charles Scribner's Sons, 1928), p. viii.

2. Adams, "The King Buzzard," in *Nigger to Nigger*, pp. 13–15.

3. See Robert F. Thompson, "African Influence on the Art of the United States," in *Black Studies in the University*, ed. Armstead Robinson et al. (New Haven: Yale University Press, 1969), p. 150. See also P. Amaury Talbot, *The Peoples of Southern Nigeria*, 4 vols. (London: Oxford University Press, 1926), 3:468–510, 754–58; and Melville Herskovits and Frances Herskovits, *Rebel Destiny* (New York: Whittlesey House, 1934), p. 4.

4. Arthur Glyn Leonard, *The Lower Niger and Its Tribes* (New York: Macmillan, 1906), p. 142.

5. Of course, the influence of slave culture in this regard must be weighed against the considerable pressures, generated by the master class, favoring disunity and treachery in the slave community. As numerous as traitors were in that community, there is reason to believe their numbers would have been greater had not countervailing forces, such as those being expressed in "Buzzard," been present. See Talbot, *Southern Nigeria*, p. 470, for a discussion of towns and the spirit.

6. For a detailed defense of this thesis, see Sterling Stuckey, *Slavery and the Circle of Culture* (Oxford University Press, forthcoming).

7. Adams, "Gullah Joe," in *Nigger to Nigger*, pp. 227–29.

8. See Robert F. Thompson, *The Four Moments of the Sun* (Washington, D.C.: National Gallery of Art, 1981).

9. Adams, "The Slave Barn," in *Nigger to Nigger*, pp. 234–36.

10. Adams, "Ole Man Rogan," in *Congaree Sketches* (Chapel Hill: University of North Carolina Press, 1927), pp. 50–51.

11. What is crucial is not the quantity of Afro-American folklore, which is already considerable, but a deeper understanding of what is available. What is available contains, in remarkable degree, African myths applied to new realities.

12. Herskovits and Herskovits, *Rebel Destiny*, p. 8.

13. Ibid., p. 4.

14. See William J. Faulkner, *The Days When the Animals Talked* (Chicago: Follett Publishing Company, 1977), part II.

15. Adams, "The Dance of the Little Animals," in *Nigger to Nigger*, p. 178; "Bur Rabbit in Red Hill Churchyard," in ibid., pp. 171–73. (The more standard "Br'er" is used here, except when quoting directly from Adams, in referring to Rabbit.)

16. Herskovits and Herskovits, *Suriname Folklore* (New York: Columbia University Press, 1936), p. 521.

17. I wish to thank anthropologist Paul Riesman for bringing Songhai burial ceremonies, and the place of the violin in them, to my attention (interview, spring, 1982).

18. Adams, "Bur Jonah's Goat," in *Nigger to Nigger*, p. 177.

19. Sir Charles Lyell, *A Second Visit to the United States* (New York: Harper and Brothers, 1849), p. 269.

20. Faulkner, "How the Slaves Helped Each Other," in *The Animals Talked*, p. 35.

21. Ibid., pp. 37, 39. For a discussion of New Orleans funeral ceremonies and their bittersweet quality, see Marshall Stearns, *The Story of Jazz* (New York: Oxford University Press, 1956), pp. 57–63.

22. Thompson, "African Influence," pp. 150–51.

23. Ibid., p. 150.

24. William A. Owens, *Tell Me a Story, Sing Me a Song* (Austin: University of Texas Press, 1983), p. 253.

25. Ibid., pp. 253–54.

26. Quoted in Melville Herskovits, *The Myth of the Negro Past* (Boston: Beacon Press, 1941), p. 151.

27. James W. Lee, "The Old South in Texas Literature," in *The Texas Literary Tradition*, ed. Don Graham, James W. Lee, and William T. Pilkington (Austin: University of Texas Press, 1983), pp. 50–51.

Part III
Historical and Contemporary Myths
about Nature, the Individual, and Social Life

ROBIN DOUGHTY

From Wilderness to Garden: Conquering the Texas Landscape

Two myths, land as wilderness and land as garden, reflect and explain the activities of many early Texans. English-speaking pioneers and European settlers modified both landscape images, which had grown from colonial experiences along the Atlantic seaboard. Newcomers saw wild Texas as an environment to be subjugated, but also to be enjoyed as home. They embellished the myth of the garden by promoting Texas-to-be as North America's Mediterranean and a place where foreigners discovered classical metaphors. A third myth, topophilia, or reciprocal bonds between man and land, represented appreciation for Texas itself. People acknowledged interdependence in nature and the need to conserve a heritage that supported settlement and had given character to the state.[1]

The wilderness and garden myth held the land in usufruct. It was a space to be expropriated, delineated, and rendered hospitable. William Newcomb demonstrates in his chapter on the American Indian mind that the Indian did not share in this technological, economic, and ethical mandate to seize land. The many Native American groups in Texas saw the same space as something to which they belonged, as an ancestral dwelling place. Land furnished them material support, but it was, above all, a physical and spiritual repository of meaning.

When Stephen F. Austin complied with his father's dying request to take up his grant, Texas was "part mission, part fort, remote and half forgotten." In 1830, the Austin colony, spanning the watersheds of the Brazos and Colorado rivers, in the buffer zone between Hispanic and

Anglo-French cultures, boasted close to six thousand settlers, who had cleared farms and plantations on the banks of major rivers and creeks. Austin regarded Texas as a challenge and an opportunity. The challenge lay in redeeming the land from chaos, from a "howling wilderness" that pilgrims had lamented much earlier in New England. On the other hand, the opportunity for exploiting a vast, largely unknown region was unique.[2]

Wilderness Texas

Austin, the first and most influential empresario, set about conquering the land. Coming to grips with the wilderness was a challenge unique to American experience. Conquest reflected individual initiative and enterprise; it also symbolized the spiritual battle of a chosen people in establishing a new civilization—a promised Canaan—in the vast, unkempt, and unfamiliar continent. Austin's frequent mention of this conflict was in the mainstream of American frontier thought, which made wilderness the battleground between forces of order and reason and those of chaos and bestiality. Texas presented a difficult opponent. Physically huge, biologically complex, and geographically remote, it was a foreign enclave in which no American citizen had settled successfully.

Through "noiseless perseverance and industry," declared Austin, the settlers would force nature to unlock its bounties, so that "the axe, the plough and the hoe would do more than the rifle or the sword." His policy of "silent" recruitment of colonists, eager to crop fertile soils— inexpensive and tax exempt—was his key to prosperity. Austin was a Boone-like patriarch overseeing innumerable details in domesticating the Texas wilderness. Despite arduous travels, imprisonment in Mexico, and misunderstanding in Texas, his sense of duty and determination never wavered.[3]

It is speculated that Austin's New England background, his education in Connecticut, and his experience with the Arkansas frontier played a role in his "redemption" of Texas. His destiny, he believed, was to establish a community of Americans in this foreign land. He was sure of his covenant. Faith was essential, faith and confidence in "the self existing, consistent and bountiful Father of worlds, of time and of

Eternity." From this perspective, Austin, the believer, was able to detach himself from disappointments of events and sleights of men and to face the future with equanimity.[4]

Considering his wholehearted dedication to turning back wild lands, we can usefully contemplate Austin's strategy. Three stages or "regular gradations" for settlement existed. First, the colonist must overcome the "roughness" of natural conditions, as a farmer clears his land "covered with woods, bushes and brambles." The next step, he said, was like "ploughing, harrowing and sowing the ground after it is cleared." It laid the foundation for advancement. The third, most important, step was "gathering the harvest, and applying it to the promotion of human happiness."[5]

Explicit emphasis on human activities is somewhat unusual. In Austin's day, opinion regarded the character of peoples as a product of the environment. Climate, temperature, and moisture determined the type and stage of culture; therefore, environmental determinism, not human agency, captured attention. The fear that a hard, often brief, life on the frontier debased people's character, values, and moral fiber was well entrenched in American literature and letters.[6]

Austin's clearance stage involved tact in dealing with disgruntled colonists, tolerance of stock thefts by Indians, and coping with floods that ruined crops or diseases that sapped body strength. Occupancy called on this empresario's remarkable skill with distant officialdom and tough, but hospitable, woodsmen. His enthusiasm grew in knowing that his colony was "a home for the unfortunate, a refuge from poverty, an asylum for the sufferers from selfish avarice." Above all, his settlers, honest as far as he could determine, nominally Catholic, resilient, and desirous of freedom and abundant land, were to "harmonize with their neighbors in the *East* in language, political principles, common origin, sympathy, and even interest." They were Americans before whom Austin set an example of "economy and plainness," and for whose character he had generally a high regard. Frontiersmen pushed back the forest's edge, constructed log cabins, and exterminated predators and Indians; they worked together as a family to realize Austin's dream of subjugating the land—whether they knew it or not.[7]

The second act of redemption, "ploughing and sowing," involved the practical necessity of setting vegetable roots, peach and plum

stones, and other produce, in addition to staples such as corn, pumpkins, sweet potatoes, and, of course, cotton. Austin recognized that
"Texas as a Country . . . may be advantageously compared with any
portion of North America." Exploration in 1821 taught him that the
region he selected near the Brazos River was especially bountiful. A
pithy comment, "very good, rolling Prairie black soil, sufficiently tim-
bered," typified his keen eye for the country. He saw luxuriant prairies, "immense quantities" of wild grapes, bee trees, game animals,
clear water, and, of course, soils—red, black, and sandy. His objective
was to exploit nature's fecundity.[8]

Contemporaries agreed with the "Father of Texas" in his clear,
persistent emphasis on reclaiming the region's wilderness. With the
benefit of hindsight and maturity, Frank W. Johnson named pioneer
Moses Morrison "a true type of the frontiersmen—bold, fearless, kind
and generous, [who] performed well his part in subduing the wilderness and driving back the savage." James H. Kuykendall's reminiscences turned colleagues into epic Texans who had battled the demons
of nature and man. Deaf Smith buried the dead and succored those
wounded by Indians. Wiley Martin made a pioneer's dent in cane-
brakes along the Brazos, where all manner of wild beasts fell to the
"Nimrodian passion of the veteran Captain."[9]

One of the very first settlers, Mary Rabb, felt disappointed when,
toward the end of her trek from the Red River, she noted at the Colorado River crossing "nothing but a wilderness, not eaven a tree cut
down to marke that plais." Such a condition demanded decisive action;
no true settler hesitated to engage such an adversary. Her menfolk, the
likes of Moses Morrison, Deaf Smith, and Wiley Martin, built a log
cabin (with a chimney) in a week and set about clearing.[10]

Wilderness: Place and Home

Traditional aggression toward the wilderness diminished as people
counted blessings from satisfactions on the frontier. First, pleasures
from hunting solidified personal and community bonds. A traveler re-
plenished his host's larder with venison or turkey; people bartered
game or used it to pay their way. Men loved the camaraderie and excitement of hunting excursions, which also lessened popular fears

about the land's hostility by making known the region's prolific biota and its geography.

The coast's reputation for being unhealthful, for example, lessened as people described a "nation of geese" swarming there in winter. Waterfowl, shorebirds, and prairie hens abounded; some judged deer, wild cattle, and mustangs common enough in the coastal zone to be a nuisance. "Let no able bodied man emigrating to Texas neglect to provide himself with a good rifle or musket and at least one hundred rounds of ammunition," recommended the Columbia *Telegraph* (May 2, 1837). "We did not kill for lust's sake, but for sport's sake," claimed an old-timer. There was no point in killing large numbers; it was too easy. The skill was in choosing the biggest buck, and in having "contests to see who would kill at the greatest distance with the cleanest shot." [11]

Travelers and new settlers often stressed the beauty of wild Texas, usually in springtime, when the land bore new life, color, and warmth. Spring, 1828, was not kind, however, to José María Sánchez, who accompanied General Manuel de Teran on a fact-finding tour. Sánchez disliked San Felipe; the atmosphere spelled trouble, he argued, and torrential rain left the route to Nacogdoches well-nigh impossible. Flooded bottomlands, mosquitoes, and the dark, closed woodland canopy wrecked the expedition. [12]

Suddenly, toward the close of his disoriented march, Sánchez came upon a clearing: "There is nothing that affords the traveller in these solitary regions greater joy than the sight of a plain after coming out of the long endless thick woods," he declared. The "parkland" aspect of interior, undulating Texas, with an admixture of clearings, pine and oak forests, and prairies, drew universal praise. Abolitionist Benjamin Lundy, en route to San Antonio in the 1830s, looked from an eminence over "a region thickly settled with farms and plantations. Houses alone were wanting to perfect the resemblance." [13] Sunlight, singing birds, butterflies, and flowers caused people to imagine a European country estate. "The lawn, the avenue, the grove, the copse, which are there produced by art, are here produced by nature," opined a Britisher. Interior Texas satisfied scenic tastes as an enormous landscape garden! [14]

A third way of coping with wilderness was to find "home" in it. In "America letters," settlers compared Texas with their homelands, discovering Germany's Rhineland in central Texas, or England's Somerset, Kent, and even Windsor Forest. Olmsted loved the "German qualities" as well; he stayed in "one of those delightful little inns which the pedestrian who has tramped through the Rhineland will ever remember gratefully." Norwegian pioneer Johan Reinert Reiersen thought that the country around Brownsboro looked like Norway. Compatriot Elise Waerenskjold agreed, saying that Amli parishioners would feel at home in nearby country, with "high ridges and large pine woods."[15]

Alexander von Humboldt, in his monumental *Cosmos*, explained misgivings about unknown places by saying, "Fearful as it were of breaking the links of association that bind him to the home of his childhood, the colonist applies to some few plants in a far-distant clime the names he had been familiar with in his native land." "Peach" lands in Texas signified first-rate soils on which a native indicator plant grew whose leaves reportedly tasted like the kernel of a peach stone. American bird names stem from the colonial era when writers labeled them after European species. The graceful scissortail flycatcher was a "bird of paradise" for many Texians, who found a resemblance to the birds of New Guinea.[16]

Birds also provided color, sound, and companionship in the midst of solitude. Daniel Shipman, one of the "Old 300," helped his family to clear and crop the land a minimum of five times before crossing the Red River from Arkansas in 1821. Like other settlers, he loved the pioneer's life, finding, as he explored the Brazos Valley, a welcome to Texas in the mockingbird's dawn chorus.[17]

Other folk had similar, special experiences that turned the wilderness into drama. Gideon Lincecum (1793–1874), "leatherstocking" and natural historian, explored Texas in 1835 before becoming a resident. In spring, he walked into Karankawa country on the coast along the San Bernard River. Toward sunset he came upon an enormous flock of swans. The vast congregation took several minutes to fly over him; their wings concussed him and "seemed to devitalize the air." This "living tornado" exhausted him; however, Lincecum felt privileged to have witnessed "the flight of the southern division of American swans."[18]

John Russell Bartlett, U.S. surveyor, enjoyed a similar experience with mustangs, whose gangs streamed by him in "long undulations, like the waves of the ocean." German paleontologist Ferdinand von Roemer was greatly moved by a buffalo herd, which he "had long cherished the wish to see." Mary Holley tarried beside a huge prairie fire near the San Bernard River. "Never did I witness in the same scene, so many picturesque aspects," she exclaimed. Such natural phenomena—"tornadoes" of swans and mustangs, prairies alive with bison or wildfire—injected color, immediacy, and excitement into life in the wilderness.[19]

The Garden

The simple metaphor of the garden was applied to the South and to Texas. As a synonym for "harvest" in Austin's final colonization stage, this myth replaced the wilderness, giving "tone, character and consistency to society." "We will arrange our cottages—rural—comfortable and splendid," said Austin, "gardens and rosy bowers, and ever verdant groves, and music, books, and intellectual amusements can all be ours." This pastoral vision of tidy farms and prosperous inhabitants, which Austin did not live long enough to savor fully, was the end product of the redemption process.[20]

On the other hand, visitors and settlers recognized Texas as a natural garden. Two factors determined this myth's applicability: climate, which affected human health, and soils, which controlled crop type and variety. Climate and health were inseparable in the popular mind, and one of the most effective communicators about them was Austin's first cousin, Mary Austin Holley, whose "Texas letters" opened up the era of travel writing. Holley and others repeatedly emphasized two virtues of climate: equability and salubriousness. Texas enjoyed a "perpetual summer," she commented, because cool sea breezes tempered the hottest months, and northerly winds in winter purified the atmosphere without really chilling it. A so-called blandness or evenness in climate, therefore, enabled garden plants to survive even in winter.[21]

Equability spelled healthfulness. Purifying winds swept miasma from wetlands, making Texas more salubrious than the moister Mississippi Valley, where agues and bilious fevers abounded. Holley minimized the disadvantages of weather and climate, but others were more critical. Britisher William Kennedy admitted that floods, high winds, and "northers" threatened life and property; but away from the coast "no part of the globe is more friendly to the regular action of the human frame."[22]

Texas soils proved generally fertile. Holley's hyperbole challenged "all other countries for a comparison, both as to quality and variety," including "clayey, sandy, pebbly, rocky, with all their intermixtures." Settlers echoed her sentiments, although they speculated about the value of prairies for cultivation. One could not fault other resources. Water was plentiful, and so was wildlife, the variety and numbers of which astonished many folk. The diversity of useful plants in the rolling zone included pines, hardwoods, and the famous mesquite grass, which provided nutritious fodder.[23]

A combination of rich soils and a year-long growing season made crop selection imaginative. Visitor William Bollaert repeated the colloquialism "If you put ten-penny nails in the ground, you will have a crop of iron bolts!" The natural fecundity of Texas compared well with other regions, surpassing most.[24]

Authors, land speculators, and agents for immigrant associations stressed the comparative advantages of Texas, which grew superior cotton, sugarcane, and all kinds of subtropical fruits and vegetables. Cattle "rolled in luxury" year round, declared one author. Kennedy published the proverb "It will cost more to raise a brood of chickens in Texas than an equal number of cattle." Poultry needed food and protection from predators, whereas stock fended for themselves.[25]

The garden myth received a fillip from editors of agricultural journals. The *Southern Cultivator*, a leading farm paper for the lower South, ran more than seventy articles about Texas, mostly in the 1850s, when circulation topped ten thousand annually. *De Bow's Review*, another monthly with a focus on the South, carried no fewer than twenty-eight essays involving Texas between 1846 and 1860. Most accounts in both journals strongly advocated movement into this agricultural emporium.[26]

The letters G.T.T. symbolized escape for ruffians and debtors but prospects for other enterprising people—the opportunity to metaphorically and literally break new ground. Naturally, some in the press were hostile. A Mobile, Alabama, newspaper called the whole thing a hoax. It noted a steamship in port with scores of immigrants aboard, some of whom appeared to know all about agues and fevers. "We have heard it said, that even chickens and turkies in that country have touches of the ague," so bad that they shake off their feathers! Nevertheless, the paper wished immigrants "God speed!" [27]

Government publications also commented on the advantages of Texas. Several residents replied to an 1845 circular to assess productivity. S. W. Kellogg, for example, described conditions between the upper Brazos and Trinity rivers. Wheat grew well in the extreme north, cotton yields were good, and Kellogg conveyed the impression that conditions were suited for all kinds of crops. "The quantity of produce raised in this extent of country may appear small," he said, "but six years ago the greatest part of it was used as a hunting ground by the Indians."

John Frazer returned statistics from Jasper County in 1848. Cotton dominated in value, with corn and sweet potatoes a distant second and third. It was clear where his allegiance lay: "The face of the country is gently undulating, and the healthiness of the people is, perhaps, not surpassed by any other country on earth." [28]

Popular journals within Texas carried the same message. No agricultural periodical appeared until the late 1860s, but the *Texas Almanac*, founded in 1857, emphasized attributes of the garden. Carolina-born Willard Richardson, the *Almanac's* probable founder, wished "to populate Texas" and published descriptions of Texas counties about which residents wrote "pridefully and a little boastfully but rather honestly." An estimated fifteen thousand to twenty-five thousand subscribers read these entries. The *Almanac* was well distributed east of the Mississippi River and copies sold abroad. It "undoubtedly greatly influenced migration to Texas," insisted one source, noting that some settlers reportedly arrived carrying a Bible and the *Texas Almanac*. [29]

The idea of Texas as a natural garden capable of nurturing and sustaining farmers, planters, and stockmen and of benefiting the nation goes back even earlier than Stephen F. Austin. In the early 1800s, Zebulon Pike judged that Texas possessed one of the best climates in the world; it was "one of the richest, most prolific, and best watered countries in North America." [30] Statesman Henry Clay argued that Texas's endowments were of greater value than Florida's resources. Austin echoed and extended such sentiments. He claimed that Texas was the best region in the South. Even Frederick Olmsted admitted loftily that Texas enjoyed "an Arcadian preeminence of position" in the nation and had an "opulent future." His disdain for the South and southern ways caused him to quibble, however; the "preeminence" was, of course, quite capable of being mismanaged, so Texans could ruin the country.[31]

Such remarks fell on deaf ears. The thought of untold acreage of fine lands quickened immigrants' pulses. Few people cared whether or for how long the fertility would last. They could always push west. It was important to get there and to start planting nature's bountiful garden. And that is what tens of thousands of immigrants accomplished in the 1830s and 1840s.

A Mediterranean Garden

The fertility and salubriousness of the mythic garden tempted human ingenuity to "improve" it. Accordingly, promoters regarded Texas as North America's Mediterranean, where villages, orchards, and vineyards dotted the landscape. Stockmen would graze flocks of sheep and goats in flower-decked pastures. These plants and animals of classical Greece and Rome would serve a similar civilization in Texas.

The Mediterranean image combined information about climate, relief, latitude, and location with the Spanish imprint. Settlers adopted Hispanic place names, architecture, food, dress, speech, and idioms. But the aphorism "the Italy of North American," not the Spain, had most romantic appeal. Some people applied it to the climate and skies, others drew from history and culture. Their future Texas was as beautiful "as are now the scenes where once a Fabius fought, a Tully spoke, and Caesar reigned."[32]

Edward Stiff's emigrant guide promoted a martial image. "The eagles of Rome, in all her glory, soared not over so fine a country," he proclaimed. Similar windy utterances had a serious purpose. They urged the settler to move to Texas to draw on the essentials for a new civilization.[33]

Optimism and enthusiasm for elements in this Texas Mediterranean persisted for at least fifty years after the Declaration of Independence. Experimentation with plants commonly associated with southern Europe (peaches, oranges, nectarines, olives, figs, and vines) made economic and aesthetic details of the Mediterranean tangible. The myth had other embellishments. The advantages of early Greece as the "Golden Mean" also belonged to contemporary Texas, as people argued that the Republic linked the U.S. manufacturing hinterland with Mexico's mineral empire. It faced the agricultural heartland of temperate North America, and South America, the outlet for tropical and equatorial produce, was across the Gulf of Mexico, "our Mediterranean."[34]

Geographer and naval strategist Matthew Fontaine Maury (1806–73) referred to the Gulf as North America's Mediterranean Sea. The drainage basin of this perfectly positioned, divinely ordained routeway was huge. It spanned the tributaries of the Amazon and Mississippi rivers. Rivers in Texas and Florida occupied a combined watershed larger than the River Nile. Their basins, he argued, were also more important, because the temperate zone was the homeland for mankind "in the true nobleness of his being." People were "neither pinched with hunger, nor starved with cold . . . nor surfeited to plethora," Maury declared.[35]

This special position on the Gulf of Mexico reminded pleasure and health seekers of southern Europe's ports. In the 1880s Texans of Italian and Greek ancestry plied inshore waters around Galveston for oysters, fish, and turtles. In the early morning, sailboats bobbed around the wharves, where merchants bargained for fish and farm goods. Onlookers heard foreign dialects and broken English amid a cacophony of sound from livestock, surging waves, and slapping rigging.[36]

Galveston assumed, for some travelers, a certain charm in the same era. It was a city in the sands, but orange trees, myrtle, roses, and oleanders, for which it grew famous, anchored the shifting substrate and added a tropical atmosphere. "In the morning the air is heavy with the perfumes of blossoms; in the evening the light, to Northern eyes, is intense and enchanting," explained one traveler. "The approach from the mainland will instinctively remind the traveller of Venice," he noted, so that while mosquitoes and questions about health remained unresolved, the visual aspects of the sea-girt city, and its Mediterranean symbolism, improved.[37]

Another comment captured the texture of the moonlit city when the whole luminescence of buildings and sandy streets produced a "weird and mystic influence in the scene." So strong was the image of

Venice that the observer looked in vain for "towers, domes and mina-rets, glittering" in the final rays of the evening sun and, more success-fully, for a cosmopolitan spirit among inhabitants.[38]

Being located in a "happy latitude," safe from extremes, meant that Texas was the best of all possible worlds, like classical Greece and Rome. Its three physical divisions provided three special agricultural opportunities. The coast's "peach" lands grew superior sugarcane. Better-drained soils produced abundant cotton, which found outlets in markets along north-south trending river systems. Tobacco, rice, and "intertropical" crops did well in the Gulf States, especially in Texas, so that there was no need to seek them in foreign regions, where heat and moisture were more oppressive.[39]

Plateau lands in Texas west of the Colorado River supported cattle and sheep, and San Antonio was to be the outlet for woolen goods. The city was to be the gateway for cattle, too, the innumerable herds of which, "happier and prettier than ever was pastured by Virgil in his pastorals," enlivened the open plains.

The rolling prairie behind the coast was the finest section of all—a "Golden Mean" within the golden mean. An entry in *De Bow's* in the mid-1850s described an almost "wanton waste of nature" in the Brazos Valley. "For many miles around the cotton, corn, and every other vege-table substance seem to overload the earth." Obese hogs, plump corn, and huge, orange-colored pumpkins proved the soil's fertility. In the north lay a granary where wheat, rye, and other small grains flour-ished. Nobody should doubt, it concluded, that Texas was destined to become "one of the brightest stars of the American Constellation."[40]

Topophilia: Care for Environment

In their rush to tap the land's fertility, most settlers ignored soil erosion, floods, poor husbandry due to monocropping, and wildlife loss due to unregulated hunting. By the 1870s and 1880s, however, resi-dents could no longer ignore those aspects of resource depletion. They faced the choice of conserving Texas soils, plants, and animals or losing many of them completely. The tale of conservation in North America is well documented. Basically, the movement represented a new under-standing that humanity was beggaring an environment that housed finite resources. People recognized that human activities simplified and despoiled, not improved, biological communities.[41]

At least half a century before legislators stirred themselves to conserve the state's natural heritage, a few individuals demonstrated concern for the environment of Texas. This so-called topophilia, or "the affective bond between people and place," focused on wildlife disappearance. In June, 1824, pioneer Randall Jones requested that Stephen F. Austin consider "an act to prevent the killing of deer and wild horses for the skins alone," as such practices wasted animals. The empresario did nothing, but less than five years later he noted that "beaver is very scarce on all the waters of the Colorado, Brazos, and Trinity and other rivers of Texas," due to too much trapping. Declines in some animals probably dated back to the Spanish period, but newcomers like Jones and Austin recognized them first.[42]

Gideon Lincecum, our "swan watcher," was one of the first to call for improvements in land use. It took a woodsman's eye to spot the problem—poor husbandry—amid the burgeoning cropland. In 1861, Lincecum wrote about the need to protect native grasses, which cattle and sheep had overgrazed. He lamented the decline of once "boundless fields of luscious pasturages" and condemned "the destructive tramp of immigration." Others saw the burnished image, too. In 1837, Andrew Muir's book described "great havoc" among deer. Some settlers shot as many as fifteen hundred annually as a business, and buffalo were "fast disappearing from the plains of the lower country." In less than fifty years, they would be gone forever.[43]

Some old-timers looked back and recognized changes. One pioneer, James H. Kuykendall, saw how floods had washed out fine bottomland and how weeds and scrub grew in fertile places. Overgrazing had taken its toll, but so had repeated crops of cotton and corn without rotation or fertilizer.[44]

Texans viewed the Texas wilderness as a challenge to be surmounted. Appreciation for the Texas garden emphasized material comfort, utility, and repose. The affection for the character of Texas for itself that appeared incipiently in Muir, Lincecum, and others was clearly expressed in the writings of twentieth-century naturalist and outdoor enthusiast Roy Bedichek. Like biologist and nature writer Aldo Leopold, whose experiences in Wisconsin suffused his appreciation for nature, Bedichek revealed a deep affection for the lesser-known plants and animals of Texas. Human kinship with other forms of life "is so deep and our sympathetic ties so strong and of such long standing," he declared, "that a sudden break with them is more serious than is generally supposed."[45]

From an almost fifty-year association with land and life in Central Texas after about 1913, this Illinois-born Texan recognized a mutual dependency—a veritable citizenship—in the biotic community. The wilderness myth reduced this reciprocity to a struggle, and the garden myth simplified dependency to material well-being. But both Bedichek and Leopold believed strongly in the educative powers of nature, which for the former were virtually indispensable to moral character. It followed, therefore, that quiet, watchful attention to nature's events and seasons and respect for all forms of life informed and expanded an individual's consciousness. This was not "nature faking," or turning mammals and birds into "little people." Rather, understanding and respect linked people to place ontologically. Place was more than a commodity; it was the repository or wellspring for nurturing human inspiration and wonder.[46]

Bedichek's recourse to nature as fountainhead made him attentive to despoliation of the land. Place demanded respect for organic and inorganic elements that unified it. Residents in this "most fence-conscious state" had "frustrated nature" with such barriers. Cedar choppers laid bare the ground. Poultrymen who raised battery-housed fowl, or "denatured chickens" as Bedichek called them, severed that link of affection between humanity and animal that domestication had unlocked.[47]

This gentle outdoorsman introduced readers to organisms that had "the pleasing habit of not getting out of your way," such as the Mexican evening primrose and Inca dove. He liked living things that "clubbed together," like the yellow buckeye and black-chinned hummer. His point was that "'nature red in tooth and claw' is only a partial view, and expresses incident rather than either plot or principle." Thus, humans should extend a helping hand to the land, not from conceit or disdain, but because "solidarity, or community of interest is after all and generally nature's most distinctive characteristic."[48]

This affective bond between Bedichek and Texas from the 1930s through the 1950s has grown in others, too. People study and admire nongame animals and rare, threatened, and endangered species, and they are prepared to muster the political and fiscal clout to protect them. In short, topophilia is coming of age. The older clichés and metaphors about the land no longer serve or satisfy. Residents are interested in the unique and extraordinary place called Texas, where their kinfolk depended on nature's resources and where nature's resources now depend increasingly on humankind.

NOTES

1. The concepts of wilderness and the garden in the American experience have engaged scholarly interest for at least thirty years. See, for the wilderness, Henry Nash Smith, *The Virgin Land: The American West as Symbol and Myth* (Cambridge: Harvard University Press, 1950); Perry Miller, *Errand into the Wilderness* (Cambridge: Harvard University Press, 1956); Peter N. Carroll, *Puritanism and the Wilderness: The Intellectual Significance of the New England Frontier, 1629–1700* (New York: Columbia University Press, 1969); and Roderick Nash, *Wilderness and the American Mind* (New Haven: Yale University Press, 1973). For early visions of North America, see Leo Marx, *The Machine in the Garden: Technology and the Pastoral Ideal in America* (New York: Oxford University Press, 1964); and Ray Allen Billington, *Land of Savagery, Land of Promise* (New York: Norton, 1981).

2. C. Norman Guice, "Texas in 1804," *Southwestern Historical Quarterly* 59 (1955): 46–56; and Nash, *Wilderness and the American Mind*, p. 26.

3. In published correspondence between 1828 and 1832, Austin makes a minimum of thirty references to his conquest of the wilderness. Only a few references exist about Texas as a garden: Stephen F. Austin to Thomas F. Leaming, 14 June 1830, in *The Austin Papers*, ed. Eugene C. Barker, 3 vols. (vol. 1, in two parts, published as the *Annual Report of the American Historical Association 1919* [Washington, D.C.: GPO, 1924]; vol. 2, published as the *Annual Report of the American Historical Association 1922* [Washington, D.C.: GPO, 1928]; vol. 3 [Austin: University of Texas Press, 1927]), 2:414.

4. Austin to Mary A. Holley, 4 January 1832, *Austin Papers*, 2:733; Eugene C. Barker, *The Life of Stephen F. Austin* (Austin: University of Texas Press, 1926); idem, "Stephen F. Austin," in *Readings in Texas History*, Barker Papers, Box 2B107, "Articles 1914–18," Texas History Center Archives, University of Texas, Austin; and Louis B. Wright, *Culture on the Moving Frontier* (New York: Harper, 1955), pp. 12, 15, 32.

5. Austin to Mary A. Holley, 14 January 1832, *Austin Papers*, 2:737.

6. Clarence J. Glacken, *Traces on the Rhodian Shore: Nature and Culture in Western Thought from Ancient Times to the End of the Eighteenth Century* (Berkeley and Los Angeles: University of California Press, 1967); and Nash, *Wilderness and the American Mind*, p. 24.

7. Austin to Holley, 29 December 1831, *Austin Papers*, 2:727; idem, 21 August 1835, *Austin Papers*, 3:101; idem, 14 January 1832, *Austin Papers*, 2:737.

8. Austin to J. L. Woodbury, 6 July 1829, *Austin Papers*, 2:227, and idem, "Journal of Stephen F. Austin on His First Trip to Texas, 1821," *Quarterly of the State Historical Association* 7 (1904): 286–307.

9. Frank W. Johnson, *A History of Texas and Texans* (Chicago: American Historical Society), 1:55, and J. H. Kuykendall, "Sketches of Early Texans," in *Kuykendall Papers*, Box 2R74, University of Texas Archives, Austin, pp. 19, 24, 45.

10. Mary C. Rabb, *Travels and Adventures in Texas in the 1820s* (Waco, Tex.: W. M. Morrison, 1962), p. 2.

11. Hunting in early Texas is covered in Robin W. Doughty, *Wildlife and Man in Texas: Environmental Change and Conservation* (College Station: Texas A&M University Press, 1983); W. Eugene Hollon and Ruth L. Butler, eds., *William Bollaert's Texas* (Norman: University of Oklahoma Press, 1956), p. 317; John T. Allen, *Early Pioneer Days in Texas* (Dallas: Wilkinson, 1918), pp. 31–32.

12. Sánchez, "A Trip to Texas in 1828," *Southwestern Historical Quarterly* 29 (1926): 249–88.

13. Ibid., p. 277; and Benjamin Lundy, *The Life, Travels and Opinions of Benjamin Lundy* (New York: Negro Universities Press, 1969), p. 42.

14. William Kennedy, *Texas: The Rise, Progress, and Prospects of the Republic of Texas* (Fort Worth, Tex.: Molyneaux Craftsmen, 1925), p. 106.

15. Ferdinand Roemer, *Texas* (San Antonio, Tex.: Standard, 1935), p. 128; Marilyn M. Sibley, "The Queen's Lady in Texas," *East Texas Historical Journal* 6 (1968): 109–23, especially p. 114; Frederick Law Olmsted, *A Journey through Texas; or, a Saddle Trip on the Southwestern Frontier* (Austin: University of Texas Press, 1978), p. 144; C. A. Clausen, ed., *The Lady with the Pen: Elise Waerenskjold in Texas* (Northfield, Minn.: Norwegian-American Historical Association, 1961), p. 28; Theodore C. Blegen, ed., *Land of Their Choice: The Immigrants Write Home* (Minneapolis: University of Minnesota Press, 1955), p. 335.

16. Alexander von Humboldt, *Cosmos: A Sketch of a Physical Description of the Universe* (London: Bohn, 1848), 1:5. See also Mary A. Holley, *Texas* (Austin, Tex.: Steck, 1935), p. 50; and Elsa G. Allen, "The History of American Ornithology before Audubon," *Transactions of the American Philosophical Society* 41 (1951): 387–591.

17. Daniel Shipman, *Frontier Life: 58 Years in Texas* (Pasadena, Tex.: Abbotsford, 1965), pp. 19–20.

18. Lois W. Burkhalter, *Gideon Lincecum, 1793–1874: A Biography* (Austin: University of Texas Press, 1965), p. 40.

19. John Russell Bartlett, *Personal Narrative of Explorations and Incidents in Texas, New Mexico, California, Sonora and Chihuahua* (Chicago: Rio Grande Press, 1965), 2:522; and Roemer, *Texas*, p. 199.

20. Austin to Holley, 29 December 1831, *Austin Papers*, 2:729.

21. Holley, *Texas*, p. 43.

22. Kennedy, *Texas*, p. 71.

23. Holley, *Texas*, p. 47.

24. Hollon and Butler, *William Bollaert's Texas*, p. 287.

25. Oxceneth Fisher, *Sketches of Texas in 1840* (Springfeld: Walters and Wilson, 1841), p. 32, and Kennedy, *Texas*, p. 134.

26. Mary J. Edwards, "Texas Agriculture as Reflected in Letters to the Southern Cultivator prior to 1861" (M.A. thesis, East Texas Teachers College, 1948), pp. 2, 5; and Frank L. Mott, *A History of American Magazines: 1850–1865* (Cambridge, Mass.: Harvard University Press, 1957), 2:338–48.

27. David Woodman, *Guide to Texas Emigrants* (Boston: Hawes, 1835), pp. 157–58.

28. Kellogg to E. Burke, 14 November 1848, in U.S. Patent Office, *Annual Report of the Commissioner of Patents for the Year 1848* (Washington, D.C.: Wendell and Van Benthuysen, 1849), pp. 557–61; and Frazer to Burke, 15 November 1848, in ibid., p. 562.

29. Stuart McGregor, "The Texas Almanac, 1857–1873," *Southwestern Historical Quarterly* 50 (1947): 419–30.

30. Cited by Kennedy, *Texas*, p. 82.

31. Ibid., p. 82, and Olmsted, *Journey*, p. 411.

32. [A. B. Lawrence], *Texas in 1840, or the Emigrant's Guide to the New Republic* (New York: Arno, 1973), p. 126.

33. Edward Stiff, *The Texas Emigrant: Being a Narration of the Adventures of the Author in Texas* (Waco, Tex.: Texian Press, 1968), p. 135.

34. George A. Ferris, "Stock Raising in Texas," in *Texas Rural Almanac* (Houston: Hardcastle, 1876), p. 99; J. V. Wright, "Fruit Growing-Central Texas," *Burke's Texas Almanac* (Houston: Hamilton, 1878), pp. 33–37; A. B. Gray, *The A. B. Gray Report* (Los Angeles: Westernlore Press, 1963), pp. 46–47; Ellen C. Semple, *American History and Its Geographic Conditions* (Boston: Houghton Mifflin, 1903), pp. 397–419.

35. Matthew F. Maury, "Great Commercial Advantages of the Gulf of Mexico," *De Bow's Review* 7 (1849): 510–23.

36. Charles H. Stevenson, "Report on the Coast Fisheries of Texas," U.S. Commission of Fish and Fisheries, *Report of the Commissioner for 1889–1891* (Washington, D.C.: GPO, 1893), p. 403.

37. Edward King, *The Great South* (Baton Rouge: Louisiana State University Press, 1972), pp. 101–02.

38. Alexander E. Sweet and J. Amory Knox, *On a Mexican Mustang through Texas, from the Gulf to the Rio Grande* (Hartford, Conn.: Scranton, 1883), pp. 21–22.

39. "Internal Improvements in Texas," *De Bow's Review* 6 (1848): 364–65; "Texas Lands," *De Bow's Review* 8 (1850): 63–65; "Our Gulf States and the Amazon," *De Bow's Review* 18 (1855): 91–93.

40. "Texas—Its Resources, Lands, Rivers, Products, Etc." *De Bow's Review* 9 (1850): 196; "Agricultural Capacities of Western Texas," *De Bow's Review* 18 (1855): 54–55; "Texas—Her Natural Advantages—Wool and Factories," *De Bow's Review* 10 (1851): 464.

41. Useful discussions of conservation appear in Robert H. Welker, *Birds and Men* (New York: Atheneum, 1966); Samuel P. Hays, *Conservation and the Gospel of Efficiency* (Cambridge: Harvard University Press, 1959); and Donald Worster, *Nature's Economy* (Garden City, N.Y.: Doubleday, 1979).

42. Yi-Fu Tuan, *Topophilia: A Study of Environmental Perception, Attitudes, and Values* (Englewood Cliffs, N.J.: Prentice-Hall, 1974), p. 4; Jones to Austin, 4 June 1824, *Austin Papers*, 1:809; and Austin to Henry Austin, 24 August 1829, ibid., 2:251.

43. "Native or Indigenous Texas Grasses," *Texas Almanac for 1861* (Galveston, Tex.: Robertson, 1861), pp. 139–43; Burkhalter, *Lincecum*, pp. 177–78; and Muir, *Texas in 1837*, pp. 75, 125.

44. J. H. Kuykendall, "Reminiscences of Early Texas," *Quarterly of the Texas State Historical Association* 7 (1903–1904): 52.

45. Roy Bedichek, *Adventures with a Texas Naturalist* (Garden City, N.Y.: Doubleday, 1947), p. 93; and Aldo Leopold, *A Sand County Almanac, and Sketches Here and There* (New York: Oxford University Press, 1949).

46. Bedichek, *Adventures*, pp. xxv, 90–91.

47. Ibid., pp. 4, 105.

48. Ibid., pp. 69, 79, 84.

SANDRA L. MYRES

Cowboys and Southern Belles

A perceptive observer once remarked that Texas is not a state as much as it is a state of mind, and it is Texas as a state of mind that can best be utilized for a discussion of Texas myths. Texas as a state and Texas as a state of mind—real Texas and mythic Texas—are a blend of West, East, Southwest, and Urban Texas, a blend of Anglo-European, Indian, black, and Mexican elements. Take a close look at Southwesterners, or Texans, historian Frank Vandiver wrote, "and traces of the South can be glimpsed clearly," but there is also a strong Western tradition, "a willingness to take men for themselves," with "traces of Spain," and a "certain canny toughness," which "comes surely from Plains Indians." Nor can these ethnic-cultural elements be separated from the geographical. "They cannot," said Vandiver, "be wholly understood apart from the land that nurtured them . . . a land of varied plenty, unhampered by too much harsh history, a place still becoming something."[1]

I

The history of Texas is a continuum stretching over many centuries from prehistoric to modern times. But mythic Texas is heavily biased toward a nineteenth-century orientation. It is bigger-than-life portrayals of Davy Crockett, Sam Houston, Charles Goodnight, and other heroes and a few, generally nameless, heroines. Mythic Texas is the Revolution, the Alamo and San Jacinto, the Republic, the Civil War, the Last Frontier, and the Cattle Kingdom, with moonlight, magnolias, and lace mantillas all touched with essence of oil.

This mythic nineteenth-century Texas—perpetuated in art, literature, folklore, and common belief—is also enshrined in many of the history books. If you doubt this, check the textbooks used in public schools and colleges. In the required junior high school course in Texas history, two of the most popular textbooks devote 60 percent of their coverage to the nineteenth century. About half of this material includes a discussion of Anglo colonization, the Revolution, and the Republic; the other half is given over to annexation, the Civil War, and the cattle kingdom. About 12 percent of the coverage is devoted to the twentieth century. The remainder is scattered over a number of topics, including geography, Indian cultures and society, and Spanish exploration and missions. This is not so much the fault of the writers, who include some of the state's best-known historians, as it is of the Texas Education Agency, which has decreed that the texts should concentrate on the periods prior to the twentieth century.[2]

College texts are not much more balanced, and there is no Texas Education Agency to blame. An analysis of the two most widely used college textbooks (Rupert Richardson's *Texas, the Lone Star State*, and Seymour Connor's *Texas, a History*) reveals that some 69 percent of the coverage in one and some 58 percent in the other is given to the nineteenth century, with no more than 20 percent to the twentieth century and the remainder to such miscellaneous subjects as geography, Indians, and the Spanish period. Unfortunately, twentieth-century Texas appears to live only in a few scholarly monographs and in novels by such contemporary writers as John Graves and Larry McMurtry.

Such skewed historical writing has had an impact. In a recent survey I conducted at the University of Texas at Arlington, fifty undergraduate and graduate students were asked to list the four most important events or periods in Texas history. Of the thirty-seven who had lived in Texas at least three years and had had at least one course in Texas history, fifteen mentioned the Alamo and San Jacinto or both, eighteen listed the Revolution or Independence, seventeen opted for statehood, and ten for the Civil War and Reconstruction. The other answers were scattered over various topics ranging from the founding of Nacogdoches to the Beatles concert. Of the thirteen students who had lived in Texas three years or less, five listed some aspect of the Revolution or Independence, four mentioned the oil boom, and three

the assassination of John F. Kennedy. Given such historical views, it is
not surprising that most Texas heroes and heroines emerge from this
nineteenth-century orientation.

Such narrow views are not confined to the state's student population. In 1982, members of the Texas State Historical Association were
asked to help select the twenty-five "most important Texans of all time"
for inclusion in the 1986–87 Sesquicentennial *Texas Almanac*. In February, 1984, the association presented the list of forty-one "finalists."
One represented the eighteenth century; twenty were figures associated with the nineteenth century; and twenty were from the twentieth century. Although this list appeared neatly balanced between the
nineteenth and twentieth centuries, it still revealed something important about Texas attitudes. The list included four white women, three
black men, three men of Spanish-Mexican heritage, but no Indians.
The other thirty-one were Anglo-European men, and all but four of
these were political or military leaders or men associated with money
and power. The other four included one writer (W. S. Porter, better
known as O. Henry), two historians (Eugene C. Barker and Walter
Prescott Webb), and one religious leader (Henry Cohen). The image
that emerged was one of tough, capable, and, especially, powerful
men. The times and circumstances of their power might differ slightly,
but the image was still the same. Historical Texas had blended with
mythic Texas to create a legendary history that portrayed the past as
the present generation preferred to remember it.

This predominantly masculine, nineteenth-century orientation of
both mythic and historical Texas has defined the role of Texas men and
women and the relationship between them. Both mythic and historical
Texas were first and foremost a place of strong, self-reliant men and
strong but submissive women. As historian Necah Furman has pointed
out, Texas myths, like most myths, are "grounded in fact" and in "the
common belief [that] Texas is the biggest and the best." The consequence, according to Furman, was all but inevitable: "This geographic
vastness, the state's frontier heritage, and its crass individualism contributed to the development of its dominantly masculine character
. . . [and its] particular brand of regional chauvinism has produced a
woman soft on the outside but with a backbone of steel."[3]

The prototypical Texan is a strong and powerful white male. Joe

Frantz notes in his book *Texas: A Bicentennial History*, that, like the state itself, Texans are flamboyant, violent, and "bigger and tougher than life." According to English professor and folklorist Joseph Leach, the Typical Texan "was bred of a union of suggestions on the stage, in the stories and novels, almanacs, newspapers, magazines, and travel books of the nineteenth century." But, Leach maintains, he was "not wholly the son of vivid imaginations. He was partly the son of truth," and he was a "lineal descendent of older American character types." Coming from a background of "peddlers, gallants, and backwoodsmen," the Typical Texan emerged in the 1860s "pretty well crystallized along the lines of 'The Wild Cowhand' and fellows like him." He was a superb fighting man, a man of much action and few words, tall, brave, strong, often violent, but always chivalrous around ladies. Even today the image of the Texan that rises most often to the surface is this picture of the Typical Texan as Wild Cowhand. He was, and is, expected "to be tall, skinny, friendly, quick-tempered, charitable toward his friends and merciless toward his enemies, shy around good women, a hell-horse with more compliant ones, and possessor of a dozen other recognizable stereotypical attributes." In other words, says Frantz, "in some ways he (or she—but the image is a very masculine one) is the epitome of the frontiersman."[4]

In folk literature the Typical Texan "is a large-sized Jabberwock, a hairy kind of gorilla, who is supposed to reside on a horse. He is half-alligator, half-human, who eats raw buffalo, and sleeps out on the prairie."[5] Or he is the Davy Crockett of the almanacs, "fresh from the backwoods, half horse, half alligator, a little touched with the snapping turtle—can wade the Mississippi, leap the Ohio, ride upon a streak of lightning, and slip without a scratch down a honey locust."[6] He is Paul Bunyan reborn as Pecos Bill.

Even when the Wild Cowhand leaves the range and becomes an Urban Texan, much of the former image remains. He may be, as Leach maintains, an oil baron, a cattle baron, a cotton baron, or barons "of other kinds who can make money like Croesus; but this is a mere detail in the overall figure that the Typical Texan cuts nationally." The Typical Texan may have exchanged his horse for a Cadillac, his range for the freeway, and his bunkhouse for a condominium, but in the popular imagination he is still bigger than life and tough as they come. Most people still want to believe that "Texas is wild and its people woolly."[7] Pecos Bill has simply moved to Dallas and become J. R. Ewing.

There are also Southern traits in the mythical Texan. The Southern heritage, as described by Frank Goodyn in *Lone-Star Land: Twentieth Century Texas in Perspective*, was made up of small pioneer farmers and planters. The farmer was a hard-working, rather colorless fellow whose womenfolk "were not ladies but mere women." Farmers of this sort rarely became part of the Texas myth except as minor players in the hard-times stories. The planter, on the other hand, fancied himself a knight in shining armor, "born and bred for war, leadership, fine arts, and luxury," and "his wife and daughters were ladies." Although the changes since the Civil War have weakened Southern traditionalism and made Texas more Western than Southern, George Fuermann and Frank Vandiver have convincingly argued there is still much that is Southern in both historical and mythic Texas: the Civil War in the past, segregation in the present, "plus the tie of geography."[8] Indeed, the most famous Western figure, the cowboy, is a "unique synthesis" of Southern and Western literary and historical traditions. His line of descent, observes David Davis, is "a direct evolution from the Western scout of Cooper and the Dime Novel" and "a recasting of the golden myth of the ante-bellum South." When the Southern myth reappeared on the rolling prairies, Davis maintains, "it was purified and regenerated by the casting off of apologies for slavery." Linked to this Southern tradition, the cowboy (or, in this case, the Texan) developed a code that was "a Western and democratic version of the Southern gentleman's honor."[9]

The mythic Texas male is a skillful blend of chivalrous Southern gentleman and equally chivalrous but more enduring Western frontiersman. He is the Returned-Confederate-Veteran-turned-Rancher, the hero of hundreds of Western films and novels. He is John Wayne in *The Searchers* and Randolph Scott in *The Texans*, not to mention characters from any number of less-distinguished films. He is Dan McMasters, the hero of Emerson Hough's immensely popular novel *North of 36*, on which three films, including *The Texans*, were based. Indeed, McMasters is the epitome of the Typical Texan. As the story opens, he is visiting the ranch of his father's old friend, Colonel Burleson Lockhart. As Hough describes McMasters, "A tall man he was . . . slender, brown, with dark hair a trifle long, as so many men of that land then wore their hair. . . . His eyes . . . were blue-gray, singularly keen and straight, his mouth keen and straight, unsmiling. He left the impression of a nature hard, cold; or at least much self-contained." [10] He has just returned from three years' service with his Confederate regiment, and he is proud of his and his family's sacrifices to the cause. He is now sheriff of Gonzales and a newly elected captain of the Rangers. He has come to tell the orphaned Taisie Lockhart (who is as much the typical Texas female as McMasters is the male, as we shall see) about a new market for Texas beef in Kansas.

Dan and Taisie hit the trail and for the next two hundred or so pages they battle each other while they confront and triumph over the whole range of villains, including carpetbaggers, scalawags, cattle thieves, and Indians. And, of course, by the end of the story McMasters's cold, unsmiling nature has been revealed as covering a more gentle soul. "His eyes were softened. The lines of chin and jaw seemed new to her," and they could ride off into the sunrise as Dan exclaimed, "'Why there is a new world after all!'" [11]

The mythmakers of film and fiction are not the only ones who have kept the Typical Texan alive. Readers want their Texans to be men of action, not men of words, and generations of Texas historians from Henderson K. Yoakum to Walter Prescott Webb have complied. Eugene C. Barker's scholarly biography of Stephen F. Austin, *The Life of Stephen F. Austin, Founder of Texas, 1793–1836*, made Austin somewhat larger than life, but he could not transform him into a folk hero, for Austin was more a man of words than of heroic actions. As a statesman whose great authority rested on knowledge, wisdom, and character, he thought too much and rode too little, even during his rigorous trips to Mexico. Sam Houston, on the other hand, fits the popular image of a Texan. Of course, the Sam Houston of San Jacinto is more renowned than the Sam Houston who unsuccessfully opposed secession—Texans are not supposed to be losers. The popular Houston is the centerpiece of Marquis James's *The Raven*, not of Llerena Friend's *Sam Houston: The Great Designer*. The tale is in the title: James's Houston is the Raven, a swooping bird of prey, a fighter, a personification of the Texas myth; Friend's Houston is the Great Designer, a builder, an architect, but not a mythic macho hero.

Texans are selective about their historical heroes. Barker's Austin was a founder, a builder, a thinker; James's Houston was a fighter, a drinker, a doer. Austin worked in the halls of government; Houston was a man on horseback. Texans remember Mirabeau B. Lamar, if they remember him at all, not as a poet or as the founding president of the Philosophical Society of Texas, but as the determined, vigorous president of the Republic who launched expeditions against the Indians in East Texas and the Mexicans in Santa Fe. His biographers, Herbert Gambrell and Philip Graham, emphasized Lamar's poetic and philosophical nature, thus condemning him to relative obscurity among the heroes of Texas. Poets and philosophers are not the stuff of which myths are made.[12]

Not only are Texas heroes the victims of their biographers, but the biographers are sometimes the victims of their heroes. Even Texas' best-known historian fell victim to the Texas myth. As Larry McMurtry and others have pointed out, Walter Prescott Webb's book on the Texas Rangers "mixes homage with history in a manner one can only think sloppy." In *The Texas Rangers*, McMurtry contends, "Webb was writing not as an historian of the frontier, but as a symbolic frontiersman," and "the tendency to practice symbolic frontiersmanship might almost be said to characterize the twentieth century Texan."[13]

The Webb book was transferred to film in 1936 by native Texan King Vidor. Vidor's movie, writes film historian Don Graham, "could hardly romanticize the Rangers more than Webb himself had done. . . . [T]he movie claimed to be based upon 'data' furnished by Webb's book, but those data turned out to be the stuff of legend rather than fact." Like McMurtry, Graham points out that Webb's "own facts about the Rangers contradict again and again his characterization of them as 'quiet, deliberate, gentle' men. . . . The difficulty was that he [Webb] could not bear to think badly of the Rangers."[14] Thus myth became history.

The interplay of myth and history is again illustrated in J. G. Masters's story of the father and son Smiths of Two River Valley. The father, a Texas Ranger, was the oldest member of the Mier Expedition, "noted in Texas for its heroism, noted in Mexico for rape and murder of civilians." According to Masters, this Smith was "a fierce, blood-thirsty killer. He was not simply a hater of Indians and Mexicans, he was, it seems, a man who believed these cultures were not human. His acts of torture are a matter of record." In contrast, Smith's son, also a Ranger, "defended with force but did not delight in it. He helped build parks, churches and government" and fought against injustice. "It is the father who is the Texas hero," Masters concludes. Indeed, he was so recognized by the State of Texas during the 1936 Centennial. But "the son is not a hero, official or otherwise. No monument or marker bears his name."[15]

II

If the gentler builders among the white male Texans get short shrift from both historians and mythmakers, ethnic men and women get even less attention, despite the best efforts of the Institute of Texan Cultures. In recent years, under pressure from the civil rights movement, they have begun to show up in the textbooks, but usually they are described in general, not individual, terms with descriptions of their "condition" during various historical periods.

There are, of course, ethnic myths, as other essays in this volume point out, but they are rarely part of the widely accepted Texas myth. There are few ethnic heroes in mythic Texas, and those who do exist are most often reflections of the Anglo myths. In mythic Texas there are few Indians except occasional "savage" raiders and deterrents to inevitable white progress. Chief Bowles and the Texas Cherokees never caught the popular imagination as did Joseph and the Nez Percé. About the closest Texas comes to an Indian hero is Quanah Parker, who can be admired as a man on horseback, a fighter in the Typical Texan mode. Black images are more Southern than Western, kindly Uncle Tom preacherman figures. Only Sam Pickens, the black cowboy and rodeo star, and William Goyens, the mulatto revolutionary, both men of action, approach mythic status. The Mexican hero is the border bandit or the *caudillo*, like the Indian, a man on horseback. Jack Jackson and American Playhouse made an effort to immortalize Juan Seguín but with little success.[16] Anthropologist Américo Paredes was more successful with Gregorio Cortez (who killed a sheriff and was hunted down by the Rangers) in his book *"With a Pistol in His Hand," a Border Ballad and Its Hero*. But Cortez, already a folk hero among his own people, also meets the criterion for a man on horseback. Unfortunately, what are probably more common images of ethnic Texans are the blatantly racist portrayals in *Texas History Movies*, which influenced generations of Texas schoolchildren, and, until recently, helped form the self-image of Indians, blacks, Mexicans, and other minority groups.[17]

Texas women have also been stereotyped by both the historians and the mythmakers. Women rarely make it into the index of most Texas history books and only occasionally into the text. Although there is a Typical Texan woman, she, like ethnic Texans, is more a reflection of the Anglo male image than a distinct entity. The Texas woman, Necah Furman points out, "is born, not made, and her birthplace is in the minds of men." The Southern myth made her "the victim of gyneolatry" and, from her proverbial pedestal, "in need of masculine protection."[18] Like the mythic Texas male, the Texas woman includes elements of both the Southern and Western heritage. The Typical Texan female is expected to be gracious and hospitable and to acknowledge male superiority, but she is also expected to be strong and capable, able to stand and fight when the menfolk are not around. Like her male counterpart, she is not given to unseemly displays of emotion. Cavaliers (or cowboys) never cry, and neither do their womenfolk. "Texas ladies do not cry," writes popular *Houston Post* columnist Lynn Ashby. "They laugh, they charm, they can whine and come on with pouts and promises and perseverance, but generally speaking, they do not cry." Frank Vandiver describes her as "not . . . like the Scarlett O'Haras, but her betters, ladies as tough, but girded in gentility." She is the Steel Magnolia, the prototypical Southern lady in Stephen Vincent Benet's poem:

> Her manner was gracious but hardly fervent
> And she seldom raised her voice to a servant
> She was often mistaken, not often blind,
> And she knew the whole duty of womankind,
> To take the burden and have the power
> And seem like the well-protected flower.[19]

Although they usually have a distinctly Texas slant, the Western images of women generally conform to one of the broader stereotypes of frontier women discussed by several modern authors. Glenda Riley

notes that frontier historians have usually cast women in either feminine terms (domestic, submissive yet sturdy, moral), the guardians of
all that is fine and decent, or in masculine terms (tough, sexual, political), women who act more like men than women. Such interpretations,
Riley maintains, have led to four basic typologies: (1) the Calamity
Jane, (2) the sex object, (3) the frontier suffragist, and (4) the saint in
the sunbonnet.[20] Folklorist Beverly Stoeltje presents a somewhat similar typology, characterizing the three types of frontier female images as
(1) the refined lady, (2) the helpmate, and (3) the bad woman.[21] I have
described (1) the helpless heroine, (2) the exploited drudge, (3) the
sturdy helpmate, and (4) the bad woman. Moreover, these authors suggest, the stereotypes, although predominantly applied to women of
Anglo-European ancestry, have been used to characterize Indian, black,
and Mexican women as well.[22]

Both the Southern and Western images occur in Texas fiction.
Southern women are the mainstay of novels by Augusta Evans Wilson,
Bertha M. Clay, and especially Susan Shubrick Pinckney of Hemp-
stead, Texas, who all wrote what C. L. Sonnichsen describes as "wildly
romantic narratives . . . of tears, heart-throbs, and melodrama." Pinckney's novels, particularly, reflect the popular notions of the Southern
Belle. These ladies all came from Southern, aristocratic families of
great wealth (before the war, of course), "had small, sweet faces with
soft eyes and delicate complexions," and understood a "love stronger
than death and death more beautiful than life."[23]

Similar women are sometimes found in Western novels. "Woman
in the 'western,'" according to W. H. Hutchinson, "was a sawdust doll
. . . had hair to her waist, when the braids 'accidentally' came un-
wound, possessed a clear complexion and lustrous eyes, she was *good*,"
an idealized maiden "genteelly skirting the whirlpool of life." "Bad"
girls also appear in the Westerns, "doomed to a miserable end—either
as an accomplice of the villain or as a lone figure stumbling off into
scorching sun or numbing blizzard."[24] Sometimes these women are a
skillful blend of Southern Belle, Madonna of the Prairie, and Sturdy
Helpmate, "equally suited to, and equally willing to become the wife
of either the curly-headed cowboy whose manner is rough and tumble
but whose heart is golden or the bookish school teacher with the thin
nose and penchant for Horace."[25]

Perhaps the most interesting blend of the Southern and Western traditions in Texas literature is the character of Anastasie (Taisie) Lockhart in *North of 36*. She can ride, rope, and herd cattle with the best of her men; she is a determined and practical ranch manager; but she is also beautiful, "rarely, astonishingly, confusingly beautiful." In the end she reverts to Southern lady and tells Dan McMasters, Typical Texan, "'You have used me like a man. I was a woman. . . .' Her fingers were warm. He caught her chin in both his hands, though still her fingers clung. 'Taisie,' said he, 'what fools we've been! Ah, what a blind fool I was! Forgive me!'"[26]

Taisie Lockhart was based on a real Texas woman, Amanda Burke, who accompanied her husband up the trail to Abilene in 1871. But there is little similarity between Taisie's trail adventures and Amanda's. Indeed, Taisie's story was so unlikely that it led several critics to deny that any women had ever gone up the cattle trails.[27] A number of women did go on trail drives, some with their own herds, but until recently they have been overlooked by historians.

Indeed, Texas historians have generally disregarded or denied the role of women in the development of Texas. Texas' leading historian, Walter Prescott Webb, ignored women for the first five hundred pages of *The Great Plains* and then included them among the "Mysteries of the Great Plains." He concluded that "the Plains repelled the women as they attracted the men. There was too much of the unknown, too few of the things they loved. If we could get at the truth we should doubtless find that many a family was stopped on the edge of the timber by women who refused to go farther."[28]

Men may have dictated the historical myths about Texas women, but women have helped perpetuate them. For example, the 1976 *Handbook of Texas* article on the status of women, written by Judge Sarah T. Hughes, includes the following statement:

> Women who came to Texas in the early nineteenth century were ill-prepared for the trials and hardships that awaited them. Courage and determination were as much required of women as of men and women helped build the houses, tended the livestock, and slept on crude beds of logs with rope or rawhide lacings for springs. A gun was always close at hand in anticipation of the ever dreaded attack from Indians.[29]

This female version of the hard-times myth is based on a number of nineteenth- and early twentieth-century memoirs, reminiscences, and autobiographies that, as several historians have pointed out, rely on a blend of selective memory and a desire to emphasize the unusual rather than the commonplace. In Texas, such accounts stress how far women had to walk, extremes of weather, shortages of food and other supplies, and "the constant fear of attack by Indians or Mexicans."[30] There were several such narratives by women in Anna J. H. Pennybacker's *A History of Texas* (first published in 1888), which, in various editions, was the major public school text for nearly forty years, and there were many similar stories in Annie Doom Pickrell's *Pioneer Women in Texas*, first published in 1919.[31] Where her subjects did not include tales of hardship, deprivation, and danger, Pickrell added a few of her own selection to make things seem right.

Most of these tales, as historian Margaret Henson has pointed out, were highly exaggerated. Certainly there were problems, inconveniences, and hard work involved in making a home on the Texas frontier, but few of the women were "ill-prepared." Most came from families with experience in frontier living, and some of the women had lived on other frontiers before migrating to Texas. Henson's study of women's contemporary letters and diaries has led her to conclude that these sources "seldom mentioned the presence of Indians or snakes and not many women talk about carrying guns."[32] Nor does there appear to be much evidence that women were repelled by the plains or were responsible for the retreat from the plains, as Webb believed the case to be. Some women hated the plains, but others found them beautiful. Nor were women the only family members who wanted to stop at the edge of the timber.[33]

In addition to stressing the hard life to which Texas women were subjected, Mrs. Pennybacker, Mrs. Pickrell, and other authors also helped perpetuate the Southern lady and the Sturdy Helpmate stories. Mrs. Pennybacker mentions only five or six women in her 1912 edition, and of these only Jane Long gets more than a passing mention or a short paragraph in the notes. Jane, of course, is beautiful and charming and every bit the Southern Lady. In Mrs. Pennybacker's account, James Long tries to give Jane a pair of gloves as a prize for winning a game of checkers. But Jane demurs: "You owe me nothing . . . ladies do not play for prizes." Then comes the narrative, familiar to generations of Texans, of Jane's trip to Texas in a "miserable boat, then on horseback in the midst of pouring rain," fleeing from Spanish forces, and a long winter on Galveston Island "with no companions save her two children . . . and a negro girl Kian."[34] Throughout her story, Mrs. Pennybacker stresses Jane's delicate health, but one wonders just how delicate it was, since the lady in question lived in Texas for many years after her husband's death and died in 1880 at the age of eighty-two.

Annie D. Pickrell's biography of Mary Crownover Rabb tells of a gently reared Southern girl of great charm and beauty (naturally), accustomed to "ease and plenty," who married John Rabb and was condemned to life in terrible Texas because she "felt a sense of wifely duty toward that husband, a sense of duty that made her desire above everything else to do all in her power to add to his comfort."[35] But the picture of Mary Rabb that emerges from her own account of her life is very different. She seems to have been a strong, determined woman, well prepared by experience and family background for life on the Texas frontier. Certainly she did not have the educational benefits Pickrell described, since she spelled phonetically.[36]

Another popular genre, the captivity narrative, portrays women as delicate victims. In these tales, males survive their captivity, write books, and become important men. Women endure captivity, write books, and die, or, rather, gracefully succumb. It is true that some women captives, notably Cynthia Anne Parker and Rachel Plummer, did die shortly after being returned to their white families. But many others did not. The stereotype is a better way to assuage fears and doubts about the "terrible things" that happened to the women during their captivity than to live with the fact that some of them, including Cynthia Anne, seemed to prefer Indian society to white.

Given these skewed pictures of Anglo-Texas women, women of other ethnic groups may feel fortunate that they have been almost completely overlooked by the historians and the mythmakers. Texas has no Pocahontas or Sacajawea, and historians generally ignore the important role played by women in Caddo society. Black women are usually seen as faithful family retainers and servants, rarely as women who accomplished something on their own (Jane Long's black slave Kian, or Kiamatia, is attached to the Long myth but is not really a part of it). Mexican-American women are usually viewed as domestics or prostitutes. Very few Texans would recognize the names of María Cavillo or Becerra Seguín, although both women wielded a great deal of influence and power in Spanish and Mexican Texas.[37]

Other ethnic women have not received much recognition either, certainly not abolitionist Elise Waerenskjold. After all, good Texas women, however much they might abhor the excesses of slavery, were not supposed to sell out to the abolitionists. To make matters worse, Norwegian-born Waerenskjold was a divorcee and supported herself quite well with her pen.[38] Nor is much said about the Japanese women displaced to internment camps during World War II, since Texans are more attracted to conquerors than to victims. Only German-born sculptor Elisabet Ney has received any significant amount of attention, and she was accused of everything from living in adultery to trying to burn her baby in the fireplace.[39]

Considering not only the myths but the attitudes these myths represent, it is, as Necah Furman concludes, "remarkable that the state has produced women of outstanding caliber at all." Yet Furman goes on to recount the accomplishments of a number of women of various ethnic backgrounds, women who simply do not fit into the Texas "collage . . . of courageous cowboys . . . and helpless damsels."[40]

Not only has mythic Texas influenced our views of male and female images, it also has influenced our image of the relationship between them. The Wild Cowboy idealized women but was alienated from them. According to the myth, "the only Texans alive were he-men on horse-back, never for long tied down by either apron strings, responsibilities or the finer points of the law."[41] The cowboy might enter a sexual relationship with one of the "bad women," but he generally eschewed marriage or being tied down to one place. Although the Southern Texan was less physically separated from women, he remained emotionally withdrawn. He put his women on a pedestal and expected them to stay there. As Stoeltje has pointed out, "Relations between sexes *within* society were based on a nineteenth-century idealization of woman, who was to be treated with 'honor' and politeness but without emotion by the cowboy or as a comrade [or helpmate] who is a nonsexual partner by the settler type." But always "it is the male who has choices and determines the nature of the relationship in terms of time and distance."[42] Texas men tolerated women as long as they acknowledged male superiority, did not try to assume male prerogatives, and did not think too much. According to the myth, in Texas men were men and women knew their place. Women were expected to take care of home and family and let men look after world affairs, politics, and business.

So prevalent were these myths that they dominated many real relationships. In her autobiography, Texas author Willie Newbury Lewis recalls that her husband simply did not believe that a woman had any business doing anything but taking care of her home and family. It was a lesson he stressed early in their marriage. When Mrs. Lewis innocently asked about a cattle deal he had been discussing with a friend, he quickly retorted, "'We were discussing business. Do I give you everything you wish for? If I do suppose you run the house and the family . . . and I'll run the business.'" "During our forty-five years of married life," Lewis continues, "I never again asked about business. . . . I simply signed the papers that were handed me and returned them without knowing what I was signing." Will Lewis's ideas about woman's place extended beyond her interference in business. "Since my husband objected seriously to my writing," Lewis reported, "I did not attempt a second book until after his death."[43]

Despite the changes in woman's place in recent years and the emergence of such notable Texas women as Barbara Jordan, Ann Armstrong, and Sissy Farenthold, many Texas women and men still prefer the old myth-dictated relationships. Images are often more comfortable than reality; myths still help assuage our fears and stimulate our fantasy.

To some extent, the Texas myth is changing. World War II, television, and the growth of the Sunbelt have all changed the Texas image. As Roy Bedichek mourned over a decade ago, Texans are finally becoming less singular, less identifiably Texans. Indeed, as the perceptive reader will have observed, most of the quotations related to the Texas myth predate 1970. Yet mythic Texas lives on, Texas as we prefer to remember it. And it still influences our images of men and women. Texas men are still pictured as strong and powerful he-men; Texas women are still "members of a double minority"—Texans and women.[44] Myths remain essential to our self-preservation, to our understanding of time and place, and to our sense of destiny and importance.

NOTES

1. Frank Vandiver, *The Southwest: South or West?* (College Station: Texas A&M University Press, 1975), pp. 47–48.

2. The texts surveyed were Jim B. Pearson, Ben Procter, and William B. Conroy, *Texas: The Land and Its People* (Dallas: Hendrick-Long Company, 1978); and Adrian N. Anderson and Ralph A. Wooster, *Texas and Texans* (Austin, Tex.: Steck-Vaughn Company,

1978). For a more complete analysis of these and other texts, see Margaret Henson, "Texas History in the Public Schools: An Appraisal," *Southwestern Historical Quarterly* 82 (July, 1979): 403–22, especially p. 406.

3. Necah S. Furman, "Texas Women Versus the Texas Myths," in *The Texas Heritage*, ed. Archie P. McDonald and Ben Procter (St. Louis: Forum Press, 1980), p. 168.

4. Joseph Leach, *The Typical Texan: Biography of an American Myth* (Dallas: Southern Methodist University Press, 1952), pp. 1–3. A similar typology is offered for Westerners in general in James Oliver Robertson, *American Myth, American Reality* (New York: Hill and Wang, 1980), pp. 135–46. Joe B. Frantz, *Texas: A Bicentennial History* (New York: W. W. Norton and Company, 1976), p. 4.

5. Alexander Sweet, "American Humor," quoted in Leach, *The Typical Texan*, p. 2.

6. Quoted in Walter Blair, "Six Davy Crocketts," *Southwest Review* 25 (July, 1940): 451.

7. Leach, *The Typical Texan*, pp. 4–5.

8. George Fuermann, *Reluctant Empire* (Garden City, N.Y.: Doubleday, 1957), p. 267. Also see Vandiver, *The Southwest*, especially pp. 7–21.

9. David Davis, "Ten-Gallon Hero," in *The Western: A Collection of Critical Essays*, ed. James K. Folsom (Englewood Cliffs, N.J.: Prentice-Hall, 1979), pp. 16–19.

10. Emerson Hough, *North of 36* (1923; reprint, New York: Pocket Books, 1947), pp. 12–13.

11. Ibid., pp. 335–36.

12. Herbert P. Gambrell, *Mirabeau Buonaparte Lamar, Troubadour and Crusader* (Dallas: Southwest Press, 1934); Philip Graham, *The Life and Poems of Mirabeau B. Lamar* (Chapel Hill: University of North Carolina Press, 1938).

13. Larry McMurtry, *In a Narrow Grave, Essays on Texas* (Austin, Tex.: Encino Press, 1968), pp. 40, 43.

14. Don Graham, *Cowboys and Cadillacs: How Hollywood Looks at Texas* (Austin: Texas Monthly Press, 1983), p. 27.

15. J. G. Masters, "The Smiths of Two River Valley" (unpublished, copyrighted).

16. Jack Jackson, *Los Tejanos, The True Story of Juan N. Seguin and the Texas Mexicans during the Rising of the Lone Star* (Stamford, Conn.: Fantagraphics Books, 1982), although in comic book format, is a serious history. American Playhouse presented a film version of Seguín's life several years ago.

17. *Texas History Movies: Four Hundred Years of History and Industrial Development* (Movie, Magnolia Petroleum Company, 1928, 1943).

18. Furman, "Texas Women," pp. 168–69.

19. Stephen Vincent Benet, "John Brown's Body," quoted in Vandiver, *The Southwest*, pp. 10–11.

20. Glenda Riley, "Images of the Frontierswoman: Iowa as a Case Study," *Western Historical Quarterly* 8 (April, 1977): 191, 194.

21. Beverly J. Stoeltje, "'A Helpmate for Man Indeed': The Image of the Frontier Woman," *Journal of American Folklore* 88 (January-March, 1975): 27.

22. Sandra L. Myres, *Westering Women and the Frontier Experience* (Albuquerque: University of New Mexico Press, 1982), pp. 1–4. Also see Shelley Armitage, "Rawhide Heroines: The Evolution of the Cowgirl and the Myth of America," in *The American Self: Myth, Ideology, and Popular Culture*, ed. Sam B. Girgus (Albuquerque: University of New Mexico Press, 1981), pp. 166–81.

23. C. L. Sonnichsen, *From Hopalong to Hud: Thoughts on Western Fiction* (College Station: Texas A&M University Press, 1978), pp. 129, 139.

24. W. H. Hutchinson, "Virgins, Villains, and Varmints," in Folsom, *The Western*, p. 34.

25. Douglas J. McReynolds, "American Literature, American Frontier, All American Girl," *Heritage of Kansas* 10 (Spring, 1977): 26.

26. Hough, *North of 36*, pp. 22, 336.

27. James C. McNutt, "Changing Images of Ranch Women" (paper delivered at the Texas State Historical Association Meeting, Austin, Texas, March, 1984), pp. 17–18.

28. Walter Prescott Webb, *The Great Plains* (1931; reprint, Lincoln: University of Nebraska Press, 1981), p. 505.

29. Sarah T. Hughes, "Women, Status of, in Texas," in *The Handbook of Texas*, ed. W. P. Webb, H. B. Carroll, and E. S. Branda, 3 vols. (Austin: Texas State Historical Association, 1952–76), 3:1125.

30. Margaret S. Henson, *Anglo American Women in Texas, 1820–1850* (Boston: American Press, 1982), p. 2. Also see Myres, *Westering Women*, p. xviii; Sherrell Daniels, "The Archetypal Reminiscence" (paper delivered at the Western History Association Conference, Kansas City, Kansas, 1980); and John B. White, "Published Sources on Territorial Nebraska: An Essay and Bibliography," Nebraska State Historical Society Publications, 23 (1956), pp. 11–23.

31. Anna J. H. Pennybacker, *A History of Texas for Schools, also for General Reading and for Teachers Preparing Themselves for Examination*, rev. ed. (Austin, Tex.: Mrs. Percy V. Pennybacker, 1912); Annie Doom Pickrell, *Pioneer Women in Texas*, reprint (Austin, Tex.: Jenkins Publishing Company, 1970).

32. Henson, *Anglo-American Women*, p. 2.

33. Myres, *Westering Women*, pp. 36, 99–102. Also see Glenda Riley, *Women on the American Frontier* (St. Louis: Forum Press, 1977), pp. 1–2, 15.

34. Pennybacker, *A History of Texas*, pp. 54–55.

35. Pickrell, *Pioneer Women*, p. 90.

36. *Travels and Adventures in Texas in the 1820s; Being the Reminiscences of Mary Crownover Rabb* (Waco, Tex.: Morrison, 1962).

37. There are few scholarly studies of Indian, black, or Mexican women. The best, Ann Patton Malone, *Women on the Texas Frontier: A Cross-Cultural Perspective* (El Paso: University of Texas at El Paso, 1983), presents an excellent analysis of black, Indian, and Anglo experiences.

38. *The Lady with the Pen: Elise Waerenskjold in Texas*, ed. C. A. Clausen (Northfield, Minn.: Norwegian-American Historical Association, 1961).

39. Emily Cutrer, "Elisabet Ney: Early Sculpture in Texas" (paper delivered to the Texas State Historical Association Meeting, Austin, Texas, March, 1984). The legends about Ney's marriage and the death of her son are perpetuated in *The Handbook of Texas*, 2:278.

40. Furman, "Texas Women," pp. 168, 170.

41. Leach, *The Typical Texan*, p. 118. Also see Robertson, *American Myth*, p. 164. The Southern myth is discussed in Keith L. Bryant, Jr., "The Role and Status of the Female Yeomanry in the Antebellum South: The Literary View," *Southern Quarterly* 18 (Winter, 1980): 74–75.

42. Stoeltje, "'A Helpmate for Man Indeed,'" p. 40.

43. Willie Newbury Lewis, *Willie, a Girl from a Town Called Dallas* (College Station: Texas A&M University Press, 1984), pp. 54–55, vii.

44. Quoted in Furman, "Texas Women," p. 167.

ELIZABETH YORK ENSTAM

The Family

FOR Texas the origins of myth lie on the frontier. Although the frontier era of older states is remote in memory, its mystique dimmed by the passage of time, in Texas some people still live on the very soil where their families first arrived in covered wagons. Depending on the area, for Texans the frontier lies perhaps three, and sometimes only two generations back. To be sure, the frontier has long been an American, and not merely a Texan, preoccupation; the scene of much of our national history has been, since 1607, one frontier after another. It was perhaps inevitable, then, that the frontier experience should become the source of a major national myth, reflecting our aspirations and projecting our values.

Wherever its locale, this American myth's functions have been similar to those of the traditional mythologies of other cultures. Among ancient and preliterate peoples, mythic narratives have served numerous purposes. Explanations for the society's origins and for puzzling phenomena of the natural world, observations about human nature, beliefs about the human relationship with the divine or with the universe, and even justifications for customs and rituals established by the people themselves—all employ narrative form in a blending of natural with supernatural. Myth, it may be said, draws experience and imagination together into a rational and coherent worldview.

For modern literate populations as well, myths may serve important functions, preserving widespread social ideals, for example, or expressing the excitement or pathos of revered experiences. By investing cultural memories with meanings that transcend the historical events or conditions that are their sources, myths may also transmit values across the generations. In this way, modern myths serve to perpetuate the traditions, customs, and practices that first gave a people their identity.

Americans possess a fertile source on which to build myth, a frontier that lasted, in one place or another, for some 280 years. Out of all that time one particular myth appears over and over in apparently endless variations, welling from a national experience that we recall, rightly or wrongly, as truly epical. Perhaps because of its importance to us, or perhaps because a mass society's demand for entertainment is almost insatiable, several media express this myth. Thousands of films, television plays, novels, short stories, and popular ballads have used different places, time periods, and characters to tell essentially one story: how the West was won. In celebrating our conquest of the continent, we reaffirm our values and goals, share common experiences despite our different origins, and sometimes even reexamine the basic tenets of our culture. Thus, though this national myth lacks the supernatural elements characteristic of traditional myths, it does achieve genuine transcendence, reaching beyond specific events or historical conditions to evoke widespread recognition and immediate understanding of its stories.

I

The American myth of the frontier has often found its setting in Texas. Familiar to every schoolchild, the legacy of the Texas frontier includes the full cast of uniquely American heroic characters who populate the mythic depictions of the frontier. The cowboy, the schoolmarm, the sheriff or marshal, the Indian, the dance hall girl, the outlaw, the pioneer woman—all approach the level of archetypes in their appeal, and all are essentially Anglo in both their origin and interpretation of the Texas experience.

Along with these, the American myth includes a rich array of powerful and evocative images of pioneer families in Texas. Indeed, the members of those imaginary families have virtually become stock characters of popular fiction set in Texas. The crusty, hard-bitten father demands too much of his virile sons, whom he really, deep down inside, loves too much. The gentle, homespun mother keeps to her kitchen and defers to her husband, but still possesses the gritty courage needed to defend the homestead whenever the men are away. Daughters are tomboys reared much like their brothers, to ride and shoot as youngsters, only to cease practicing (but never really lose) these skills once they don long skirts. The sons often rebel against their father and compete with their brothers, then forget it all whenever an outside force threatens family and ranch. Attractive for their familiarity, these images of Texas families convey a strong sense of values— cooperation, belonging, and family loyalty, despite incidental rivalries, personal conflicts, and dangers from the raw land.

Popularity, however, can lead to exaggeration, and the images of Texas families have often been distorted into stereotypes. These images, nonetheless, draw their power from historical reality: the primary agent in the settlement of Texas was the family. That is, the basic appeal of these fictional families lies in their relationship to real Texas families. According to the census schedules, the families brought to Texas by pioneers from the older states were usually nuclear in form.[1] Relatively small, with three to five children, they were what scholars now call the "modern family," which first appeared in Western European cities by the seventeenth century (and some scholars insist, earlier still). The *Mayflower* and the *Arabella* first brought this type of family to the New World, and pioneer families, whether moving from Europe to New England or from Tennessee to Texas, remained small and nuclear until the children grew up and married. In the second generation, these families often became both larger in size and extended in form, housing three generations under a single roof.

Memoirs and family anecdotes, though tinged with sentimentality after the passage of many years, provide glimpses of day-to-day interactions among the members of those frontier families. Pranks and practical jokes, quarrels and rivalries, fatal accidents and terrible illnesses all reveal traits and relationships that the census could never record. By law, custom, and appearance pioneer families were patriarchal in structure, with the father designated as the head of the household. By dint of necessity or the interplay of human personalities, they were often egalitarian and sometimes even matriarchal: father was the head of the family, as the old Texas saying went, but mother was the neck.

Contrary to the predominance of single male characters in films, television series, and popular fiction (as well as too many history books), families and not single men built the communities, towns, and cities that became Texas. Homes and businesses, churches and schools, indeed, ranches and farms were long-term endeavors. These institutions were not built by drifters or adventurers, but by men and women who married, reared children, and stayed to struggle against drought and dust and pests and wind and mortgages and, in eastern Texas, through civil war and its aftermath. Without them, the most fabled of all Texas heroes, the cowboy, would not have found employment, and the bloody exploits of Rangers and scouts and bluecoats would have been unnecessary.

Despite their strong appeal to the American public, the traditional images of Texas families omit important elements of the state's past. Oil and cotton, both highly significant to Texas' economy, fade in the myth before ranching. Cities and towns, always necessary as markets and distribution centers, hardly appear to have existed. Indeed, in the popular culture the sole function of the urban frontier was to provide an infinite number of identical main streets where sheriffs and marshals could shoot it out with every imaginable type of bad guy. Instead of an inexhaustible population of "shootists," however, the majority of the residents of Texas frontier towns were usually members of families.

In the early urban areas of Texas the form of families differed somewhat from that of rural areas. The first families to arrive in the new towns were married couples and their children, nuclear families like those of rural areas. After a few years, when the early arrivals had drawn some relatives west, these families' relationships were extended in nature, even though they often continued to reside in several households. During the 1870s and 1880s, for example, members of the McCoy family of Dallas lived at four separate addresses, but were in almost daily contact with each other and regarded themselves, all together, as a family. Only family papers and stories can reveal the actual forms and relationships of such urban extended families; the census schedules list separate households, which were, of necessity, nuclear in appearance.

Despite the omission of urban families, the most serious flaw in the popular image of Texas families lies in their identity. "Texan" has come to mean white pioneers from the United States, who are now commonly included in the term "Anglo." The nearly total exclusion of the Tejano (or Mexican Texan), Indian, and black, as well as of the immigrant peoples from several European countries, has resulted in a one-dimensional view of historical demography in Texas. Yet, much of the drama, fascination, and, ultimately, the meaning of Texas history comes from the non-Anglo peoples and the tension that resulted from the clashing and blending of competing cultures. The richness and variety of the actual experience of family in Texas may be seen in the several forms that the family took during the state's past.

The Tejano family, for example, like that of the Anglo pioneers, was essentially European.[2] Patriarchal in structure, with its origins among the Spaniards who arrived in the eighteenth century, well before 1800 the Tejano family had developed beyond the pioneering nuclear family to become, especially in rural areas, extended in form. Despite the similarities with Anglo families, Tejanos often shocked Protestant immigrants from the United States. Offended by the sensuality of the fandango and by entire families swimming nude in rivers and streams near public roads, Anglos considered the Tejanos "irresponsible." Indeed, many descriptions of Tejano families by Anglo travelers and settlers pictured only groups of people, often women and their children, without recognizing the structure and relationships that distinguish families in any culture. Engaging perhaps in wishful thinking, Anglo men chose to see Tejana women as having "roving eyes," and speculations by Anglo writers on the "various shades and features" of Tejano children implied that the women were promiscuous, the men "no account" for not controlling "their" women.

Yet the same Anglo observers also commented on the open affection displayed, often in public, between Tejano parents and children. Anglos were impressed by the everyday kindness exhibited in Tejano home life, especially toward the elderly. Tejanos were "clannish" in their fierce loyalties, these Anglo observers noted, with intimate and close family relationships.

Blacks in Texas, as in other Southern areas, had maintained their family ties throughout the long years before the Civil War. Before 1865 the marriages of black people lacked legal standing. Worse, black families faced the constant threat of separation through sale, estate settlements, hiring out, or emigration by one spouse's owners. Still, blacks considered their marriages to be both serious and permanent. Their families were not, in their view, matriarchal in structure, even though whites counted the black families as consisting of mothers and their children. As a means of compensation for the general insecurity of their position, early in their American history, blacks developed strong networks that would provide support to individuals who lost their kin. When blood relatives were not present, the entire black community of the plantation functioned as an extended family. Within black families the oral tradition kept alive the memories of family members, including those of past generations and those residing in other states. Thus, after 1865 blacks in Texas had strong family bonds on which to begin community life.

Along with communitywide support, the evolution of an Afro-American culture, separate from and alternative to the dominant white ways, helped black families to survive the rigors of slavery. In a complex intertwining of African memories, white influences, and adaptation to stressful and often dangerous conditions, black people found strength and solace in their own forms of recreation, songs, children's games, and folktales. With a form of Christianity that was less Calvinistic and more tolerant than the religion practiced by whites, after 1865 blacks nonetheless often exhibited, even in rural areas of Texas, values very similar to those of the white community. In Washington County, former slave Nellie Carr reared her family within the Protestant work ethic with a strict, old-fashioned discipline. "We cut wood; we hauled it," her daughter remembered many years later. "We picked [cotton], we hauled to gin. . . . When [mamma] sent you to the spring [for water], she'd spit an' you better be back time it dried."[3]

In nineteenth-century Texas towns and cities blacks found themselves under the same strains of urban life faced by whites, plus racial prejudice. The church became, even more than for black rural residents, the center of community life. Ministers and church leaders stressed the importance of family relationships, regular employment, and ownership of a home. Women who took in washing or worked as domestic servants and men who found jobs as laborers, servants, porters, or teamsters saved their money and purchased land to build their homes. Whenever possible, black women were homemakers who raised fruits and vegetables, as well as cows, pigs, and chickens in their back-yards. If they had to earn money after marriage, they preferred to take in washing rather than to go outside their homes to work. Thus, if at all possible, black women lived according to the ideal of home life espoused by the white middle-class culture. Along with their acceptance of certain white values, blacks retained the good habit of community support and sharing that they had practiced on the plantations. In hard times black families provided each other with personal support and shared food and clothing.

Of all the inhabitants of nineteenth-century Texas, the Indians had the most complex family structures and the most explicit regulations for family relationships. Regardless of cultural differences, the rules of kinship and etiquette were much the same among all the Plains tribes. These similarities appeared within the Texas Indian cultures, from those of fierce nomads like the Kiowas to more advanced Caddoan peoples like the Wichitas. Both of these tribes were essentially warrior cultures in which men played the most prominent public roles. Women's importance lay in the basic social structure, that is, in the family. The Wichitas were matrilineal and matrilocal, organizing the tribe around the women and placing women at the heads of families. Among the Kiowas, more prestige went to the male line. Though Kiowa men usually lived among their wife's relations, the family tipi, shield, and band name were usually patrilineal.

Among both peoples and, indeed, among all the Plains tribes, terms of kinship implied specific economic and social functions, as well as biological relationships. Mothers and fathers, sons and daughters, aunts, uncles, grandparents—all had well-defined duties to each other for survival. If someone was not available to meet the customary responsibilities, the appropriate relative would perform his or her duties. Thus, a child addressed mother and mother's sisters alike as "mother," and father and his brothers as "father." Among the Wichitas the father's sister also was "mother." One of these relatives would assume the functions of the parent in case of a parent's death. Certain other relatives had special designations and status. The mother's brother, for example, was not "father," but was addressed by a special term showing his added importance as maternal uncle as opposed to father's brother. In general, Kiowas used kinship terms more explicitly than did Wichitas to distinguish the male and female lines of the family.

Both Wichitas and Kiowas observed very specific codes of behavior for daily interactions between family members. Just as women never addressed their fathers-in-law directly, men had to speak to their mothers-in-law through another person. Both sexes were allowed to have familiar, even risqué, conversations with sisters- and brothers-in-law, who might one day be their spouses. Children observed polite, almost formal relationships with their parents. With grandparents, by contrast, they exhibited openly affectionate, even raucous behavior, often teasing and joking in ways considered very inappropriate with parents. Despite this almost distant behavior toward their children, Kiowa and Wichita parents treated the young so leniently as to deserve the designation "permissive," whether compared with nineteenth- or twentieth-century white standards. Never disciplined by threats or corporal punishment, Indian children learned appropriate behavior by example. Those who were slow to learn found themselves the targets of adult sarcasm and ridicule and of the pressures of tribal opinion. Rarely did Indian parents have to resort to stronger means.

The result of these relationships was a cohesiveness within the villages that went much beyond the support systems provided even by an extended family. Indeed, Kiowas and Wichitas experienced a sense of family that was virtually tribal in extent; they knew a kind of community long vanished among peoples of European descent and culture. Of all nineteenth-century inhabitants of Texas, only Afro-Americans had anything like the Indian familial organization.

The complexity of Texas' history, then, has provided rich possibilities for the development of a myth of the family. Within the differing experiences of actual families in Texas, a narrative or cluster of narratives could have emerged into a myth of the family for one or more of Texas' major peoples and certainly for the Anglo-Texans, with their origins in the larger American culture. Such a myth would project familial values beyond specific situations or events, present an inspiring model for other families to emulate, and in general idealize the role of the family within the wider culture.

Because family occurs at the very base of human experience, the search for such a myth must begin with the ways people spontaneously express their view of the world, with their unconscious assumptions about being human, and with the kinds of things they puzzle over in their daily lives. The purest sources for such thinking lie in the indigenous art forms. Each of Texas' major cultures produced a rich body of folklore, which recorded memories, expressed values, and generally philosophized about life and human nature. Composed primarily as forms of entertainment, these stories, songs, and legends provided all four cultures with models to solve difficulties, teach lessons, and amuse or warn through the fates of characters who met with various degrees of disaster. Often the central figures of this traditional lore had relatives, sometimes as allies and on other occasions as antagonists or even enemies.

But perusal of the stories, songs, and fables, and even the superstitions and tall tales produces no ideas that could be seen as contributing to a myth of family. Folklore centered its attention on individuals. Whatever the importance of relatives in such stories, the family rarely, if ever, appeared as a group with shared interests and emotional bonds. For all four cultures, family, as opposed to relationships between individuals, played little or no role in folktales and failed to produce stories that ever reached the stature of true myth.

The reasons for this puzzling fact must lie both in the situations of people's lives and in the nature of myth. The very importance of family causes it, in normal circumstances, to be taken for granted as a part of the natural world. For this reason, something extraordinary must happen to direct people's attention to it. Myth also requires unusual circumstances. One motivation for the development of myth is a question or problem troubling enough to demand an explanation or the visualization of a much-desired goal and the ways to work toward it. Thus, for any people to produce myths about the family, something must inspire concern and caring for it, whether consciously or unconsciously. A hazard must imperil the family, perhaps, or threaten the quality of family life, or under extreme conditions, endanger even the family's existence. In other words, without some reason to idealize family, a people would have no cause to formulate a vision of family life, to seek ways to strengthen the family, or even to ponder what a family should be.

The Indians, for example, apparently perceived no danger to family life. Wichitas and Kiowas did not take their relatives for granted as far as feelings and affection were concerned, but if one died, another would take over the deceased's responsibilities to children and to the tribe. Texas Indians thus had little reason to examine their family relationships. Similarly, Tejano folklore showed no particular evidence of concern about the survival or integrity of their families. As contacts with Anglos increased, traditional Tejano family relationships served to provide solace, support, and status to those individuals who had to venture into the Anglo world to earn a living. Wishing to preserve their own cherished traditions, Tejanos may inadvertently have strengthened family relationships in the process.

For blacks, also, family became a haven from the daily stresses of dealing with the hostile whites, who dominated the sources and the means of livelihood in Texas. Although their aspirations had always included strong families, black people focused their strivings on individual achievements, especially for and by their children. As among the Indians and Tejanos, the images of family and family life in black folklore remained incidental, without the focus or purpose of real myth. For Anglo Texans as well, the family as an entity played little role in popular stories and tales. Anglo folklore flourished mainly in rural areas, where traditional values and relationships met few threats and experienced little change. The folklore of all four main Texas cultures exhibited little or no consciousness of the nature, purposes, or functions of family: family simply *was*.

II

Although folklore failed to produce a real myth of family, the Anglo culture in Texas suggests at least three other sources of values, standards, and ideals conducive to formulation of such a myth: the family as idealized in nineteenth-century women's fiction; Southern traditions of veneration for family; and the image of dynasty. Of these three, the ideal family in women's novels had the broadest base, coming as it did from American society as a whole.

During the nineteenth century—during, that is, the years of Texas' settlement—industrialization and the rapid growth of cities were changing the American economy and with it the family. These trends occurred first in the Northeast, then spread into the Midwest and, after 1865, the South. With industrialization middle-class women gained a great deal of power within the home. The new jobs in factories and offices drew husbands and fathers away from their homes, thus depriving them not only of the companionship of family life, but also of the ability to control household affairs and the behavior of family members. Instead, mothers now took primary responsibility for the day-to-day teaching, training, and disciplining of the children.

On the other hand, work in the manufacture of household items and clothing had been among the very first industries to be mechanized around 1800. Not only did this development draw young, single women to work outside the home, but it also began to tear away the homemaker's traditional economic functions of producing food and clothing for her family. Middle-class women felt keenly a loss of status and a sense of bewilderment as they became less important in the home economy. By 1830 a nagging question plagued many women regarding their roles in the home: if a woman was no longer a provider for her family, what was she? More, factories began drawing entire lower-class families, including mothers, into twelve- and fourteen-hour work days, thereby threatening family life and indeed the family itself. Many Americans found genuine cause for alarm about the nation's future.[4]

During the next thirty years a solution to that problem appeared. Articulated first by women writers, a new definition of woman's role placed the mother in the heart of family life. Leaders in this new view of motherhood were writers like Catharine Beecher, who defined a new "science" of homemaking, and Sarah Josepha Hale, who edited the first American mass circulation magazine, *Godey's Lady's Book*. They saw mothers as nurturers of children, comforters of careworn husbands, overall managers of households, and spiritual centerpieces of homes. The husband, of course, was recognized as head of the family, but the new concept of woman's role gave women a status within the family that was distinctly higher than in earlier American generations. An outpouring of books, pamphlets, tracts, sermons, and articles took up and promulgated this view of family life. Chiefly a middle-class phenomenon, its influence pervaded American culture as it reached even into the schoolbooks and became the ideal to which working-class women aspired.

Spread initially during the 1830s and 1840s with an outpouring of didactic literature, by the 1850s and 1860s domesticity and its companion concept of Victorian propriety were inspiring romances and domestic novels. Written by women for women, this new genre of enormously popular fiction explored the entire range of familial experiences and, in the resolutions of these stories, buttressed women's new role in the family. Thousands of fictional heroines defended their ideal families from various kinds of threats as they worked out difficult relationships between themselves and their husbands, parents and children, in-laws and outsiders. Each heroine found a way to keep her family intact and successful according to the ideals of domesticity and of what a family should be. By means of such stories, the domestic novels single-mindedly advocated a specific form and structure for the family. In so doing, they instructed nineteenth-century women in the age-old ways of myth and functioned to perpetuate values and standards and to justify women's familial roles, however recently defined.

This myth of the family immigrated west into Texas with the women pioneers from the United States. While they were imbued with its standards from early childhood, women added to it another vision as well, the goal of turning their homesteads, their own little patches of wilderness, into gardens. In the best traditions of American real-estate promoters, early Texas immigrants like Mary Austin Holley had written of Texas itself as a garden, just waiting to make people rich and comfortable. Women, as a general rule, were less dazzled than men by such sales pitches, even those written by other women. However appealing its physical beauty, the land would yield a decent livelihood only after years of labor and suffering and isolation. Women recognized the West for what it was—a psychological and emotional wilderness, as well as a physical one. As much as the men, they needed visions—their myths—to give them reasons for so much effort. Despite their awareness of the hardships ahead, they came, many of them, with enthusiasm and high hopes for the kind of lives they could shape from the raw land.

For those who were Southerners the new myth of the family was enhanced by sectional traditions. Family already exercised a special hold on Southerners, and to some degree this veneration for family had grown along with the South's historical development. After 1831 the best Southern minds turned almost solely to the defense of slavery and in the process sought to glorify a way of life and institutions that depended on human bondage. Threatened by the abolitionist crusade and by the rapid industrialization of the North, Southerners searched history and literature for justification of their system. They developed a special fondness for medieval times as portrayed in the novels of Sir Walter Scott. In a climate of opinion that thus looked backward, it was hardly surprising that Southerners developed a regard for family that would come to be one of their culture's chief traits.

Especially after the Civil War, dispossessed and displaced Southerners found solace in the deeds and personalities of their forebears and, more, a sense of reality and a hope, in the midst of defeat, for a future in which their traditions could survive. Family memories and stories provided a sense that their relatives were linked with something higher than ordinary experience, that they had, so to speak, entered the realm of archetypes. Such stories and anecdotes thus were more than fond memories. Their recounting became a means of entry into a mystical reality that contrasted boldly with a hopeless, careworn present and served to enhance the family beyond even the importance already ascribed to it by American culture in general. For many nineteenth-century Texas pioneer women, then, a Southern background united with the cult of domesticity and its literature to provide an image of the family that approached the level of myth.

In less than two generations this myth of the family withered. West Texas would seem to offer the most obvious reasons for its demise. The challenges of this dry, windy land must have affected human intentions and not merely work habits and methods. If tools and implements had to be adapted to the plains, surely ideals and dreams had to alter also. As often noted by scholars, the frontier did not respect gender-based roles, much less the conventions of propriety. To get the work done, women had to live, much of the time, in two worlds, their own and that of men. Life on the frontier required a fine balancing of necessity and propriety and, often, acceptance of a way of life for which women had not been prepared. Did the myth, then, falter in the face of such intransigent realities?

In truth, West Texas family life did have a way of taking courses for which no prescriptions existed. The Bosworth family, for example, lived for most of a twenty-four-year period in a covered wagon, moving each time the father heard of a place that might be better than the one they had. This family became settlers only when Mrs. Bosworth, in one final effort to have regular schooling for their eight children, refused to leave Texas. She left her husband and took the family to Stephenville, then to Ozona in Crockett County. Her husband wandered into New Mexico and did not rejoin the family for nearly a decade.

Few Texas families lived like the Bosworths, but many faced situations that could grind away at anyone's ideals. On occasion Texas families were headed by women, a situation diametrically opposite to what family was supposed to be. For forty-five years Henrietta King ran the famous ranch founded by her husband; for forty-one years Cornelia Adair ran the five-hundred-thousand-acre JA Ranch in the Panhandle. Hundreds of other women all over Texas found themselves the widowed owners of ranches and farms, and thousands more in towns and cities, as well as rural areas, routinely managed the family property alone while their husbands traveled on business.

For women on the West Texas frontier, loneliness must have launched the severest and most unexpected assault on the myth. Images and ideals, if they are to develop into myths or even endure within myths, require constant nourishment from the sharing of dozens of unconscious, perhaps hardly noticeable, patterns of behavior that make up a way of life. The lack of companionship and emotional support from others enduring similar experiences may have exacted its greatest toll on educated women, who had most thoroughly imbibed the ideas about appropriate family life through their schooling and their reading. Women clung successfully to the code of propriety in their personal behavior, but the realities of West Texas simply would not nurture the tender images that the cult of domesticity had fashioned into a myth of the family.

But there have always been families that wandered and women left as widows with property and family responsibilities to carry alone. Other frontiers also meant isolation and debilitating loneliness for the settlers. In general, the Texas frontier environment was harsher and less colorful than we care to remember, but it produced no results on families that could not be found elsewhere in the nineteenth-century

United States. Thus, the frontier cannot be blamed for killing off the myth single-handedly. Rather, the underlying reasons for its demise may be found in East Texas.

The myth of the family should, by all expectations, have flourished in the eastern and southern areas of the state, where settlement occurred earlier and under less difficult conditions than in the arid West. Indeed, the strength of Southern culture and family ties, and above all, family traditions and stories should have buttressed the myth. This could not happen, and the reasons lie as much, perhaps more, in the family itself and in American values as in anything that occurred on the Texas frontier. Indeed, the very lack of a myth of the Texas family helps to illuminate both the attitudes of nineteenth-century Texans (and Americans in general) toward family, and several significant characteristics of family as institution.

The most basic function of any family is to rear children and, while rightly expecting love and loyalty in return, to prepare the children to deal with the world beyond the family. Directly related to the larger society, family is by nature an open-ended institution that changes whenever any member dies or marries. Marriage, especially, alters a family, for each new in-law brings additional influences, traditions, and, perhaps, values. Within those family traditions, stories help to provide the children with models of appropriate behavior, with examples of laudable deeds, with an identity, with the security of belonging in the family group, and, perhaps with a sense of status. But while some families have anecdotes of heroism, others have a fair share of scandal. Family stories, then, tend to appeal only to the particular family that produced them. Myth, by contrast, functions within the common experience of a people.

In frontier times, Texas society in general was inhospitable to a real myth of family. While individual men undoubtedly treasured their homes and family relationships, day-to-day tasks and idealized visions of family were left to the women. Home, after all, was woman's sphere. Most men, it would appear, took family for granted or saw their families as the means to specific ends. As Willie Newbury Lewis wrote in her autobiography, her husband had married not because he wanted a family and family life, but "sons to carry on his name and success."[5] However generously Will Lewis met the financial responsibilities of family, he was rarely involved with the lives of his wife and children in Dallas. Instead, his real home lay with the men he hired to work his ranch in Dickens County. Men's interests, as a general rule, lay beyond the family, in work or in the public realm. This was the separation of male and female spheres that people expected, with the men dominating public life and defining public policy. Thus, the values and goals of frontier Texas and of nineteenth-century America, were not those of family, even though families provided the support systems and the means by which men's own plans would be accomplished.

To survive, myth must find acceptance by those whose purposes shape the society and by those who express its fondest ideals. The most gifted writers of the nineteenth century explored individual experience, not the problems or accomplishments of families. Women's concerns were shared only with other women, whose lives were circumscribed by custom, tradition, and law. Private and inaccessible to the men who created the national fantasies and the men who made public policy, women's experience did not enter the mainstream of American interests. Male readers and male writers, both of serious literature and of pulp fiction, disdained and ridiculed the female novelists who examined family life and relationships. Well into the twentieth century, those who shaped American ideals, like those who controlled public life, largely ignored the family. The subject apparently failed to excite Americans as a people.

More important, the very origins of the nineteenth-century myth of the family were inconducive to its survival. Consciousness of, indeed, rationalization of, the family with a specific definition of its form, structure, relationships, and functions appeared only when the American family began to change with the social forces unleashed by the economic effects of industrialization. With this awareness of change came, as early as the 1830s, the sense of being threatened. After that, two decades of didactic literature expressed people's opinions of what family should be. Only after the goals had been clearly enunciated did the fiction appear with examples for dealing with the various aspects of family life. This process was too rational, too deliberate. Enduring myth wells directly from the subconscious minds of storytellers to combine with values and aspirations assumed by their listeners. By contrast, the myth of the family brought to Texas by the Anglo women pioneers had shallow roots in a specific historical situation and could not survive when customs, traditions, and the American world view changed after 1900.

In the twentieth century also, individual male heroes, not families, have dominated expression of the American myth. The protagonists of films, television plays, and popular novels include cowboys and gamblers, assorted lawmen, trappers and trail scouts, wagonmasters and mountainmen, and enlisted troopers in the army. For such characters, wives and children and homes would hamper depiction of the imagined independence of frontiersmen. To be sure, family often provides some degree of background for these adventures. The hero may have, or at least once have had, parents and perhaps brothers and sisters, but they are usually far away or dead and therefore no impediment to his wandering life-style. Family might provide the context of such stories as the footloose types defend them from various hazards, though without lasting involvement with, much less commitment to, the family. Once in a while family provides the rationale of the story, as in a search for vengeance against a relative's killers. In the "adult westerns" of the 1950s, the central character could have a real, grown-up love interest and even, sometime in the future, after the story ended, a marriage. For the most part, though, fully drawn fictional families have been rare in twentieth-century vehicles of the American myth.

Even when westerns have been stories of families, they have mostly concerned struggles against an external force like the climate, the weather, white outlaws, or Indians. Very few, if any, of these films have investigated the frontier's effects on family life and family relationships. Conflicts within the family might add tension to the dialogue, but these matters are incidental to the real story and serve only to make the characters more sympathetic, sometimes by giving them more resemblance to twentieth-century people than historical accuracy allows. Without portrayal of the internal stresses on pioneer families, without consideration of the family's central role in settling, indeed conquering, the West, these stories also fail to produce a myth of the family. In the mythos of Texas, then, as in that of the United States as a whole, the family plays only a supporting role, evoking images that are at times vague and at others, vivid and haunting, but almost always merely a part of the scenery. However value-laden, the images of family remain fragmented and shallow, unable to convey more than suggestions and hints about family life in Texas.

In serious literature, too, family has not found its way into myth. When Texas women writers in twentieth-century mainstream fiction have pondered the familial experience, they have used Texas settings to provide insight into human relationships, not to convey any didactic messages or to propagate a particular view of family. In exploring the conflicts and subtleties of family, their stories have lacked a common theme for family life, much less any familial goals.[6]

If women's visions and Southern veneration could not produce an enduring myth of the family, what then of the relatively recent image of dynasty? This concept might, one would think, fit Texas better than any ideas brought from the East. The very terms that describe Texas connote bigness, even grandeur—herds and gushers, spreads and spaces. In the vastness of Texas, surely, the natural course for a family was to expand into a dynasty, originally envisioned as being built on an empire of cattle and land and, more recently, on wealth from oil. Has this image not provided the inspiration for a genuine myth of the Texas family, giving real families a set of standards and values as the way to achieve an ideal?

Again, the answer is negative. The image of the Texas family as dynasty is very recent, appearing only after 1945. Traditional folktales and legends of Texas lack the dynasty image altogether. Anglo Texans have told stories of the frontier—of the endurance of hardships caused by climate or weather, of encounters with Indians or Mexicans or outlaws, of practical jokes played on neighbors. Best known, perhaps, are the tall tales about colorful characters whose fantastic adventures match the size of Texas. In short, Texas folklore has celebrated the lives of ordinary people. If some of those people should chance to be extraordinarily wealthy, well, they are still who they were before they made all that money, and they go out of their way to let you know that they have not changed a bit. As H. L. Hunt's favorite song goes, "We're just plain folks."

Whatever the private ambitions of Texans about "making it big" (an American and not just a Texan goal), the image of dynasty comes mostly from forms of entertainment about Texas produced by non-Texans for non-Texans. Instead of reaching the stature of genuine myth, the dynasty image has produced only caricature and parody. The Benedicts of *Giant*, flawed as heroic characters by insensitivity, if not by outright callousness and bigotry, have degenerated into the Ewings of "Dallas," with a plethora of complexes, neuroses, assorted vices, and greed. The twentieth-century non-Texans who have written stories about Texas have chosen to portray the corruption sometimes brought by enormous amounts of money; they ignore any realistic, much less visionary, assessments of the future of families in Texas.

The single most peculiar fact in a search for a myth of family in Texas, then, lies in the neglect, by Texan and non-Texan storytellers and writers, of the rich and varied sources that might have produced and, indeed, possibly could still produce such a myth. The raw heroism of everyday life on the several Texas frontiers; the stark, grimy toil of people who wrested their living from the miserly earth; the triumph of Texas' minorities in preserving spirit and identity and pride through so many years of Anglo hostility and abuse; the age-old tragedy of free peoples conquered and their cultures erased by an overwhelming enemy—Texas has a world of memories and experience on which to base a myth of family.

But this very diversity may only hamper the formulation of myth, especially of family. The images of genuine myth seek to enhance remembered experiences and to inspire future generations to take up the values that made such actions and endurance and effort humanly possible. With public life now the scene of competition between and among the groups that once clashed on Texas battlefields, the state's peoples lack the shared goals and immediately understood themes that can coalesce into myth. Folktales, tall tales, family stories, fables, legends, traditional songs—all still serve their customary functions of providing entertainment, conveying values, and linking past with present. Although they share some of the purposes of myth, they remain discrete within their own cultures and unique to their own specific historical experience, unable to inspire Texans in general.

The family in Texas is hardly distinguishable from the family in the rest of the United States. The lack of a myth of the family (as opposed to images, fantasies, and ideals) strongly implies that we value most our traits as individuals. Perhaps this is not entirely detrimental to the family. In a rapidly changing society, family also must be able to change, to meet unforeseeable conditions and satisfy new needs. Myth might actually hinder the family's ability to do these things. It transcends the uniqueness and individuality of history by investing specific events and actions with a level of meaning that reaches beyond consciousness and reason into the unconscious, the assumed, the unquestioned. Thus, once formulated, myth often has a remarkable power to dominate a people's vision, even in the face of blatant, contradictory reality. It must not lock a society into the past, however admirable that past might appear. Foreseeing the future is not a function of myth, and perhaps more than any other institution, family must serve present and future.

NOTES

My thanks to Raynal Barber, Jacquelin M. McElhaney, and David J. Weber for their comments and suggestions. Works that influenced this paper include: Herbert G. Gutman, *The Black Family in Slavery and Freedom, 1750–1925* (New York: Vintage, 1976); Julie Roy Jeffrey, *Frontier Women: The Trans-Mississippi West, 1840–1880* (New York: Hill and Wang, 1979); Annette Kolodny, *The Land before Her: Fantasy and Experience of the American Frontiers, 1630–1860* (Chapel Hill: University of North Carolina Press, 1984); and Allan R. Bosworth, *New Country* (New York: Harper & Brothers, 1960).

1. For studies of the frontier family in Texas, see George M. Blackburn and Sherman L. Richards, "A Demographic History of the West: Nueces County, Texas, 1850," *Prologue* 4 (Spring, 1972): 3–20; Seymour V. Connor, "A Statistical Review of the Settlement of the Peters Colony, 1841–1848," *Southwestern Historical Quarterly* 57 (July, 1953): 38–64; and Blaine T. Williams, "The Frontier Family: Demographic Fact and Historical Myth," in *Essays on the American West*, ed. Harold M. Hollingsworth and Sandra L. Myres (Austin: University of Texas Press, 1969).

2. Arnoldo de León, *They Called Them Greasers: Anglo Attitudes toward Mexicans in Texas, 1821–1900* (Austin: University of Texas Press, 1983), pp. 9–10, 37–40, 43. Also idem, *The Tejano Community, 1836–1900* (Albuquerque: University of New Mexico Press, 1982), pp. 126–27, 130–31; and Mario T. García, *Desert Immigrants: The Mexicans of El Paso, 1800–1920* (New Haven: Yale University Press, 1981), pp. 197–99, 202.

3. Kenneth Foree, "Dynamo at 107," *Dallas Morning News*, 30 June 1946.

4. For an account of the changes in women's roles, see Nancy Cott, *The Bonds of Womanhood: "Woman's Sphere" in New England, 1780–1835* (New Haven: Yale University Press, 1977), especially pp. 19–100; and Gerda Lerner, "The Lady and the Mill Girl: Changes in the Status of Women in the Age of Jackson," in *The Majority Finds Its Past: Placing Women in History* (New York: Oxford University Press, 1979), pp. 15–30.

5. Willie Newbury Lewis, *Willie, a Girl from a Town Called Dallas* (College Station: Texas A&M University Press, 1984), p. 78.

6. Lou Halsall Rodenberger, ed., *Her Work: Stories by Texas Women* (Bryan, Tex.: Shearer Publishing, 1982), introduction.

NICHOLAS LEMANN

Power and Wealth

THE idea that the mythology of power and wealth might be exaggerated as a defining characteristic, or maybe *the* defining characteristic,
of Texas culture, is immensely appealing to Texans today. Proud of our
state's diversity, we would like to think of it as a place where very different peoples have peacefully joined together, without caring who
dominates, to form a society. We are worried that as rural Texans have
moved to the cities, and as urban Americans from elsewhere have
moved here, too, the state has lost its essential character, which is
rural. Driving between the biggest cities, we see a rural Texas that
appears pastoral and imagine the whole state to have had that spirit in
its best days. There must be hardly a person in the state who has not
been annoyed at having the popular television show "Dallas," with its
scheming millionaires, held up all over the world as the essence of
Texas life.

So it would be nice to be able to write that Texans in fact are not
enthralled by the mad pursuit of power and wealth—that deeper,
more sinewy country values lie at the heart of the life of the state. To
some extent it would be true. Certainly the majority of fifteen million
Texans don't have either power or wealth, and if they want them, it's as a
matter of an abstract longing rather than a ceaseless quest. As is often
pointed out, the depictions of Texas life that most strongly stress the
themes of power and wealth seem to come from non-Texans.

Since I'm going to argue here that, nice as it would be to say all
that, it wouldn't be completely honest, I might as well also own up to
not being a native Texan. I am a fifth-generation Louisianan, have lived
in Texas six years, and have come to know Texas firsthand mostly
by working as a reporter covering urban Texas. Maybe I've missed the

real Texas, though I don't think so. What I see is a state that is, in fact, distinguished from the rest in large part by how strong a part of the mythology power and wealth are. Yes, they're part of our national mythology, but more so in Texas.

T. R. Fehrenbach argues eloquently in *Lone Star* that Texas—Anglo Texas, anyway—was characterized from the start by a view of power fundamentally different from that which prevailed in the rest of the country:

> The Mexican-Indian warfare, taken together, spawned an almost incredible amount of violence across west and southwest Texas. . . . Because of this history, the dominant Texan viewpoint was not that Texans settled Texas, but they conquered it. Many other Americans have never been able to rationalize this in terms of a mythical North American mission in the world. Texas was never a refuge for the lowly, or oppressed, or a beacon proclaiming human rights. It was a primordial land with a Pleistocene climate, inhabited by species inherently hostile to the Anglo-Celtic breed. Some North Americans chose to conquer it, and in the process unquestionably came to look upon themselves as a sort of chosen race.[1]

Elsewhere Fehrenbach says that in this way, Texas is more like the rest of the world than it is like the United States. Anyone who has read the works of the settlers and founders of the nation side by side with those of the settlers and founders of Texas couldn't help but agree. Stephen F. Austin, it is true, was a man of peace, and even a statesman, but his purposes in founding his colony were nothing like those of the founders of the Massachusetts Bay Colony; he was an empresario interested in making a good and bounteous living for himself and his colonists. Sam Houston, though a man of war, was dovish on the question of subjugation of nonwhite races, especially Indians—but these views came to the fore after he had done the military work that made him the greatest Texas hero, and his own people didn't listen to them. Texas has had more than its share of towns founded with explicitly utopian aims, such as Sisterdale and Post, but this is because of its vastness and newness more than any other reason. The utopian strain is not to be found at the center of the enterprise, as it was in Massachusetts or Pennsylvania. The words that stand as the crystalline essence of Texas as a cause are from William Barrett Travis's letter from the Alamo: "I shall never surrender or retreat . . . VICTORY OR DEATH."

Power preceded money in Texas by many years. But the view of power that was shaped on the frontier was easily applied to money when, with the coming of oil and later of big cities, that became the prime means by which power relationships were expressed. In fact, the long time of little money combined with an admiration of the exercise of power surely must have created pent-up furies, which were unleashed when the state did at last become a commercial society. Texans have always been a self-selected breed, down to this day—people who have been willing to forsake a more secure and communitarian existence for the opportunity and lack of rigid social structure of the frontier. The tremendous and real importance of landholdings for so much of our history (which has its residue in the tremendous psychological importance of landholdings today) made the toughness and sheer acquisitiveness it took to amass land crucial qualities. If, in effect, people had to be a certain way to decide to come to Texas, the process of making the journey and getting established made them even more so. It is indicative of the character of nineteenth-century Texas that the Texas Rangers, who to today's gentler sensibilities seem almost like storm troopers, became our great mythic figures, probably more so within Texas than those other mythic Texas figures, the cowboys.

Texas liberals have tried to construct what historians call a usable past for themselves by pointing out a long tradition of mistrust of centralized power in the state, starting with the colonists and running through the Populists, Ma and Pa Ferguson, the early Lyndon Johnson, and Sam Rayburn. Jim Hightower, the present agriculture commissioner, has been the most assiduous proponent of this view in recent years. He pointedly calls himself a Populist, and it must be said that while so doing he won a statewide race against an establishment conservative by a huge margin. My own view is that this strain is in the Texas character, but it must be carefully defined and distinguished from liberalism as it exists elsewhere in the country.

Populists were, first of all, always small entrepreneurs, mainly farmers and skilled artisans. Their complaint against power was not so much that it existed as that it existed elsewhere, and was exercised to

their disadvantage. American liberalism has embraced the perennial
Populist cause of an increased money supply only cautiously, and only
in the name of lower unemployment. The Populists themselves had no
appreciable social-welfare agenda, and what they intended to do with
an inflating currency was borrow it to bring themselves material prosperity. Texans have never resented the rich man as long as he is self-
made and a Texan, and they never had national liberalism's desire to
redistribute wealth away from capitalists and to wage-earners; in fact,
national liberalism is so bound up in the social dynamics of large-scale
industrial capitalism as to be practically untranslatable to Texas. To
some extent, rural and small-town Texans can be aroused to resentment
of big-city Texans, but even this does not imply a mistrust of all forms
of power. Latter-day East Texas Populists like Rayburn and Wright
Patman were good friends indeed to small-town bankers and merchants. What has always united Texans is a resentment of power exercised over Texans by non-Texans, especially New Yorkers. One hears
this sentiment today from half-section farmers and corporate chief ex-
ecutives in almost the same words. Hightower himself was careful to
direct his Populist fervor outside the state, at such venerable bogey-
men as Wall Street, Washington, and "the middleman."

Texas was most liberal in the national sense when it was poorest,
and when the wounds of Reconstruction (the worst episode of Yankee
power-wielding) were still fresh enough to keep the state bound root
and branch to the Democratic party. Even today, Texas voters swing
back to the left when times are a little hard, as happened in the 1982
elections, in which the Democrats swept in at the nadir of the oil bust.
The liberal Texas view of the federal government, though, was as a provider of infrastructure—highways, railroads, electric lines, dams.
These were Johnson's great causes in his liberal days, and they are typical of what a colonial economy wants from its government (it is also
typical that government becomes an important part of the accumulation of private fortunes, as it was for George and Herman Brown in
those days).

Two other issues that are an essential part of national liberalism
show how unliberal Texas has always been, precisely because of its
view of power. Even in its most liberal days, Texas was (as it still is)
strongly supportive of the military, and out of conviction rather than

economic interest (the opposite is true in California), because the great lesson of Texas history is that strength and force are the foundations of our society. And on the other hand, Texans have never been (and still aren't) generous about the social welfare system. Sympathy for the downtrodden isn't a part of our history; within Texas, people have had to fend for themselves under harsh circumstances, and there has not been much dissatisfaction with the results.

The marriage of Texas' tough notions of power to an ethic of monetary wealth was made by oil; before oil, the number of families wealthy from cattle, cotton, rice, or timber was far too small to give a sense of definition to the state. It took half a century after the gusher at Spindletop for the power-money ethos to reach its full flower, but with hindsight progress toward that ethos looks inevitable and inexorable. The first great oil fields near Beaumont made relatively few Texans rich because they quickly came under the control of Eastern interests—hence the present-day Gulf and Texaco. Even the company that was considered the quintessence of the home-grown oil business, Humble, was wholly owned by the Rockefellers' Standard Oil of New Jersey from the teens onward. But with the big West Texas oil boom of the twenties, especially in the Permian Basin, and even more so with the East Texas boom of the thirties, the wealth began to spread more widely among Texans. By the early fifties that Texas archetype, the fabulously wealthy, right-wing, tough, uneducated roughneck-become-oilman, was a dominant figure, both in the life of the state and in the reputation of Texas elsewhere. It was over an oil issue, the Tidelands, that Governor Allan Shivers broke with the national Democratic party and established Texas as the conservative force in the nation that it is today.

The most famous of the Texas wildcatters—H. L. Hunt, Sid Richardson, Clint Murchison, Hugh Roy Cullen—were all typically Texan in their rural Southern backgrounds, their practical-mindedness, their ruthlessness, and their settling into community life relatively late. Also, just as the plutocrats of the Northeast's Gilded Age felt comfortable wrapping themselves in the ethos of the small-town, early-nineteenth-century Middle West, the oilmen considered themselves the legatees of the Texas spirit. Possession of land, often by rough means, was crucial to them; they were instinctive, feisty, uncomfortable indoors. It was common among these men to have as their single scholarly interest a near-obsession with frontier history. They collected art depicting frontier life, collected Texana, and bought ranches (meanwhile, of course, virtually all the large-scale ranchers in Texas became rich from oil royalties, thus strengthening the marriage between nineteenth-century tradition and twentieth-century business). They found it easy to transfer the Texas Populist mindset to ultraconservatism, in part because the putative enemy was the same—the Eastern Establishment, which over two generations had gone from laissez-faire to liberal. By the same token, Texans by and large did not resent the oilmen—they had exploited the land, not their fellow Texans. Today there seems to be no one in the state who does not look forward to boom times in the oil business.

Had there been no oil, Texas might have, despite its history, by now developed a genuinely skeptical, or at least rueful, view of power and wealth; this has been the case in much of the rest of the Confederacy, where until recently references to the Lost Cause were almost a daily part of life. Today the Deep South seems finally to be wearying of its obsession with the Civil War, but for generations there was a real hostility to economic development on the grounds that it was culturally Northern. Even the famous apostles of growth for the South, like Henry Grady, saw its source as unavoidably Northern business interests. Texas, rougher and more independent anyway, found in oil a way to boom that won nearly universal assent—and also in a way that seemed culturally anticolonial. Rather than begging the North to build factories here, we were demanding and getting bushels of its money so that it could run its factories and cities *up there*. Oil meant a degree not only of economic independence, but of revenge. I remember being shocked when I moved here to see the bumper stickers that said things like "Drive 70, Freeze a Yankee"; I'd expected that such raw resentments would be kept below the surface.

What might be called the current period in Texas history, during which our attitudes about power and wealth took on their present form, began, I think, with the oil embargo in the fall of 1973. The price of a barrel of oil, which hadn't changed drastically for years, immediately doubled, then rose steadily, then six years later suddenly doubled again, then continued to rise for nearly three more years before it finally ebbed and the life of the state seemed to settle down a bit. During this time Texas became, by the Census Department's measurement, more than 90 percent urban, and Houston and Dallas, in particular, took on the feeling of major metropolises. The population of the state, which had stayed remarkably flat in the sixties, rose steeply—immigrants streamed in from the West, the Midwest, the Northeast, Mexico, Central America, and even Europe and the Mideast. Texas became a rich state statistically (that is, as measured by per capita income) as opposed to poetically for the first time in its history. And sophistication, hard to measure but impossible to miss, rose probably more steeply than these other indices, finding its expression in urban amenities, in cultural institutions, even in dress and speech.

During this period, it seemed to me that both Texans and non-Texans thought they saw the state becoming homogenized, losing its distinctiveness. I often heard visitors—not real immigrants, who soon came to know better—complain that Texanness was just a self-conscious veneer, a pretension. Some people here wore cowboy hats and boots as a pose, the argument went, but really they were living in a place that had become much like other places. Native Texans made the same point, only elegiacally, and intellectuals made it more fervently than almost anyone else. Houston and Dallas could just as well be Minneapolis and Kansas City, they said; there were no more ties to the land; Texanness was fundamentally rural and untransplantable to the cities. One would frequently hear, for instance, that Larry McMurtry had been a Texas writer of the first rank in his twenties, when he was writing about the small towns and ranches of West Texas, but had sold out in his thirties, when he had moved to and begun to write novels about Houston, which in this view was Anywhere, U.S.A.

To my mind the cities, and especially Houston, were extremely Texan, in large part because a distinctively Texan mythology and set of values prevailed in them (as it did, for that matter, in the small towns). First of all their link to the country, being fresher, was more apparent than elsewhere. People of all walks of life made a point out of acting "country"—for example, driving pickup trucks, using colorful rural figures of speech, and professing a simple, basic, un-neurotic view of life. Many parts of Houston and Dallas look like small towns set end to end into infinity, and the symbolism of rural life is everywhere in the cities. The Texas cities in the seventies had among the highest divorce rates, murder rates, and rates of church attendance in the country, all conditions typical of the fast first generation of urbanization.

Also, the rural-to-urban progression (or regression, in the view of Texas intellectuals) is universal in the whole developed world and just happens to have occurred more recently in Texas than in the rest of the country; there are things transcending rural and urban that make Texas Texan, and many of these pertain to power and, perforce in an urban society, to wealth. The pursuit of wealth is openly the basic theme of urban life in Texas, more than elsewhere. Status in the big cities is much less complicated here, because it correlates almost exactly with money. The inheritors of fortunes are considered much less admirable figures than the makers of them here, which is exactly the reverse of the situation in the East. Among the vast not-rich majority, the idea of getting rich is a far more nearly universal dream than elsewhere (hence the symbolic import of the famous freeway sign in Houston that says "Business Cards in Eight Hours"). Among the rich, ostentation, as shown in outrageously unrefined and public tastes in art, housing, dress, and politics, prevails because there is no sense of anything to be played down. (If Texas were really rural in its soul, then the rural-born-and-raised millionaires of River Oaks would be rich austerely, in the authentic style of country wealth.) Prominent cultural figures in Texas cities, such as symphony conductors, the preachers in the biggest churches, and museum curators, do not dare assume the pose of their New York counterparts, that of critics (and finally redeemers) of money and power; instead, they celebrate those things, and it is clear from the interactions between wealth and culture who is subordinate to whom.

Even all this doesn't capture the extent to which the pursuit of money permeates the air in urban Texas. I used to take the earliest flight from Austin to Houston a lot, at the end of which the cargo of businessmen would burst out of the plane as if it were a starting gate; sometimes the stewardess, after saying goodbye over the public address system, would add sweetly, "Hope y'all make a lot of money today." Texas is the only place I've been where one hears it said of someone, in a quiet tone of sympathy mingled with pity, "Ol' Norman works for a salary." The owner of the Eastern magazine I work for now is a wealthy real-estate developer who yearns, it is said, to be permitted to mingle socially with journalists; in Texas, the socially ambitious journalists I know try to mingle with real-estate developers. Denton Cooley, one of the world's most famous surgeons, before whom heads of state bow and scrape, told *Forbes* magazine in some detail and with great pride about his business dealings, explaining that it is according to them that his success will be measured in Houston. The ranching mythology has been almost completely taken over by the rich, because it's so hard to make money with cattle these days; Cooley's arch rival, Michael DeBakey, is one of many prominent Texans of whom I've heard it said that he owns a ranch he's never seen, because it's an essential status symbol.

These attitudes toward money and power give urban life in Texas a distinctive tone. The rich—and to some extent, the citizenry generally—have been fearful of letting the cities get into the hands of the politicians. The result is that city politics is relatively unimportant here, and city politicians relatively powerless. Typically, the mayor and council members will be minimally paid, which guarantees that they'll be of the business class and work part-time, letting a technician-manager run the show. The great civic goals are efficiency and boosterism, found in different proportions in different places. The idea, so crucial to the history of Boston or New York or Chicago, that power struggles between groups with opposing interests are an essential characteristic of city life, and that the course of city government closely follows those struggles, is still anathema here. Even so mild an acknowledgment of pluralism as single-member council districts had to be rammed down Texas cities' throats by the Justice Department, and you still hear longing talk about their abolition. Power struggles are supposed to take place in the business world, not in local politics, and the winners are supposed to be allowed to have their way in other areas.

As Americans, and perhaps even as Texans, it's hard for us to accept that an ethos of power and wealth can be entirely good, or that it can prevail unremittingly everywhere. Are there significant pockets of rebellion in Texas? Are we ultimately going to ruin ourselves unless we adopt different values?

These are questions of such broad implications that one can't do much more than poke around them, but that's worth doing. I think, first, that power is exercised by different people at different places along the spectrum of (in Max Weber's terminology) traditional-to-rational. At one extreme would be the South Texas *patrón* who makes all the rules himself, holds his power personally and absolutely, and trades total protection for his workers' total loyalty; at the other is the head of a big publicly traded corporation whose parameters are tightly controlled by federal law, the stock market, and his competition, and whose exercise of power does not personally involve him in the lives of his employees. Roughly speaking, this distinction correlates with rural and urban, but only roughly; there are many owner-managed big businesses in Texas where the chief is a figure of personal as well as corporate authority. If these people begin to fade from the scene, it will be hard for power to retain its sense of moral authority and justification in Texas myth, and therefore pluralism might increase. Also, as one instantly sees watching a session of the Legislature, different interests—rural and urban, for instance—struggle bitterly against each other. But I don't think the outcomes usually have a broad effect on the culture.

As for subcultures where the prevailing ethos is genuinely different, I don't think they are significant. Clearly, in its day the Indian culture in Texas was truly a challenge not only to Texans' power but to their notions about power; Texans responded by wiping it out. Hispanic culture has in the Catholic church a major institution that acts to countervail capitalism probably more than do the Protestant churches, but this should not be taken as a sign of overall opposition. As an example, the leading Hispanic politician in Texas (and the country), Henry Cisneros, espouses views that are classically Texan: probusiness, promilitary, admiring of worldly success and ambition, seeing government as ideally an engine of prosperity, not social reform. Black culture in Texas is notable, to my mind, for its strong entrepreneurial streak. I was pleasantly shocked when I first saw McGregor Way in Houston, a black neighborhood of columned mansions such as exists in almost no other big city. This is not the life lived by most black Texans, but it is the side of black Texas life most obviously different from black life elsewhere. To some extent the city of Austin and various small towns around Central Texas—Buda, Fayette, Wimberley—are havens for people who have consciously laid aside the pursuit of worldly success, especially in its Texas definition. What we do not have, though, it seems to me, is a major slice of the state that has decided to give up the individual pursuit of power and money to pursue those things collectively, in the manner of Detroit automobile workers. Hence the lack of a powerful challenge to the ethos.

It seems intuitively true that a society in which power and money were wielded unhesitatingly, and widely admired, would not be a good one; this is why non-Texans assume Texas is essentially venal. Is it possible to defend Texas *as Texas*, that is, without making it sound like Vermont? I think it is, at least for now. Were the rest of the world truly noble, Texas might look bad; as it is, Texas only looks more honest. Because such primal passions lie too close to the surface of life here, life here is hardly ever dull. Perhaps I show my professional biases. A novelist can do great things by teasing out the subdued passions that lie beneath the orderly surface of a more restrained society than ours, but as a journalist, you've got to get them to tell you about it, and this is far easier in Texas than elsewhere.

Also, to the extent that life in Texas has the quality of an ongoing melee, it is redeemed by the sense—it still exists—that everyone is starting even and fighting fair. The collective memory of the state remains blue-collar or shabby white-collar. One feels that the no-holds-barred atmosphere gives a Vietnamese boat person or a roughneck or a door-to-door encyclopedia salesman a greater chance than he or she would have elsewhere. I'm not saying that Texas is social-Darwinist. It's one crucial step away. The feeling is more, "I made it out of the oil fields on my own hard work, dammit, but I know there are a lot of good men still back there," as opposed to, "The men still back there had their chance, and if they haven't made it, it's their just deserts." There is a constant danger that a state that worships winning will treat losers with contempt. I think Texas doesn't yet, mostly because its class system is still in nascent form, and the self-made know on some level how lucky they were, in a way that inheritors cannot.

So I think that favorite Texas worry—is Texas still Texan?—works out in a tricky way. If a mythology defines Texas, then Texas can't be ruined by cities, or by Yankees, but only by a new mythology. In a way this should make Texas secure, but it does seem hard to imagine that the Texas mythology can really last another 150 years. The pursuit of money and power sooner or later brings money and power, as is happening now; and concentrations of the real thing, as opposed to the chase, attract the impulses of a society to civilize, to modulate, to impose order. The better Texas does at its own game, the more it invites this happening. I think it will happen, but very slowly. A similar process took a full three generations in New York, but because Texas has such a different history and economy it could take much longer here. In the meantime, we ought not to deny ourselves the chance to enjoy the show. One day the Houston and Dallas of today will be getting the same elegiac treatment that the Floydadas and Waxahachies of a generation ago (when they must have seemed nothing but dull and typical) get now.

These thoughts may sound abstract, but most of them grew from seeds planted six years ago, when I was in full flight around Texas, driving from city to city in a yellow Volkswagen, stopping back at my apartment on Saturday nights to check the mail, and otherwise living in motel rooms. This period reached its crescendo in the summer of 1979, which I spent in Dallas. I was staying at a place called the Dupont Plaza, wedged between Stemmons Freeway and Industrial Boulevard, where one wall of every room was a giant mirror (whether intended to make the space seem roomy or sexy, I couldn't tell).

Dallas has a small group of self-assured rich people at its apex—its legendary Establishment—but a vast population of people hustling like crazy to get a piece of the action. I found myself wandering into this world.

Dallas is in a way the least Texan place in Texas—it's flat and featureless, completely nonregional in the way it looks, and economically a mercantile, rather than a frontier, city. Whereas in Houston one feels oil in the air, and in San Antonio ranching in Mexico, and in Fort Worth the vastness of West Texas, in Dallas one has intimations of the approaching Midwest. In the Houston airport I used to see middle-aged sharpies armed with rolls of quarters working the pay phones before the flight boarded, pitching oil deals, the modern Texas version of A. J. Leibling's telephone-booth Indians—"Del, these are *proven* reserves." In Dallas there were, instead, people pitching a line of pantsuits to buyers from small-town department stores at the Apparel Mart.

Still, the more I saw, the more I asked myself, "Where else could this possibly be taking place?" That was the summer of the gas lines and President Carter's malaise speech, and the mood of the whole country was strange. Dallas was even stranger. The shortages created a mood of free-floating panic in a city so totally dependent on the car and so hot—one spent hours sweltering in the lines, and met all sorts of hoarders, black-marketeers, and tipsters who had sprung up overnight like mushrooms. At the same time, the price of oil was soaring and there was a feeling of incipient boom in the air. The real estate market was getting superheated. People were moving to town to take their shot—people from all over the place, though Dallas was usually their first big city.

I spent a good deal of time making the rounds of the self-improvement industry, for which Dallas was a great headquarters. The combination of the gold-rush feeling and the sense that success in Dallas depended on nothing as concrete as finding oil but rather on salesmanship, aggressiveness, contacts, and a pleasing appearance made people feel they needed a training course to go over the top. I met people who taught courses in how to dress, how to talk, how to walk, how to think, how to sell, how to keep a marriage together, how to make money as a Christian. Here was all this rogue energy and opportunity in the air; they would teach you how to harness it, how to get in tune with it, how to make it work for you. All you needed was a Positive Mental Attitude and Goals!

These courses' main product was cassette tapes, called "motivational tapes," which you were supposed to listen to in your car on the freeway while driving to work. I worked up a pretty good collection of them, and I would listen myself. There was a quality of self-hypnosis about them. The speaker always had a low, soothing voice and he always told you to listen ten or twelve times, so that you would *really absorb* the message. Then you were supposed to repeat key phrases over and over to yourself. The content of the tapes was pure American folklore, part Benjamin Franklin, part Napoleon Hill, part Dale Carnegie, with a dollop of Jesus thrown in. Henry Ford, you would be told, was a failure at forty. So was Winston Churchill. Jesus Himself was not widely acclaimed in His time. But the words "I can't" were not in these people's vocabularies. They thought positive. They dared to dream. Cripples learn to walk. Hunchbacks straighten up. Sales records are broken by one-time losers. Etcetera. In the morning traffic I would see people behind the wheel terrifically dressed up, furiously chewing gum, mumbling to themselves, and I would imagine that all of us were getting our little motivational fix before starting to work.

My other project in Dallas was following around a twenty-nine-year-old commercial real-estate broker named Sherwood Blount as he cruised the freeways in his pearl-gray Cadillac, making deals over his car phone. Moving to Texas from an education and professional training in the East, I had been amazed at how widespread the desire to make a fortune was among bright young people. People I knew in the East who were ambitious wanted secure, high-paying jobs, but they didn't want to get rich. In Texas this was the universal dream, and to its credit, one met many more people who had moved way up the ladder in a short time than one did in the East. I wanted to write about such a person and, after shopping around a little, I found Sherwood, who was the son of a Dallas fireman, a former middle linebacker for SMU, and, at that moment, was worth $2,194,800 (he told me so). He agreed to let me spend a few weeks with him.

Just before we joined up he had brokered the sale of a maize field way, way out north of Dallas (in "the magic corridor," as the realtors called it), from its longtime owner to a homebuilder named Jerry Don Stiles. His great cause while I was with him was to persuade Stiles to resell the same land right away to another homebuilder named Peter Shaddock, with Stiles making a fast profit and Sherwood a fast commission. A subplot involved his trying to get the owner of the adjacent property—the mad heir of the original settler of the land, by now entirely surrounded by suburbs but still holding out—to get into the deal, too. This man, though crazy, was what one thought of as a Texan, but the notion of his getting homogenized didn't stand the test of reality; Sherwood was spiritually more purely Texan than the landowner, even though he was the agent of suburbia.

Amid much intrigue, the deal fell through. Late on one long day of machinations, the director of the Campus Crusade for Christ came to visit Sherwood in his office. His name was Bill Bright. What he wanted from Sherwood was a million dollars.

He began his pitch: "You know," he said, "Dallas and Houston are the two most strategic cities in the world, in terms of Christ. Dallas is one of the most *blessed* cities in all the world."

"Amen," said Sherwood.

"People talk about the healthy economy of Dallas and Houston," Bright continued, "and I think the business climate here is blessed because God has blessed it. Because the people believe. Now, New York City, New York, is one of the most corrupt, decadent cities in the world. It's a Sodom and Gomorrah. And that's why its economy is declining. It's a cesspool. It's a garbage pail. And it'll continue to be a millstone around the neck of this nation because of its decadence."

He went on: "Now, Sherwood, we've militarily become a paper tiger. We're impotent. We're in a great spiritual crisis. There's no optimism anywhere. There's no hope. We need an awakening. And frankly, that's why I've come here today. My one great objective is to mobilize men, Sherwood, like yourself. I'm looking for a thousand men like you who will put their shoulders to the wheel. It's always only a handful of people."

Sherwood said he didn't have a spare million just then, but he would see what he could do later. After Bright left he was walking on air. "Imagine that," he told me. "Him asking an old East Dallas boy like me for a million dollars." I thought I had finally arrived, mythologically speaking, at the exact center of Texas: say what you will about lonely towns and oil rigs and barbed wire and doing the two-step in beery dance halls, this was the heart of the matter, the place where all the yearnings that propel Texas converged.

His moment of reflection over, Sherwood stuck his head out in the hallway, looking for the other brokers who worked for him. "Alden?" he said. "Rick? Y'all make any money today?"

NOTES

1. T. R. Fehrenbach, *Lone Star: A History of Texas and the Texans* (New York: American Legacy Press, 1968), p. 447.

GILBERT M. CUTHBERTSON

Individual Freedom: The Evolution of a Political Ideal

TEXAS, myth, and politics easily interact, since they are complementary concepts. The cowboy *is* part of his horse, just as the Indians believed the Spaniards to be. The intimate relationship is similar to that in a primitive or prenational community in which myth legitimizes and supports the holders of power. During the Republic, Texans mobilized myths behind the cause of their national revolution. The "folk memory" of this great mythmaking period has never been lost. Although popularly viewed as a false belief, *myth* is more appropriately defined as a metaphor, a model, or a story that leads to truth and possesses a potential for both rational appeal and emotional development.

Underlying this essay are three central theses relating myth to the politics and governance of Texas. First, myths are reflected in the stories of cultural heroes in each period of Texas history. Political leaders, because they are popularly elected, usually embody the ideals and values of the state at any particular time. They also shape the direction in which the political system and its myths develop in response to changing social and political conditions. Myth, power, and values interact to define politics. Second, myths perform the primary function of educating Texans in their fundamental values and of reinforcing power in the community. Because of this function, educational policy and the manipulation of myths are vital to the mythmaking politician. Third, the primary value contained in the Texas political mythology is that of individual freedom, symbolized by the lone star and exemplified by the defense of freedom at the Alamo. Although the content of freedom may change, the form of freedom persists in Texans' attachment to tradition.

In this essay I shall first identify specific Texas political heroes and the functions of various political myths in the formation of Texas as a state and society, and then concentrate on the evolution of the key value of freedom. In general, Texas political myth focuses on a dominant personality, a hero or heroine, who embodies the prevailing cultural values. For example, the spirit of that *éminence grise* of Texas politics, Colonel E. M. House, might be said to have dominated the Democratic party even after he died. The presence of LBJ still wanders along the Pedernales to remind Democrats of old wounds and older victories. The spirit of Sam Houston eternally points to San Jacinto, although the general himself consulted oracles either more bibulous or more patriotic than the Witch of Endor. Table 1 summarizes the most common heroes and villains of Texas' political mythology.

The only possible exception to the continuity of great political mythmakers and heroes is during the period of the War between the States. Texas failed to produce a single major figure of the stature of Sam Houston, although "Old Leathercoat" Throckmorton, who voted against the Secession Ordinance but later became a Confederate general, and "Old Roman" Reagan, the postmaster general of the Confederacy, came close. From the standpoint of political mythmaking, this absence of heroes is somewhat unusual, since periods of great political unrest are generally great myth-creating periods.

Almost all of the early heroes are political to some extent, although Stephen F. Austin might have wished to avoid politics and might be distinguished as a statesman. However, there is a tendency to move from military achievements during the period of the Republic and the Confederate brigadiers to the criterion of economic success in the more recent periods of Texas politics. Moreover, Texas heroes have become increasingly prominent nationally, and other role models (astronauts, physicians, and movie stars) now compete with politicians, who are viewed as a mixed blessing at all times.

The ambivalent attitude toward politicians is also reflected in the bipolarity of the heroic myths. There was a pro–Sam Houston and an anti–Sam Houston party from the period of the Republic through the

TABLE 1. Political Heroes and Villains

Historical Period	Heroes	Villains
Revolution and Republic (1836–1845)	Stephen Austin Sam Houston Mirabeau Lamar	Mexicans
War between the States and Reconstruction (1861–1876)	John Reagan J. W. Throckmorton	E. J. Davis Yankees Outlaws Republicans
Populist and Prohibitionist (1880s-1920s)	Jim Hogg	Gold gamblers Railways Breweries
	Ma and Pa Ferguson	
Texanization of national politics (1900–Present)	E. M. House Sam Rayburn John Garner Lyndon Johnson	Ku Klux Klan Federal government Communists

1860s. During Reconstruction, Governor E. J. Davis was viewed as a hero by radical politicians and blacks, but as a villain by the former Confederates. In the same manner, Governors "Farmer Jim" and "Ma" Ferguson in the 1920s were idealized by their supporters and vilified by their opponents. Senator Joseph Weldon Bailey and Governor Jim Hogg were likewise controversial figures. More recent Texas politicians have not had their mythological roles stabilized, although LBJ's political exploits are already mellowing with age.

Performing the same role that heroes do in more primitive communities, the Texas political hero must liberate the people from a variety of evil forces. (This aspect of the hero's function will be considered later in the essay in treating the value of freedom.) In the earliest myths, for example, the hero must conquer the land itself, which is simultaneously a utopia to be achieved and a villain to be conquered. Similarly, there are changing stereotypes of the minority subcultures with which the politician must deal. For example, Mexicans, who were villains in the early period of the Republic, are now hyphenated and "Tex-Mex" is even a distinct dialect. Because of the migration of Yankees and Republicans to Texas, these former villains are also being integrated into the mainstream of Texas culture. Railways, which were the bane of the Populists, are no longer considered especially harmful.

Myths also perform certain functions for a society. The functions of Texas political mythology evolve in fairly distinct chronological stages. As the needs and demands of the system change, the myths also change, as do the corresponding culture heroes. During the earliest stages, Texas existed both as a threat in the minds of Eastern politicians and as a promise in the minds of Southern ones. Complicated by the slavery issue, the problem of legitimizing American settlement became Texas' first crisis. The mythological response was based on Manifest Destiny and "racial superiority," in which the Anglos discovered a justification for their rule. Both myths and institutions reinforced the dominance of "the children of light" and the subordination of "the children of darkness." After the Texas Revolution, the politicians had to translate political upheaval into stable, legal forms of power. Hence, the new mythological emphasis was upon law and order, and education. The Alamo was in no sense forgotten but was incorporated into the folk traditions as a symbol of the individualistic freedom that gives continuity to the Texas heritage. The Alamo as a physical building was almost swept away in the great surge of economic "progress" that swept Texas after Reconstruction. Judging from the "Davy Crockett Craze" of the 1950s, a part of the building's salvation lay in its new potential as a symbol for commercial enterprise. Since the 1880s, myths have placed an increasing stress on wealth as a source for political power. Whether the elite was composed of oilmen, cattlemen, bankers, or cotton or lumber magnates, the corresponding myths have stressed the desirability of wealth and its conversion into power. Table 2 summarizes some of these functions of Texas' political mythology.

There is, of course, a countermythology that portrays the corruption of the trusts and corporations, the exploitation of the farmer and the rancher, the downtrodden "little people." In addition, intermediary stages exist between the extreme idealization of wealth and the negative image of corruption in stories of loners: wildcatters who made good in the oil fields, cowboys who worked hard on the ranch until they could own their own spread, and individuals who worked their way up within the system in the "school of hard knocks." By stressing the

TABLE 2. Functions of Political Myth in Texas

Function	Description
Legitimizing	Texas was initially a "state of nature." It became a "state of mind." Noble Savages had to be Christianized and the land conquered, for the Devil had slipped into Paradise. Legitimacy was found in the idea of Anglo-Saxon superiority, Manifest Destiny, the liberal ideas of the Mexican Constitution of 1824, and the need to destroy tyrants to protect natural rights.
Legalizing	Legal myths are reflected in the various constitutions of the state. Law and order is symbolized by the Texas Rangers, "the gentlemen in the white hats," who appear as "*los Rinches*" in the Mexican-American mythology.
Reinforcing	Education uses certain heroic models of virtue and patriotism to reinforce cultural values. A synthesis of models taken from classical history, the frontier, and the American Revolution support the tradition of individualistic freedom and the government itself.
Justifying	Myths also support the social and economic establishment of the state, the economic power-holders based on oil, cattle, banking, and cotton.

potential for upward mobility within the system, the power holders protect their own positions. By stressing "the common stake" in their institutions against federal bureaucrats and regulators, the myth insulates and unifies the system. "Texas oil for Texas homes" has a suitably patriotic ring; "Texas First" has a protectively nationalistic sound, as does "Made in Texas by Texans." Why should others prey on Texas' natural resources and victimize Texans with their socialistic schemes? Texans have not gone quite that far. These slogans are merely examples of the process by which political and economic power mobilize myths and symbols in their support. Parallel illustrations could be drawn from any period in the state's mythological development.

The heroes, myths, and mythmakers of the Texas past make up an awesome cavalcade. To join the "ghost-riders" the searcher needs a good Mexican saddle and a *riata*. He or she needs what earlier writers spoke of as a *fraenum potentiae*, "a bridle on power," in a different sense, to control the winged horse of mythology. Then the searcher can visit the great shrines of myth with Archibald MacLeish in "You, Andrew Marvell":

> And strange at Ecbatan the trees
> Take leaf by leaf the evening strange
> The flooding dark about their knees
> The mountains over Persia change
>
> And now at Kermanshah the gate
> Dark empty and the withered grass
> And through the twilight now the late
> Few travellers in the westward pass.[1]

Traveling west, he might have stopped at Masada and Thermopylae and would have ended up at San Antonio—"For at the Alamo, the line. . . ." He would have heard the blood-curdling war cry of the wars with the Moors, the *deguello*. He would have seen the blood-red flag of "No quarter." He would have seen General Santa Anna's commanders, riding like riders of the Apocalypse, converging on the old mission: General Cos from the west, Colonel Romero from the east, Colonel Duque from the north, and Colonel Morales at the very gate.

Brian Huberman and Ed Hugetz in their television special, "Remembering the Alamo on Film," have brilliantly examined the analogy of the Alamo myth to the old Puritan "city on a hill."[2] The place is a focus of power, like a magic mountain. It is a gateway to myth, along with other places, Enchanted Rock, for example. A conservative, entering the Alamo gateway, would see the symbol of rugged individualism on the frontier and the need to defend America, whereas a liberal would see the struggle for a sense of community, justice, and civil liberties. This latter version would have been especially noticeable to the Tejano defenders who fought for equality for all Texans, the Constitution of 1824, and justice within the system. Both interpretations lead to true insights regarding politics. America is the Alamo, and so is Texas.

Although there is only one genuine Alamo, that "mere corral," as the Mexican reports termed it, has become not only a symbol of Texas but a universal symbol of freedom. The Alamo is at the heart of Texas myth. It is the symbol that lends cohesiveness to an otherwise motley group of defenders, including Bowie, Crockett, Seguín, and Travis. As

Huberman and Hugetz indicate, the moment at which Travis drew the line is central to the heroic legend. Here the men freely chose to resist against overwhelming odds, with Bowie carried across in a stretcher.

Now the irony is that no one would know of the "line" had it not been for one Louis Rose, "the man who left the Alamo," whose tale was reported in the *Texas Almanac* for 1873 in an account supposedly related to W. P. Zuber. The courage of the defenders could only be known and the myth preserved because of the cowardice (or prudence) of Rose. Zuber, in fact, later retracted the part about the line, which some historians had doubted all along, but as the great myth-historian of Texas, J. Frank Dobie, pointed out, it doesn't really matter whether the line is historically true. It is the way Travis should have behaved. It is mythologically true. It is morally true. Sacrificing one's self-interest for the good of the community provides an excellent educational model. Myths are expected to function in precisely this manner.

Just as the Alamo serves as a gateway to myth, myth itself is a gateway to the understanding of religion, science, and politics. Myth allows us to free ourselves from the real world and enter the realms of human imagination. Gateways need not be places; they can be heroes or even events. The black celebration of Juneteenth, Emancipation Day, is a gateway commemorating freedom. The Cinco de Mayo *fiestas patrias* commemorate the liberation of Puebla from the French in 1862 by Juárez. The frontier, symbolized by the cowboy, opened the vision of limitless space on the plains. NASA, symbolized by the astronaut, is a gateway to the new frontier of space. Even the Texas Constitution of 1876, under which Texans still live, celebrates the psychological and political liberation from Reconstruction. It is, in short, this general concept of freedom that unites all Texans.

But this concept of freedom has undergone subtle changes in meaning over time, in light of changing historical circumstances. Table 3 summarizes the evolution of the idea of freedom and hazards a guess regarding its future changes.

In each of the historical periods, the prevailing myth reflected changes in the idea of freedom. In the early period of the frontier, freedom was sometimes viewed as something negative, as freedom from something feared, Indians and Mexicans, for example. The counterfears of these groups were unsympathetically reported by the Anglos, who

TABLE 3. The Evolution of the Idea of Freedom in Texas Politics

Historical Period	Concept of Freedom
Frontier (1820s–36)	The frontier is prepolitical. Texas is a gateway to freedom that allows an escape from the past. Freedom is really limited to Anglos. In fact, Indian "freedom" is a threat. Settlers discover the TANSTAFT principle, or "There ain't no such thing as a free lunch in Texas." Freedom is viewed as freedom from hardships.
Republic (1836–45)	Freedom begins to be translated into political terms of constitutional and human rights, freedom from Mexican oppression, freedom to expand territorially and to take control of the community's own affairs. The struggle for freedom reenacts that of the American Revolution, with the themes of the "pursuit of happiness" and government by consent of the governed.
War between the States and Reconstruction (1861–76)	Freedom from the Union ironically means support of the institution of slavery as the war inverts and confuses fundamental values. The countermyth urges Texas to free itself from the Confederates. The Reconstruction period marks Texas' effort to free itself from carpetbaggers and the like. The cowboy enters with the "freedom of the range."
Democratic dominance: "The old politics" (1870s–1970s)	There are several themes, which occasionally contradict. There is freedom from economic oppression in the form of the corporations and freedom from economic inequality. There is freedom from the national government, bureaucracy, regulation, and interference with the individual.
Two-party system: "The new politics" (1980s–2050)	Freedom includes more meaningful political choices, removal of obstacles to political participation, and the broadening of the base of the electorate, so that Texas by the year 2050 stresses increasingly not only the toleration of eccentricity, which has always characterized its political culture, but toleration of diversity. Space and technology open up new frontiers for maximizing freedom and the democratic process. There is a continuing split between the liberal concept of freedom as moral permissiveness and the conservative concept of freedom as moral responsibility.

thought they were dealing with people who were "half devil and half child." At the same time, Texas became a positive symbol of natural freedom, a gateway that enabled the emigrant to escape the past and get a new start. Mexico performed this function for slaves because slavery was illegal there, although peonage was not. Texas is even today a powerfully liberating myth for thousands of illegal aliens, who see it as the realization of a dream. They are the current "children of Coronado."

An early Texas story recounts the feats of the "blue nun of the Jumayos," who was capable of being among the Indians at several places at the same time. She could visit the sick at one village while feeding the hungry at the next. This is a religious myth of piety and virtue like that of Our Lady of Guadalupe, yet it also reveals a fundamentally human desire to transcend time and space and to conquer hunger and poverty. Eventually these aspirations translated politically in terms of Morelos and Padre Hidalgo. Again, however, it must be stressed that tremendous contrasts exist in the *gritos*: "Tierra y libertad," "Set my people free," "Remember the Alamo," "Don't fence me in," and "Turn Texas loose." Still, the use of myth to effect individual freedom serves as a link for all aspects of Texas' political culture.

Another way of examining the concept of freedom in relationship to the Texas political mythology is to see exactly from what the people are to be freed. What do they fear most? The classical heroes dispatched assorted dragons, wicked kings, and evil sorcerers. Since the forms of tested heroism are fairly constant, modern politicians dress themselves in shining armor to attack their opponents as malignant windmills. With all the tools of modern technology available for campaigning, they occasionally make it very difficult, say, in a Texas senatorial race, for voters to separate heroes from villains. Furthermore, since Texas has been spared the reality of dragons, politicians find it necessary to create the illusion of their existence.

Early Texas was idealized as a free state, where the Wild Man of the Woods disported himself with the wilder woman of Navidad. It was a world just waiting to be populated by mythological beasts, half-alligator, half-mountain lion, the Crockett of the *Almanacks*, the exemplar of frontier individualism. Bowie and Colt had rendered the human condition one of perfect equality. Only a few Mexicans spoiled the perfect society.

In succeeding stages, instead of Mexicans depriving the individual of freedom, Yankees, the federal government, banks, and other suitable villains filled this role. Reconstruction Governor E. J. Davis was symbolized as a diabolical figure, a substitute for General Santa Anna, who in turn had understudied King George III. Texans of the old politics distrusted authority profoundly, at least if someone else had it, and claimed to fear nothing alive. Texans of the new politics claim to fear "nothing but fear itself," although they are beginning to worry about the new Republican menace enough to advertise on their automobile bumper stickers, "Texas Democrat"—but not yet "Texas Democrat, Endangered Species," mind you.

For the Texans of the old politics, demands for limited government and fiscal responsibility were enshrined in the Texas Constitution of 1876. That this venerable showcase of Texas traditions still serves as the mythological form for the governance of the state is testimony to the document's durability, due more to its mythological character than to its political utility. In comprehending how Texas governance operates, one must recognize the process by which a fear is magnified into a myth and converted into an institution. Political power in turn reinforces the myth. For example, the very real fear of Indians on the frontier is reflected in the power of the governor to call out the state militia. Myths rooted in the raids of the Comanche moon are too deep-seated to be dislodged by constitutional reformers, even though there is no Indian threat. The fear of blacks, appearing in the Colorado County slave rebellion, the Gainesville hangings, and the expulsion of blacks from Comanche County, was institutionalized in the form of the "white primary," which excluded blacks from voting. This institution, manipulated by the Ku Klux Klan as a source of power, was abolished only in 1953 by a U.S. Supreme Court decision. The Texas Constitution also articulates fears regarding abuse of power, fiscal irresponsibility, and public education. It requires virtually an "act of God" to transfer funds from one educational institution to another.

In the 1880s the issue of barbed wire and the fencing off of the range became a highly emotional issue during the "Fence-Cutting War" and Governor Ireland's administration. The issue was again freedom. Texans do not like to have lines drawn; when they are drawn, they like to be able to cross them.

Political heroes are expected to liberate their people. Thus Governor Hogg freed Texas from the railroads. Colonel House was working to free America from Kaiserism abroad, and a series of governors attempted to rescue Texas from Fergusonism at home. Meanwhile, the Governors Ferguson attempted to free the state of both the Klan and the University of Texas, even if they had to free large numbers of prisoners from Huntsville in time for the election. Later, Governor Shivers tried to save the state from federals and Communists; Governor White saved Texas from the Republicans and the Public Utilities Commission. Although it is useful for politicians to focus their attacks on a highly visible enemy, inflation, unemployment, corruption, and nuclear power will also serve.

One of the most important tasks of successful political mythmakers is to symbolize powerfully the most pervasive fears of their constituents. Since elections only tangentially have the effect of selecting the best candidates, their primary function is as a safety valve for discontent and a ritual displacement for more violent forms of settling succession to office. Similarly, football on Saturday displaces actual violence while providing entertainment. Texans like their football so intensely that the U.S. Supreme Court has recently had to settle a dispute regarding eligibility rules in a Houston high school case. One of the few things that the Texas observer can be certain of is that elections and football will still be the source of controversy in the mythology and politics of 2050.

NOTES

1. Archibald MacLeish, *Collected Poems, 1917–1952* (Boston: Houghton Mifflin, 1952), p. 50.

2. Brian Huberman and Ed Hugetz, "The Myth of the Alamo: Remembering the Alamo on Film" (an educational documentary broadcast over KUHT-TV Houston in 1984).

C. W. SMITH

Changing Visions of the Good Life

dem Ersten Tod, dem Zweiten Not, dem Dritten Brot

For the first generation, death; for the second,
deprivation; for the third, bread.

Old German adage concerning immigrants

I often think while I'm jogging—it makes running less of a chore—and
one day while my running partner and I were pounding along a side-
walk, I was trying to remember, for the purpose of writing this essay,
my reading of at least twenty years ago in a college philosophy class,
Plato's parable of the cave and his notion about The Good Life. "What're
you thinking about?" asked my partner. "The Good Life," I said. "Well,
that's appropriate," he said, grinning and looking about.

We had wound our way into Dallas's Highland Park and we were
surrounded by two- and three-story homes with impeccably trimmed
lawns and circular driveways built to display vehicular trophies—your
BMWs, Caddies, an Excalibur or two.

This was not precisely what I had in mind, but his quick, unconscious presumption that this is The Good Life confirmed for me what I
suspect to be most people's definition of it: material success, material
comfort, the tangible signs of wealth and power. Money is life's report
card, it's said. We were a long way from Plato, and, indeed, a long way
from what some others who have lived on, or crossed over, the land
now temporarily being called Texas have considered The Good Life.

I have no way of proving anything I might write about myths of
The Good Life in Texas; rather, what follows here should be taken in
the spirit of suggestion made after an informal inquiry into Texas his-

tory and inference drawn from personal observation. My purpose here is to trace roughly what might be called an evolutionary or historical change in what various cultural groups have considered to be The Good Life over the course of the past two hundred years or so and to suggest that we can see a trend toward defining The Good Life in ever more narrow materialistic terms as monetary rewards for individual enterprise. Beyond that, The Good Life has perhaps even come to mean the possession of wealth without regard to how it is accumulated. If the Protestant work ethic was, to John Calvin, a way for Christians to get to heaven through "good works," he and his Puritan followers also clung to the notion that any enjoyment of the fruits of such labor was sinful. Today, that work ethic has produced its own moral antithesis— that the purpose of work is to produce the means for greater carnal pleasures on an ever-escalating scale, and the man who can lay claim to the greatest accumulation is viewed by society at large as an example of heaven's blessing.

I

Elsewhere in these pages, W. W. Newcomb in his essay on the Native American mind has outlined some of the major conflicts between the Native American and European-American concepts of land and property. Whether they were farmers like the Caddoes or nomadic hunters like the Comanches, says Newcomb, "no Indian people in Texas regarded the varied lands they hunted over or raised corn on as commodities to be bought and sold, or to be held or owned by individuals. The majority, at least implicitly, regarded themselves as belonging to or as part of the natural world. Often the earth was regarded explicitly as Mother. Many consciously sought to live in harmony with the earth, with the animals it nurtured, and the forces that created it all. None regarded themselves as its conquerors or exploiters."

Newcomb also outlines the well-known aboriginal communal concepts toward personal property, spoils of the raid or hunt, and fruits of harvest and notes that these attitudes of communal reverence toward the land and concern not for the welfare of the individual but of the tribe "undoubtedly contributed to the relative ease with which many of them were dispossessed" by "land-hungry farmers and ranchers" who would "appropriate it for a higher purpose."

That "higher purpose" was, of course, the European notion that land is to be claimed, owned, tilled, drilled, mined, or grazed by nations or individuals who may stake out inviolable and exclusive claims to it. Land is to be owned and exploited, whether for the glory of God, the pope, or the king of Spain, or for the use and abuse of a redneck who, although he might be running from the Tennessee constabulary, is the first white man to declare this piece of Texas his and therefore considers it his exclusive domain with unimpeachable rights to use and abuse it.

In discussing the Scotch-Irish immigrants who poured out of Appalachia during the eighteenth and nineteenth centuries and headed for Texas, T. R. Fehrenbach makes an interesting and useful distinction between how they came and how the Spanish colonized lands under their dominion. Contrary to the eighteenth-century Spanish concept of conquest, incorporation, and exploitation, the "Anglo-American historical experience was to be this: the people moved westward, on their own, and they sucked their government along behind, whether it wanted to go or not."[1] This suggests to me that to the Anglos, The Good Life contains more than a little anarchism, meaning that it is the life least fettered by institutions, whereas to the Spanish and their descendants, institutions are regarded with far less suspicion. Indeed, the Hispanics literally grouped about the mission churches all across the West; their church—the institution, the religion, and the edifice—was indispensable for The Good Life.

For both the Anglos and the Spaniards, land had no inherent value. Unlike the Native Americans, who held that the land contained a spirit, the Europeans considered it only a commodity. Individuals and governments may buy and sell or trade it. This profound historical shift in the concept of property brings us to one of the most fundamental myths of Western civilization—the Myth of Ownership.

The settlement of Texas by people of European extraction repeats for the most part the earlier pattern of colonization on the Eastern seaboard, and it is a commonplace observation about our history that many early Texans were fugitives of one sort or another for whom the possession of land was secondary. As even the most casual historian knows, the initials G.T.T. stand for "Gone to Texas," an expression which came into use in the first half of the nineteenth century when Texas had the reputation for producing and harboring outlaws. The letters were often chalked on the doors of houses in the Southern states to tell where the occupants had gone," and at some point "people in other states appended the symbol to the name of every rascal who skipped out."[2]

An 1831 letter from an early settler to his correspondent in Tennessee declares, "Every one who is driven from all other places flies to this country as a city of refuge." The writer tells his listener, "It would amuse you very much could you hear the manner in which the people of this new country address each other. It is nothing uncommon for us to inquire of a man why he ran away from the States! but few persons feel insulted by such a question. They generally answer for some crime or another which they have committed; if they deny having committed any crime, and say they did not run away, they are generally looked upon rather suspiciously."[3]

For others like the horse trader Phillip Nolan, this territory seemed to hold the promise of adventure, profit, and an expansive arena to suit his thirst for the "free" life. Nolan obtained permission in 1791 from the Spanish governor of Louisiana to capture wild horses in Texas but ran afoul of the Spanish in San Antonio:

> I was soon spoken of as a spy. I was not imprisoned, but I was cheated out of all my goods, and in less than one year, reduced as poor as any Indian who roams the forest. Disappointed, distressed, tired of civilization, and all its cares, I was about to abandon it forever; the freedom, the independence of the savage life, was always congenial to my nature, and I left the Spaniards, and wandered among the Indians, that live between the Illinois and St. Antonio: this life, however, I found less pleasing in practice than speculation. I was a favourite with the Tawayes and Cammanches;—successful in the chace, victorious in little feats of activity, but I could not altogether *Indianfy* my heart.[4]

For the fugitives and men such as Nolan—the traders, the trappers, the frontiersmen—this territory, which lay outside the United States, must have constituted not so much an opportunity to discover The Good Life of the farmer and rancher who must lay claim to a specific plot of the earth necessary to this success, as *freedom from re-straints*, including, one supposes, the restraint of law and the restraint of having to stay put. As Ellis P. Bean put it, "At the age of seventeen years, I had a great desire to travel, and see other parts of the world. To see some foreign country was all my desire."[5]

But to most of the Anglo-Americans who poured out of the South and the Appalachian region of the United States to settle in Texas during the nineteenth century, Texas meant land that could be claimed individually and used or exploited. It was a wilderness to be tamed, conquered, and "redeemed," as Robin Doughty puts it elsewhere in these pages.

As much as we are fond of the notion that they were all somehow self-reliant, individual pioneering families, who walked onto a location and began ploughing and cutting down trees, the truth seems to be that an early sort of developer brought a larger number of them here. The large colonization grants wrested from the Mexican government by Stephen F. Austin, DeWitt, Peters, and some thirty-seven other em-presarios had to be populated to be fulfilled according to the contracts. In at least one case—Robertson's Colony—the land that included some twenty counties or so of modern Central Texas was literally purchased by the settlers from the empresario Robert Leftwich, who negotiated the deal in Mexico under his own name. Leftwich double-dealt the Tennessee subscribers who had sent him to Mexico City, and he never bothered to save a parcel of it for himself, taking a cash settlement instead.[6]

Whether they were brought here by self-seeking entrepreneurs or more altruistic empresarios, the Anglo-American and European settlers were led to believe—or they presumed—that the land was an Eden lying fallow, a veritable unspoiled Garden. Myriad accounts encouraged them to uproot themselves from Kentucky, Ohio, or Germany and try their luck here. "In the present day, so many of the inhabitants of the old world, as well as of the new, are turning their attention from their land worn out by constant tillage, to the flowery gardens of the sunny south-west that a history of that country has long been desired," declares the editor in the preface of an 1852 collection of letters previously mentioned. Her Texas correspondent, W. B. Dewees, one of Austin's Old Three Hundred, packs his letters with rhapsodic descriptions that must have plumped the hopes of many a luckless or landless American looking for a new home:

> You, in Kentucky, cannot for a moment conceive of the beauty of one of our prairies in the spring. Imagine for yourself a vast plain extending as far as the eye can reach, with nothing but the deep blue sky to bound the prospect, excepting on the east side where runs a broad red stream, with lofty trees rearing themselves upon its banks, and you have our prairie. This is covered with a carpet of the richest verdure, from the midst of which spring up wild flowers of ever hue and shade, rendering the scene one of almost fairy-like beauty. Indeed it is impossible to step without crushing these fairest of nature's works. Upon these natural flower gardens feed numerous herds of buffalo, deer, and other wild animals.[7]

That—1822—must have been a wet year. In 1830, the same settler speaks of the "northwestern and western portion" of Texas (we must presume he meant northwest and west of his location around Columbus): "The valleys are rich and covered with high, waving grass, the mountains high, and abounding in every variety of mineral productions. Here abound the finest streams of clear crystal water bounding over deep cascades and rolling on in great rapidity through a country of unrivaled beauty." In 1831, the writer committed himself to a claim that today might be punishable by the Federal Trade Commission:

> You desired me to tell you in what manner we spend our idle hours. In doing this I shall tell you how a good many spend most of their time, our country being so rich as to require but little time to till the ground. This is an excellent country for game and fish. On the coast we find beds of oysters, fishes of various kinds, and all manner of fowls. Up the country our rivers abound with various kinds of fish . . . in the smaller streams,   ·
> trout may be found in great abundance. In hunting and fishing we are able to while away many an idle hour. We frequently make up parties of men, women and children, and start out on a hunting or fishing expedition and are gone for several days. These excursions are very pleasant, as we are able to find plenty of honey, kill game, catch fish, and amuse ourselves in looking at our beautiful country, our clear water courses, and in contemplation of the future, for as the past has been full of bitterness, we of course look forward to future happiness, since our land is so well calculated to be a land of ease and luxury.[8]

By 1850, the same writer declares that he has "awakened to the stern and sober realities of life" but only a handful of sentences later crows, "We have been blest far beyond our deserts! Prosperity and plenty have abounded! We need want for nothing; all that is necessary for our comfort and happiness is to be found at our very doors! Wealth has flowed into our coffers and we have nothing for which to mourn."[9]

The German pioneers who were brought to the Fisher-Miller land grant on the upper Colorado and Llano rivers by the Society for the Protection of German Immigrants in Texas in the 1840s were peasant farmers. "The German economic and social system of the mid-nineteenth century placed a low ceiling on their potential for achievement, and the males faced lengthy service in the military. . . . Germany offered no real hope for further progress. . . . To these recently freed, newly literate peasants, the noblemen of the Society offered a chance of escape, a chance to . . . improve their economic position." The society made the "exaggerated promise that a land of milk and honey awaited them here and that they could easily establish a new Canaan in the Promised Land."[10]

However, it was not as easy to wax eloquent about that portion of Texas lying west of the ninety-eighth meridian, called by the naturalists in Major Stephen Long's 1820 expedition part of "The Great American Desert" and declared "wholly unfit for civilization, uninhabitable by a people depending on agriculture for their subsistence." James Abert's 1845 probe confirmed that impression. Nevertheless, a few decades later boosters in new hamlets such as Plainview, Clarendon, and Mobeetie were sending brochures to prospective settlers back East, and some newspaper editors were once again painting a picture of that mythical Eden: "Come to the Panhandle for cheap lands; come for rich and productive soil; come for health; come for seasonable summers and balmy winters," urged the editor of the *Tascosa Pioneer* in 1887. "Come and raise cereals, fruits and vegetables, sorghum, grains, grasses and forage; come and raise cattle, horses, mules, sheep, hogs, goats and poultry." These words spoke to the land hunger of the American East, and the same editor a year later found himself describing how "a half-dozen immigrant wagons, loaded with women, tow-headed progeny and other plunder, passed through yesterday morning."[11]

Out on the Llano Estacado, the farmers came in part because the railroads had come. Encouraged by the state's gift of gigantic tracts of land and knowing that economic health depended on population, the railroads became land agents, laying out town sites and farmlands as well as promoting and selling acreage—many times in cooperation with (or in conspiracy with) the town and ranches along the right-of-way. The railroads established tours that included transportation to and guided walks through demonstration farms, where the prospective buyer was told he might become "sole Monarch" of a "little Empire," his wife "Queen of the Realm," together the "royal pair" growing happy and rich. After the boosters of Plainview discovered irrigation, they made a lake beside the train station and imported giant bullfrogs from Louisiana as well as cranes, swans, and peacocks to grace the water and its banks.[12]

If the Myth of the Garden-Already-Made underwent a severe test out on the Llano Estacado, it was replaced by another: that the land was *becoming* an Eden, could be *made* into one. Settlers in the Panhandle believed that the notion of this land as a desert was wrong and that the country was growing more "seasonable." In their view, they had come in dry years and the natural annual rainfall was comparable, according to one deluded editor, to Chicago's. They came to believe that when they plowed the ground, the earth could hold its moisture better, thereby creating more evaporation and thus making more rainfall—"rain follows the plow," they said. They thought that growing crops would make more rain, as if nature's distribution were made according to need, and that by planting trees they could break the wind, create shade, and protect the crops. Thus more rain would fall.[13]

They also thought that the electric currents in telegraph wires would bring more rain to the region, likewise the steel rails of the trains. Smoke could do it, so could shooting off cannons and shotguns. Like us, they believed in the Myth of Technological Progress, though it went by the more colorful name of Yankee Ingenuity. It had brought them barbed wire, which allowed them to fence in a land where neither stone nor timber were available, and the windmill, which allowed people to water their stock and gardens, even when their land lay miles from surface water. It had produced the Colt .45, which so many believed was ultimately responsible for the defeat of the Comanches. It wasn't too much to expect a new twist in technology to change the climate. Then, decades later, and much too late for many, came the irrigation pump, a mixed blessing.

Naturally, in such an atmosphere of bubbling optimism, disappointment and disillusionment were common. The German farmers brought by the Society of Nobles found "no land of milk and honey. Instead of the Eden described in the advertizing brochures . . . they encountered hunger, cholera, malaria, dysentery, drought, hostile Indians, poisonous snakes, and a hundred other hazards." [14]

One unidentified Frenchman, writing around 1858 from the ill-fated Fourierist colony known as La Reunion, near Dallas, had a long litany of complaints to make against the land to which he had come looking for a better world. His complaints included rare rainfall (punctuated by torrential downpours), intense heat, and poor soil. Yet, in spite of that, "it offers a great many opportunities for living well." As for the false hopes raised in the colonists by Victor Considerant, the man who had led them here, "he had only questioned the Texan realtors who had self-interest in praising their country, which acquires value only through settlement. The American reports, cited in the works of said Considerant, have all been made by individuals who had purchased, for almost nothing, an immense amount of land, and who, also, had all the reason in the world to find Texas the most beautiful country which exists." [15]

These ballooning hopes rising on the winds of optimism, these bitter plummetings to earth—they speak of a desperate dependence on things beyond their control. Those early farmers and ranchers, grounded in an agricultural economy, where their sustenance, their security, and their self-esteem depended on the vagaries of climate and seed and soil, derived their notions of The Good Life directly from the earth.

II

That Anglo-Americans who settled Texas in the nineteenth century brought their own version of the Protestant work ethic with them will surprise no one. In their appeal to the Mexican government in 1822 for the colonization grant that later became Robertson's Colony, the seventy members of the Tennessee and Kentucky Texas Association asked collectively for the right to settle "for the purpose of supporting and maintaining our families by the cultivation of the soil." They claimed that "the common pursuit of our people is that of labor, which banishes idleness and the vices connected with it, it renders man patient, sober, economical, and adorns him with these precious qualities the sources of individual, domestic, and social virtues."[16]

In the 1870s, a young Englishman, Willy Hughes, immigrated to Kendall County to learn sheep farming. Exuberant letters sent to his relatives in England display an unabashed reveling in work:

> From daylight to late at night we are kept "a-going," I assure you: first it's cooking breakfast and milking, and separating newly-born lambs and their ewes from the flock, then turning out the flock and drafting the older lambs with their ewes into the field, and holding refractory ewes for the lambs to suck; then there's ploughing or planting all day; then the flock comes in, and more new lambs to "fix," and more suckling and feeding; then supper to cook and washing-up to do, and by the time one has finished supper, one feels as though one could fall to sleep at the table. It's glorious fun, though; and we enjoy the life immensely.

Elsewhere, Hughes says that "I seem to be blest with a very small share of difficulties, and if any block does occur it worries me to discuss it with any one, as it has always been an intense pleasure to me to do everything for myself without help."[17]

Gilbert Jordan, in his memoirs of growing up around Mason in a family of German Methodists, says that his father always had

> his head upright, looking the world straight in the eye. He always worked hard, tending to his cattle, horse, sheep, and hogs, plowing and cultivating his field, building and repairing fences, hauling supplies, scraping the sand to dig for water in the creek, butchering and preparing meat for the family, building and repairing barns and sheds, hauling and storing fodder, hay and grain for his livestock, rounding up, doctoring, branding, and dipping cattle, and working at hundreds of other tasks on the farm and ranch. He believed in the old German saying, *Arbeit macht das Leben süss* ("Work makes life sweet").[18]

In discussing the Scotch-Irish forebears of those Appalachians who eventually made their way to Texas, Fehrenbach outlines a sensibility and worldview perfectly in keeping with the marriage of Protestantism and capitalism:

> They were enormously self-disciplined, both by their Puritan ethic and the warlike borderer's life. They had three public virtues: thrift, because they had always been poor and Knox taught poverty was a disgrace; self-

reliance, because in the new Reformed world every man felt himself something of an island; and industry, agreeing with St. Paul that who did not work should not eat. They interpreted the New Testament mainly as a moral destruction of aristocracy and beggardom. The quality of social mercy was not strained, but the idea made Scotch-Irish uncomfortable. Calvin, through Knox, extolled material success and despised human weakness. He had destroyed the old Christian concept of a station in life and built a new cosmos in which men and women should have no place, but functions. The act of being was thus meaningless; action was everything, and the work of any man could only be judged by what he did.[19]

For these people, The Good Life afforded an opportunity for work that both redeemed the soul and allowed them to practice self-reliance. The Good Life of work also allowed them to avoid poverty, which is not precisely the same thing as allowing them to get rich, a point that will be returned to later in discussing our contemporary twists on these legacies. The point here is that work was not merely considered a necessary evil or merely a means to success: work encouraged and fostered virtue in the individual who performed it. The Good Life was the righteous life, the busy life.

Not all Texans were, or are, white Protestants, a fact a good many of our older history texts have largely ignored. The notion that The Good Life consists of claiming, holding, and using a plot of good land and building a "little Empire" on it was far beyond the reach of, say, the black slave who was brought here to do much of the work. Now and then, in perusing the early accounts of life on the Texas frontier, we are inadvertently given disturbing and ugly glimpses of the lives of slaves, as we see in the journal of Ann Raney Coleman, whose husband gave her a servant specifically for use in caring for her newborn son:

> I was very glad of this as I found her very handy about the house. Sometimes she was disobedient and did not mind what I said to her, then I would threaten to whip her. Presently afterwards, she was missing, and I would have to nurse myself that day. In the evening she would have to be brought home by some of the field hands, having found her hiding in some woods in the field. She got a whipping from my husband on the first sight of her.[20]

This servant was six years old.

Or, there's this, from an account written over a century later of a Dallas black woman still living in 1984, who describes how, in 1922, the white owner of a Navasota County plantation came in the middle of the night to "whup" her stepfather for saying "something out of line that wasn't for black people to say at that time." Warned of the imminent attack, the stepfather hid out, so the man attacked the women:

> And you know, Old Man Morrett whipped her, and Bud Jones holding her. My mama couldn't walk for 13 weeks. And they broke my arm. . . . I had to hold my arm in a sling like this two or three times a day. . . . And Old Man Morrett broke my sister's nose with a pistol. Mama had to take paper and tear it up, and put it up her nose so the wind could go through it, and it could heal up. By being broken here and knocked apart, by keeping it pressed open, it made it grown funny. I'm sorry I'm crying. That was the way. That is what happened long time ago.

Later, the same speaker says, "This Old Man Morrett came at my sister one time and took her off and kept her five or six hours. He had sex with her, raped her. That's all it was, because she wasn't willing. Oh, my sister like to went into hysterics. She never did get over that."[21]

It seems clear that for many, the foremost definition of The Good Life must have meant freedom from terror and oppression.

Nor were, or are, all Texans here in pursuit of individual enterprise and the accumulation of individual material wealth. There were attempts at monastic or communal life, in which The Good Life meant the life of shared belief apart from any secular concerns. A group of Quakers formed the colony of Estacado in the Panhandle, and by 1890 it numbered two hundred persons. A group of Methodists in 1913 founded a colony known as The Burning Bush one mile southeast of Bullard, in which "all wealth was held in common, and everyone who lived on the land ate from the common table." A small band of Mormons in 1847 formed Zodiac four miles east of Fredericksburg; another clan of utopians formed Icaria twenty miles south of Justin in Denton County in 1848. Still another: "In search of a Promised Land, the Canadian sect known as The Flying Roll, or Israelites, settled on a 144-acre tract in East Texas. The vegetarian group that followed the Mosaic law recruited 75 local families around 1900. They built a church which they named the New House of Israel. The male members had long hair and braids."[22]

Perhaps the most curious and interesting of these experiments was a group of celibate, married women in Bell County, who apparently shunned their husbands to form the "Women's Commonwealth" under the leadership of a Pentecostal named Mrs. Martha McWhirter. "Most of the original members were married women of well-to-do families with their young children. Their communal tendencies developed gradually as they rebeled [*sic*] against the authoritarian doctrines of their local churches, and they asserted financial and sexual independence from their husbands. The commonwealth women were successful in the hotel business."[23]

By far the most grandiose experiment in Texas during the nineteenth century in pursuing a notion of The Good Life that ran counter to prevailing attitudes was the French Utopian Socialist community known as La Reunion near Dallas, which began in 1855 and lasted a few years before disintegrating for a variety of reasons, including mismanagement, the climate, a hostile press, lack of adequate preparation, poor morale, insufficient capital, and a lack of firm leadership. The leader of the colony, Victor Considerant, was a disciple of Fourier and adhered for the most part to the latter's concept of the cooperative agricultural *phalange* (phalanx), in which people voluntarily lived and worked in common dwellings and were made satisfied and harmonious through the fulfillment of their natural desires for company and variety. Considerant's own vision of The Good Life as it would be lived by his fellows was that,

> instead of a life consumed by cruel anxieties, we shall have conquered at last the right of Freedom from Care, which results from the blessed sentiment of solidarity and which gives to each the consciousness that his individual life is integrant of the social life. It is the right to social life, the right to a harmony between the elements of life, and the being who lives. Each one here feels himself a member of a social body founded for his faith and by his faith, destined soon to realize this in its plentitude, and recognizes himself as an associate and an active agent in a work whose grandeur penetrates him deeper and deeper every day.[24]

Significantly, these alternative communal societies all seem to have been predicated on the notion that work has value only in its contribution to the social welfare of the group.

III

Many more of us Texans now live in cities than on farms and ranches, and that's been true for some time. The shift in population from the country to the city and the corresponding shift from an agricultural to an industrial or multibase economy has had profound effects on the way we live, on the way we think, on what we expect from the future.

It seems obvious to me that for most of us, ownership of a parcel of land to be used for providing our sustenance is unimportant. We might buy the town lot that's under our house, but that, too, grows increasingly less important as we turn to purchasing condos and townhouses with zero lot lines. Those of us who are wealthy might purchase a second home on a lake or a river. But, in any case, we will not depend on the land: it will not support us; we will work for *it*. That land is not the source of our physical or spiritual well-being; in the scheme of what we need for our good life, it is irrelevant or, at best, merely tangential to our ongoing lives, serving perhaps as the seed of some vague dream of escape or rest for a future good life on a five-acre retirement ranchette. The myth that the land has anything to offer is an anachronism to most Texans, unless they are ranchers or oilmen, and for most of the state's urban peoples, the state exists mostly as collections of exploitable humans gathered in large groups called cities.

We've replaced the need for land as the foundation of our good life with the need for careers and jobs. And here, Sunbelt Texas still sends out that spangled aura of promise of opportunity to cities like Detroit, as we've seen since the recession of the late 1970s, when streams of Michigan Joads came pulling their U-Haul trailers and created a furor by setting up tent cities in our state parks. That blue-collar migration has slowed some, but the white- collar workers from the East and Midwest are still coming, following their firms. The boom has soured for the moment in Houston, but Dallas is still the prosperous Oz (which may have had something to do with its having been chosen as the site of the 1984 Republican National Convention), whose totem bird is the construction crane.

The land has become irrelevant in the search for The Good Life, but work is still the religion here, albeit a secular one. During the 1984 convention, a heterogeneous group of anti-Reaganites stood outside the famous fence to protest against a broad range of social, economic, and foreign policies while a group of young, well-groomed, white students kept yelling at them, "Get a job!" Although the students seemed

to miss the point, they were unconsciously expressing a rather antiquarian point of view concerning the secondary function of work: it re-
lieves idle hands. Get a job *and you'll be too busy to worry about El
Salvador*; get a job *and you won't worry about the nuclear arms race*;
get a job *and you'll be too busy thinking about making money to care if
anybody else is poor*; get a job *and you'll forget about pollution*.

In the February, 1984, issue of *D Magazine*, one of the state's slick
and glossy upscale-consumer magazines (these periodicals are for us
what the Sears-Roebuck catalogue was to farmers in the earlier decades of the century), several of the city's "most eligible bachelors" describe their assets. One, a Porsche salesman whose work earns him "an
annual six-figure salary," says, "I'm success motivated. That's why I'm
fit for this city. Success is what makes people thrive here." Another, a
land broker to development firms, says, "I don't want an excuse to stop
working. There is no thrill like being on the chase of the deal." Another claims that "Dallas is still the best place in the world to make
your fortune." Our local role models—H. Ross Perot, Mary Kay Ash,
the various Hunts, Tom Landry, Trammel Crow—are always quick to
extol the pleasures, if not the virtues, of work, and newspaper accounts
of their philosophy invariably attach a price tag, presumably as a sign
of the wisdom of their words.

Most of the hard, dirty work in Texas cities is done not by descendants, metaphorical or literal, of the Anglo-Americans who settled
in Texas or by proponents of supply-side economics, but, rather, by
Mexican-Americans and Mexican nationals who have crossed the border illegally in search of work and a better life for their families still in
the home country. I have no statistics to support this, but a casual tour
of construction sites, restaurants, body shops, factories, and yards of
boomtown Dallas certainly suggests to me that the *bracero* may well
be the person closest to our old pioneer settlers in spirit and motive,
although the Southeast Asians are running a close second, if ability and
willingness to work for a better life count for anything. A student of
mine who spent a year working construction sites in Dallas said, "The
Mexicans work hard and keep their mouths shut, the blacks work hard
and gripe about it, and the few white guys around only show up about
half the time, and they're usually drunk or stoned." Now and then our
newspapers run feature articles on recent immigrants (French, South-

east Asian, or Iranian) who have bent themselves to the task of becoming Americanized in a hurry and who have managed in a short time to own a house in North Dallas, a chain of businesses, and (usually) a Mercedes. Those who merely work are granted no space; to enter the pantheon of American success, it is not enough to be thrifty, fruitful, and hard-working (as no doubt many thousands of *braceros* are)—wealth must be present as proof of labor. The work ethic requires the accumulation of wealth as the completion of the equation.

Naturally, a good many middle-class blacks and Mexican-Americans have adopted the WASP sensibility regarding The Good Life as it applies to bigger and better homes, appliances, and automobiles, but I suspect that to most of the immigrants from Mexico, The Good Life means not only prosperity but also *life with their families*. You see them by the dozens lined up at the post offices on Saturdays buying and sending money orders across the border: for them, Dallas must be the temporary means to an end, and they cannot fulfill themselves here the way a Porsche salesman can—Dallas cannot be an arena for the enactment of their fundamental vision of their place in the world at large. With their strong ties to Catholicism and to family, their jobs are a painfully necessary means to sustenance, and they are here at the risk of danger and at a sacrifice.

Most of our popular publications—our mass market magazines and newspapers—have, in the last ten years or so, shied away from examining issues of substance and have become glossy shopping journals. They perceive, rightly or wrongly, that their readers have grown uninterested in anything outside the walls of their individual households. The September, 1984, issue of *D Magazine* contains dozens of pages of advertising for fashion and furniture, and an article on business will counsel you to invest your oil money in the Caymans.

I think we are at present living in an era that is extraordinarily secular, materialistic, and areligious. Our contemporary myth of The Good Life is for the most part a hazy and altogether unexamined belief that we are all here in Texas for one reason: to make as much money as we possibly can as quickly as we can. The connection between our enterprise and our religious beliefs seems to be that work is a moral undertaking only when wealth is present to give proof of the effort, that comfort is tantamount to being blessed.

To some extent, The Good Life has always meant prosperity to those who came voluntarily, of course. Describing the life of some early settlers, Ann Raney Coleman says: "They worked thirty hands, and several negroes lived together in one cabin. This was the way most of the wealthy planters lived when we first arrived in Texas. A double log cabin with an entry running through the middle was their residence. To make money was their chief object, all things else were subsidiary to it."[25]

But never, I think, have objects been so necessary for The Good Life. If anything tangible has replaced land as that sine qua non for The Good Life, it is that plethora of utensils, tools, toys, clothing, and heretofore undreamed-of appliances that our Myth of Technological Progress, our electronic wizardry, will next present to us as the thing without which we cannot possibly live. We have surrounded ourselves with these objects and cannot seem to get enough of them (I'm writing this on a word processor, and this year I bought a videotape recorder). Those ten-foot-tall stacks of goods rising from the aisles of our local Target stores represent the depository for our fondest dreams. Roger Staubach does Rolaid commercials presumably because he wants more money (he cannot really need it, can he?), proving to millions of young athletes that their careers are only a means to the end of becoming rich celebrities. During the recent Olympic games, one of the most common discussions about the careers of potential gold medalists was how much those medals would be worth as a means to another, entirely unrelated, end.

Beyond that, what I sense in my college students and even in my own children is that we are headed for still another step away from the notion that work has its own value and that good work, hard work, is the best (most efficient, most respectable) means for attaining wealth. Afoot in the land is an impatience with the idea that The Good Life means working to get rich. Their role models are celebrities who owe their wealth and status to no old-fashioned notion of initiation-by-labor: Michael Jackson is not a thing to do, he is someone to be, all the better if you can get it while you're still a teenager and bypass the boring stuff.

For land, then, we have substituted consumer goods; for labor and work, we have substituted wealth and fame. That's indeed a long, long way from what Plato, or Calvin, had in mind. To the early Puritan, the man who lived for himself and wallowed in comfort and riches was, in essence, evil. And that very man has now become our measure of heaven's approval. Recently, the members of the First Baptist Church of Dallas gave their pastor, the Reverend William Criswell, a $40,000 Mercedes as a token of their appreciation. The event was publicized in the local papers without, apparently, any embarrassment to either the donors or the recipient. Nor was there the slightest indication that the car would be given away. When our own religious leaders honor such invidious tokens of success, it can only suggest to their congregations that heaven approves of personal aggrandizement at the expense of the poor, and that a life without such comforts is sinful.

It seems to me that our own age is so spiritually poverty-stricken that to call a collection of gadgets and a big bank balance The Good Life is as much as to say that our myths—that body of belief that has sustained human energy and effort for countless centuries—seem to be drying up at the source; the source is that mysterious human need for something that transcends the limits of the things we touch and use and know only with our senses. The Good Life might have once meant "the right life" or "the righteous life" or even "the fulfilling life" or "enriching life," but now it does not mean homage to God, service to humanity (in the movie Risky Business, four high school students snicker when one says, as a joke, that he wants to "serve his fellow man"), or intellectual and spiritual fulfillment. For the most part it now means only "the comfortable life." I also suspect, but naturally cannot prove, that a society that lacks any firm belief in anything but creature comforts can commit cultural suicide much more readily than a society that has a deeper, richer view of the world, and, indeed, may even secretly welcome it.

NOTES

1. T. R. Fehrenbach, *Lone Star: A History of Texas and the Texans* (1968; reprint, New York: American Legacy Press, 1983), pp. 89–94.

2. Walter Prescott Webb, H. B. Carroll, and E. S. Branda, eds., *The Handbook of Texas*, 3 vols. (Austin: Texas State Historical Association, 1952–76), 1:658.

3. W. B. Dewees, *Letters from an Early Settler of Texas* (Louisville, Ky.: Hull and Brother Printers, 1854), p. 135.

4. Malcolm MacLean, ed. and comp., *Papers concerning Robertson's Colony in Texas*, 11 vols. (Fort Worth: Texas Christian University Press, 1974–), 1:6–7. See also John Edward Weems, *Men without Countries: Three Adventurers of the Early Southwest* (Boston: Houghton Mifflin, 1969).

5. MacLean, *Papers*, 1:44.

6. Full details of the story are in MacLean, *Papers*, vol. 2.

7. Dewees, *Letters*, p. 28.

8. Ibid., pp. 130, 136–37.

9. Ibid., p. 305.

10. Gilbert Jordan, *Yesterday in the Texas Hill Country* (College Station: Texas A&M University Press, 1979), pp. 3–4.

11. Frederick W. Rathjen, *The Texas Panhandle Frontier* (Austin: University of Texas Press, 1973), pp. 110–15; Donald E. Green, *Land of the Underground Rain: Irrigation on the Texas High Plains, 1910–1970* (Austin: University of Texas Press, 1973), pp. 11, 63.

12. B. R. Brunson, *The Texas Land and Development Company: A Panhandle Promotion, 1912–1956* (Austin: University of Texas Press, 1970), pp. 44, 68.

13. Green, *Land of the Underground Rain*, p. 69; Walter Prescott Webb, *The Great Plains* (Boston: Ginn and Company, 1931), p. 378.

14. Jordan, *Yesterday*, p. 4.

15. "The Fulfillment!! or Twelve Years Afterward," in *Documents Apostoliques et Prophéties*, ed. Jean Journet (Dallas: DeGolyer Foundation Library, 1963), pp. 4–5.

16. MacLean, *Papers*, 1:367–68.

17. Thomas Hughes, ed., *G.T.T. Gone to Texas: Letters from Our Boys* (London: Macmillan, 1884), pp. 6, 138.

18. Jordan, *Yesterday*, p. 17.

19. Fehrenbach, *Lone Star*, p. 87.

20. Ann Raney Thomas Coleman, *Victorian Lady on the Texas Frontier*, ed. Richard C. King (Norman: University of Oklahoma Press, 1971), p. 77.

21. Ruthe Winegarten, ed., *I Am Annie Mae* (Austin, Tex.: Rosegarden Press, 1983), pp. 51–54.

22. Green, *Land of the Underground Rain*, p. 8; Donald S. Fogarty, *Dictionary of American Communal and Utopian History* (Westport, Conn.: Greenwood Press, 1980), pp. 194–95, 219, 231.

23. Fogarty, *Dictionary*, p. 206.

24. William and Margaret Hammond, *La Reunion: A French Settlement in Texas* (Dallas: Royal Publishing Company, 1958), pp. 107–15, 61. There were many Fourierist-inspired communities in the United States during the period, the most notable of which was Brook Farm. Ben Capps's excellent but sadly neglected novel, *The Brothers of Uterica* (New York: Meredith Press, 1967), tells the story of the La Reunion colony in fictional form.

25. Dewees, *Letters*, p. 26.

T. R. Fehrenbach

Texas Mythology: Now and Forever

The *Encyclopedia Britannica*, admitting that there probably is no one definition that would please all scholars and still be understood by lay people, defines *myth* as follows:

> Myth is an extremely complex cultural reality, which can be approached and interpreted from various and complementary viewpoints. The definition that seems least inadequate because most embracing is this: myth narrates a sacred history; it relates an event that took place in primordial time, a fabled time of the "beginnings." In other words, myth tells us how, through the deeds of supernatural beings, reality came into existence, be it the whole of reality, the cosmos, or only a fragment of reality—an island, a species of plant, a particular kind of human behavior, an institution. Myth is always an account of "creation"; it relates how something was produced, began to be.

Contributors to the *Britannica* are undoubtedly trained in the classics and know that "myth" and "history" were the same root word in Greek. The Greeks considered their mythology, as we call it now, to be their very ancient history, set down by storytellers and poets. That mythology explained how the cosmos was created out of chaos, how gods afflicted human beings, and how heroes and demigods occasionally saved them, explicating how most things came to be. Of course, by about the close of the fifth century B.C. educated Greeks no longer believed any of this, regarding mythology in the same light we do: interesting, if nicely done, perhaps still believed by the hoi polloi, but not by us better-informed folks.

Myth has also entered our language in other ways. In a recent

New York Times one writer mentioned "the mythic" Frank Sinatra, another a "mythic" Gilbert (of Sullivan fame). Since both of these are real people in real time, the reference is obviously to those myths or untruths spawned by their careers and lives. In this sense, myth is used in place of fad, fashion, rumor, or notion—all mistaken, of course.

All this causes me to approach the subject of "Texas myths"— which are becoming almost as popular a subject as child abuse or pornography in some circles—with trepidation. Is there such a thing as a Texas mythology, and if so, by popular definition, must it be untrue?

I

By the classic, encyclopedia definition there is no such thing as Texas myth. Texas—Anglo-Texas, in this case—is a region and state of the American Union formed by our recent ancestors in recorded time, not a mystical realm forged and inhabited by demigods. The beginnings are not laid down in any sacred book, nor did any early Texan ever try to explain the cosmos. By classic definition there is certainly a Greek mythology, and a Jewish mythology, and a Christian mythology—though no Texas scholar, especially a subsidized one, is going to explore the last two in this day and age.

But yet, if history and mythos at root are the same, then we have to take another look. The Texas past, as set down in factual and fictional literature, as passed on in song and cinema, is related as a sort of semi-sacred history. The early events were almost always poorly or sketchily recorded—no one knows precisely what happened within the walls of the Alamo or inside the minds of its defenders. The Rangers made terse reports or none and kept few records; nineteenth-century empire erectors weren't men of words but of action. And although none of the pioneers were supernatural beings, many of them have always seemed larger than life to us. Their deeds, rarely self-explicated, cried out for elaboration and embellishment.

Although Anglo-Texas came into being only yesterday, the beginnings already seem far back in time, almost in another universe. Official and unofficial Texas historians keep trying to explain, while they exalt, this "creation." So there may be a true Texas mythos, stemming like that of the Greeks from the beginnings, a creation. But it never tries to explicate the cosmos; Texans brought all that with them from across the water. However, Texans have worried much about the creation of this particular fragment of reality, Texas, and worried even more about the particular forms of human behavior involved in it. Why did Travis and Bowie court extinction in a grim Spanish fortress when they had excellent advice and the means to avoid it? Did Travis draw or not draw a line on the dust, and, either way, what are the implications for the soul of man, struggling in this messy universe?

In any event, something called "Texas myths" is now fair game for discussion and dissection, and this makes me a little uneasy, too. For we are dealing, in the case of true mythology, with an "extremely complex cultural reality," which can be interpreted from all sorts of viewpoints. And the one thing I would not want us to do with Texas history-mythology is to demythologize it.

When and if a culture does that, its past becomes neither so pretty nor so satisfying—poets and fable spinners not only write better but have a far better understanding of the human spirit than do social scientists—and worst of all, it fails to make sense: As Jung wrote, "True mythology has become so completely alien to us that we have lost our immediate feeling for the great reality of the spirit." The problem is that modern science knows no more about the cosmos than about archaic Greek poetry—and a lot less than Texas school children know about the heroes of the Alamo.

If a Texas mythology has sprouted to fill in the interstices and bare spots of recorded Texas history, it doesn't hurt to trim it a bit, pull the really noxious weeds. But one must be careful not to damage the whole growth, or attempt to expunge history itself. For although history, like mythology, is sometimes grotesque and often quite unpalatable to changing tastes, only a sense of history gives human beings cohesiveness; and without a sense of common history, people are unlikely to hold a sense of common destiny. Too much history may saddle us with archaism, an inability to get the past off our backs, but too little leaves us with the twin corpses of futurism and nihilism, in which there is no comfort at all.

What Texas myths, then, shall we study and dissect for learned purposes, and from what view shall we approach them? By the broadest definitions there probably are as many Texas myths as there are Texans, and more are being spun every day. But the real mythology, the formative mythology, I think, can all be traced back to the era of the Texas creation, a period lasting roughly from 1825 to 1875, during which the Republic and state and people and institutions of Texas were made.

Since we have records, albeit imperfect, we have to start with Texas history. It at present is Anglo-Texas history, and like all national or ethnic histories, it has been embellished with useful insights and accretions. If we do not know exactly why some men stayed at the Alamo, we have to put some ideas—ones that make sense to us—in their heads. If we do not quite understand why other men went rangering for beans (if they were lucky), we have to discover some logical reason. And if we wonder why any cowpoke joined a trail drive, or was willing to be killed at some disputed waterhole for ten bucks a month and found, it becomes almost necessary to "legendize" the fact. Further, what we call "history" is always a construct; nobody ever has, or ever can, capture events for posterity exactly *wie es wirklich gewesen*, to quote a great German practitioner of constructs.

Texan accounts of the creation, Texan history, real and written, in its starkest form—events—are generally undisputed, however. Some thousands of Americans, by invitation, colonized the empty Mexican province of Texas, where in ten years they carried out more civilized development than the Hispanic world had been able to do in three hundred and came to outnumber the Spanish-speaking settlers ten to one. Aside from some inevitable frictions, the colonists remained loyal to Mexico, which had granted them great tracts of free land, until the Mexican government, alarmed at their progress, began to impose forms of rule hateful to American culture and sensibilities, such as taxes, customs duties, and military garrisons. Then, very much like their own forefathers, who had revolted against Great Britain, they declared independence, and after marches and massacres that were the very stuff of legend, they made it stick.

Thereafter, the people in twenty-odd thinly settled counties mostly east of the Colorado continued as an improbable nation for ten years, defending themselves against both Mexican governments that never accepted the de facto independence won at San Jacinto and Indians along a running, bleeding frontier. These border wars were both defensive and aggressive in character, marred by atrocities on all sides. In Texas, American settlers impinged on the Indian frontier as they had in the seventeenth and eighteenth centuries; the Indian wars lasted two generations, reaching an intensity and generating hatreds not seen since earlier centuries. However, the removal of the Texas Indians, warlike and peaceable, was only a culmination of a process that began on the Atlantic slopes much earlier.

In the course of these border struggles, Anglo-Texans made significant adaptations to both their enemies and their new environment. They developed "ranging companies" for frontier defense, learned horsemanship, acquired repeating pistols, and seized and used the cattle culture of northern Mexico in those parts of the state (more than half) where water and wood were naturally scarce. The dynamism of American culture, compared with Indian or Mexican, allowed Texans to take and hold the land.

Texas logically entered the union of American states, precipitating the war with Mexico that secured the Southwest for the United States. Since in 1861 Texas was still economically, culturally, and politically an extension of the cotton South, it joined the Confederacy and lost its second war for independence, suffering the same consequences as the other subdued states.

Texas was only half-settled, however, with huge areas of harsh but virgin lands to be distributed. This frontier drew immigrants, and the cattle kingdom in some sense replaced the exhausted cotton kingdom, while Texans exploded their adaptation of the Mexican cattle culture, now organized as a business, over the entire West.

This whole history, aside from the unmistakable patterns of violence—Texas had to be conquered, not merely settled—was essentially a prolonged land rush, marked by periodic land booms and land busts. The great lure of Texas was free, or almost free, land in quantity. The reason most families came to a raw, rough country was to get property. Consequently, a vision of landed empire always shimmered before settlers' eyes, and the ethos of Texas was a property holder's or seeker's ethos.

The conscious collective desire of this people, as far as it had any collective desires, was to create an Athenian or Jeffersonian democracy, that is, a male, slave-owning democracy of property-holding citizens. At times the dream was nearly fulfilled, though always thwarted by natural, economic, or political conditions beyond Texans' control.

These facts and events, duly recorded or laid down in documents or constitutions, are not seriously disputed, even by those who prefer the Anglo-Saxon Conspiracy Theory—which overdignifies the process; Texans were never sufficiently united in anything to carry on a successful folk conspiracy.

But this history, even without the cracks, seams, and bare spots being embellished by "usable" legend, presents latter-day Americans with some genuine philosophical problems. It is very much a tribal history. Like the Alemanni or the peoples who called themselves *Englisc* (and others *Welsc*, or outsiders), the Texans came from mixed origins, but in the process of entering, taking, and holding a territory, they made themselves into a distinct tribe, or very nearly a tribe. The frontier and enemies who were also racial and cultural enemies created Anglo cohesiveness out of many different elements.

Once troubles began with Mexicans and Indians, it was Them or Us, each war having serious ethnic and cultural connotations. This made them wars between civilizations, not just between nations, which might be settled without utter domination or extermination. The struggles for Texas involved not right and wrong, but several rights in collision—and the conflict between two rights has always been the most difficult for human philosophy to resolve. In fact, philosophy has never resolved one, from Texas to modern Israel. They are usually settled by force, and only time can give the result legitimacy.

The creation of Texas had an Old Testament ring to it. A people chose this land, entered it with their families and servants, conquered and held it against both human and natural obstacles, and tried to erect their version of Jerusalem on it. Out of any such history must come, and came, notions of blood and soil, notions of racial and cultural superiority and inferiority. Texas as a fragment of reality was not created on the sixth day or by covenant or in any peaceful way; it was made by the flash of flintlocks at the Alamo and San Jacinto, by the cowing of the Mexican nation, and by the near extermination or removal of the aboriginal owners. All that is fact, not mythology.

The problem Texas poets and historians have always faced is to make that history lovable, or at least palatable. To repudiate it is impossible; repudiation would destroy the essential meaning of the conquest, and of the whole Texan people. And Texas poets and image makers, amateur and professional, have generally succeeded splendidly. They, like the frontier's harsh necessities, have shaped both actions and attitudes. Those Texans descended from the frontier experience, the creation, see history and society very differently from Americans whose background in adventure was to arrive in steerage and then engage in economic or social struggles within the context of an already formed, orderly government and society.

II

Now, whatever mythos, or explanation of the "creation," arose in Texas, it was derived mainly from the human figures who made these events happen or were caught up in them. Texas came about in a heroic age, and all heroic ages have Heroes. Texas threw up an entire pantheon; let's call them, for convenience, Tribal Heroes. These Heroes did not lead the people into the Wilderness (those who did are still regarded dubiously), but they did deliver them from bondage.

There was the grim Bowie, his life sidetracked by personal tragedy to glory, the determined, visionary Travis, failing at everything except his finest hour on the walls of the Alamo, and the Greek-tragedy character Fannin, getting himself and hundreds slaughtered as a result of his flaws. There was Sam Houston, a perfect case of *palingenesia*, or heroic withdrawal and return—all Texas Heroes in some sense in Texas became "born again."

Texas had its brutal Ajaxes and sullen Achilleses, sulking in their tents while the Republic nearly went down the tubes. And it had a whole horde of lesser heroes, the members of the tribe who, rallying round the Heroes at last, either died gloriously or turned an improbable venture into a nation.

Above all, Texas had its martyrs, who, as martyrs usually do, carried the day as successfully as the charge at Buffalo Bayou. Martyrs do not merely signify, they justify. The Mexican armies not only lost the war, they lost posterity by giving no quarter at the Alamo and by the injudicious legal murders of Fannin and his followers. But above all, those sacrifices were absolutely necessary. Without them, the story could not be complete; it would lack its mythological, poetic perfection.

No matter how embellished or exaggerated, the core of all the heroic acts is true. Some did stand and die at the Alamo; the supposedly civilized Mexican nation carelessly made heroes and statesmen out of backwoodsmen; the gods gave vengeance at San Jacinto. Texas was born, like most nations, in blood and iron, and without men of blood and iron it would have been stillborn.

The creation forged by the Tribal Heroes had to be maintained and made complete. This required the aggressive patrolling of the new frontiers, and eventually, the extermination of Indians who could not fit into the New Jerusalem. The Indians deserved extermination because they did not fight by "civilized" rules; even the Mexicans did not torture women and children to death. But here there were crimes on both sides; the Texan wrath, like rain, fell on both the peaceable and the warlike. The Texans never doubted the necessity or validity of this conquest, any more than Romans latinizing Gaul or Iberia. And the Texans did not make a desert to call it "peace"; they went into the desert to make it bloom.

Protection of the tribe, extension of the frontiers, called up a new swarm of heroes. These were Rangers, pistol-empowered riders rounding up the remaining varmints, variously understood as Indians, Mexican bandits, and indigenous cow thieves. The Ranger could not assume the stature of the original creating Hero, but in most ways he was a more satisfying heroic symbol. The great Tribal Heroes were obviously all uncommon men, if not a bit odd before called to apotheosis. The Rangers, however, were common clay, true folk heroes thrown up by the frontier itself. Nearly every able-bodied male in Texas between 1836 and 1861 went rangering at some time, or stood on call. The Texan nation never paid for these services, but all could identify with them.

The Rangers were uncommon, however, in courage and certain deadly skills. They offered opportunity for that type of man who does not mind, and even enjoys, riding with danger, for the frontiers made them necessary. And what Rangers did best, kill Indians and cow border Mexicans, the whole society saw as meet and right.

Police work, however, is brutal business at bottom, especially

if the police are armed and dangerous; however necessary or applauded, it .can never assume the heroic prospect of remaking the
world by revolution. Therefore, the Texas Ranger from the first was
more vulnerable, however originally indispensable, than the indis-
putable Tribal Hero.

The hard core of the Ranger force, which normally consisted of
unstable and occasional bands brought together for ad hoc solutions to
border problems, consisted of the Ranger captains. These were men
culled from the ranks because they were the best thinkers, the dead-
liest men available. Usually without uniform and pay, they were utterly
professional where it counted. They learned their business, and they
did it so well they burned an indelible impression into both the frontier folk and most Americans, who read about their exploits in newspapers. Forced into dubious and usually unequal battle with more
numerous foes from whom they could expect neither quarter nor
mercy, these captains forged the legends of "one-man armies"; they
performed deeds of sheer, calculated daring that still make us gasp.

The best Rangers possessed that Roman trait of knowing how to
emasculate, not just defeat, their enemies. Webb saw them as rough
but keen psychologists. They studied Indians, so that they knew how to
fall upon unwary Indian camps and demoralize them by "magic"; they
also knew how to demoralize and emasculate Mexicans or the wild
bunch. This was as useful as the weapons put in their hands by the
workshops of civilization in the East, the famous Colt revolvers, or the
armor of moral certainty their own society granted them. Good captains never rode like paladins into battle with the enemy; they sneaked
up on him. But at the last minute, they went into action with devastating and disconcerting boldness. Attacked by overwhelming numbers,
they counterattacked; accosted, they shot first and asked questions
later. They played on every moral and psychological weakness, until
their very legend inculcated terror. The saying that a Ranger never
ordered anyone to do something twice is largely true; legends are not
made through dialogue.

Hays took "Indian" warfare to the Indians. Caldwell and Ford
psyched out Comanche medicine and ruined it, before destroying Comanches in hordes. McNelly took absolutely nothing from the bad
guys, whether telegraphing a bigshot suspected of ordering murders

that the next time a killing happened he would personally call him out, or offering to gut-shoot a Mexican border official if stolen cattle were not returned beginning now. When McNelly rode south of the Rio Grande in the pursuit of rustlers, starting a small war and causing no small international incident, long-suffering frontier Texas slapped its collective thigh with glee. Ranger "subtlety" was something a frontier society appreciated; probably a frontier-descended society still admires it secretly.

The Rangers may have done their hard job too well. They killed a few outlaws, more Indians, and drove even more out of the state. But genuine atrocities against Mexicans, both during the Mexican War and in border incidents, built up a residue of hate. Worse, the deliberate instillation of feelings of inferiority, and the technique of refusing to talk with a rhetoric-loving culture that liked to debate niceties, made Texans and Mexicans despise each other. Brutalization may be forgiven; humiliation is much harder to forget.

Much of the modern distaste for the Ranger "image," however, has nothing to do with the border wars of the nineteenth century. More arose from the border fracases and incidents of this one. The old breed, the real warrior types, mostly passed out of the service by the 1880s. Newer Rangers were often a lesser breed, politically appointed. They were now constabulary, and in no time and place are constabularies popular with whatever underclass exists, in Dublin or Del Rio. The ethnic Mexican underclass created along the border hated them, with reason: they upheld a hated status quo. But even the political hacks with badges got blamed for things they never did, although they not only tarred the legend but almost got the whole corps officially abolished; it could be salvaged only by placing Rangers under a new, sanitary Department of Public Safety in the 1930s.

Only those versed in Texas-Mexican Spanish seem to understand that *rinche* did not mean Ranger exclusively, but every official from sheriff's deputy to commission constable in Texas. Thus when *rinches* have been accused of crimes, it is often impossible to pin the perpetrators.

Despite the later tarnish and recrudescences of racism among lawmen too dumb to understand that what was useful along a violent and thinly settled border does not go down when sizable numbers of

Mexican-descended Texans vote, Ranger history-mythology survives. Its real strength among Anglo-Texans can best be judged, perhaps, by the earnest efforts of so many people to discredit it.

Legends die hard. I remember an incident when I was young, when people in the brush country still sometimes walked around openly armed. A Ranger who was heckled by a pistol-wearing loud-mouth turned, and quiet and squint-eyed, told the man to draw or light out. He lit out. That ploy broke seventeen official rules and codes of conduct, no doubt, but it got the job done—and I suspect a Texan's reaction to it depends on his or her emotional and intellectual distance from the ancestral frontier.

The final heroic, mythmaking figure of the creation is the Cowboy, who got in just under the wire before the frontier closed and Texans began to live more or less like Kansans. Like the Tribal Heroes and Rangers, Cowboys stamped themselves into both the Texan and American consciousness, maybe forever. But here, because by the 1870s there were far more writers and more magazines and newspapers on the scene, there was even more mythic embellishment and elaboration.

Now, good cowmen, unlike stalwart Tribal Heroes and keen-shooting Rangers, were first and foremost businessmen. Charles Goodnight handled Comanches by avoiding them, waiting for the army to clear the range. The Waggoners were planners, not trailblazers. Cowmen also were as pragmatic in their way as Rangers. If Rangers adopted Indian-style warfare, cowboys took over the entire panoply of the North Mexican cattle culture—costume, life-style, and jargon—along with the longhorns left behind by Mexican ranchers. And this lent glamour to a quite arduous and grungy business.

The honest cowhand was loyal to boss and brand, a semifeudal notion adopted from the Mexicans, just as the honest Ranger remained loyal to the society that sent him forth and paid him miserably. Other values coincided, because they were all frontier values. The cowhand had to have physical courage, herding half-wild stock in lonely places. But the good cowboy was never reckless. Although the imagery is filled with hair-triggered buckaroos and young pins "wild as the West Texas wind," the cowman didn't wear a badge and didn't have to look for trouble, and the lore indicates clearly that the wild ones invariably came to a bad end. But there was a key code the cowhand had to obey: no respectable man backed away from a fight if some fool thrust it on him.

If the cowhand became and remained a sort of hero, the cow owner was the man who made this culture run. The owner or manager of a huge spread might be a Glasgow accountant or a Chicago capitalist, but he was usually a true survivor. He let the army and Rangers wage the war of extermination against the Plains Indians, moving westward after it was over. The smart ranchers never had anything against wire or railroads; that war was started by the sentimental environmentalists of the day as well as by those cowmen who forgot the real reason everyone came to Texas in the first place—to acquire land. Many great ranchers donated land for town sites, knew railroad presidents on a first-name basis, and organized local banks; the more nesters that arrived, the more they prospered. Ranchers usually did better than land speculators, save those few who actually believed in their own product and held on to some. Those who unloaded Texas land continually vanished from both the soil and history; the descendants of those who held on through drought and dust and dismal markets still have presence on the land.

By the conventional wisdom, the creation ended with the closure of the true frontier around 1880. This leaves no room in Texan mythology for the oilman, or for the erector of great corporate enterprises, utility, insurance, or whatever. Despite the mighty economic engines that now dominate the state, this seems a fair assessment. The character and self-imagery of Texas were formed before Spindletop. The oil booms and oil boomtowns, from Wichita Falls after the Electra field to 1980, when nearly every stockbroker in Dallas got in the drilling business, have always held a smell of chicanery that almost obscured the scent of empire. The "world's littlest skyscraper," erected in Wichita Falls in 1919, is still a sort of monument. Promoters promised investors a four-story office building and built one four stories high, but measuring only 10 x 16 feet, a high-rise outhouse. The last time around, bankers who didn't know a drilling rig from a pump jack got taken. And in most cases, the landholders have always been the true winners, the inheritors, for oil is merely another product of the soil.

The old West Texas saying that a man's word is his bond unless he's in the oil business, in which case you should bring a passel of lawyers, indicates that the fictional J. R. Ewing is not all that far-fetched.

Of course, many other figures and cultures figured in the creation. There was the Cotton Kingdom, which actually ruled Texas in the antebellum years. But this, like the later timber baronages in the Piney Woods, was an extension of the Old South to its natural limits. The hoeman and tenant farmer won only a Pyrrhic victory over the lordly planter in the Civil War. The planter induced a certain mimesis in half of Texas, at least in manners, that blended oddly with the rough culture of the cow camp. But the dirt farmer could not create heroic images or memories. His descendants, most of whom fled to Dallas to escape starvation, retained chicken-fried steak and religion, but put most of the rest of it behind them. They are survivors once removed.

We should not forget the lawyer; then as now, Texas was infested with the breed. But the very lawyer image clashes discordantly with the other kinds. Many Texas heroes were actually men of the bar, but they aren't remembered for their lawyering. After all, there was no filing of briefs over the Alamo, or court foreclosures of Comanche territory. However, as the land defeated generation after generation of new hopefuls, there were all too many foreclosures of landowners in frontier history for the lawyer ever to have a favorable image in nineteenth-century mythology. Literature cannot dredge up a single admiring reference. In folk memory the lawyer is a hired gun, usually arrayed against the poor-but-honest. Texas was the theater of the world's most horrendous title litigation in the last century, what with Spanish land grants, treaty assurances of title, Republic head rights, and state land sales all encroaching on each other, to say nothing of less-than-scientific surveys. The lawyer was useful, but he couldn't fit into any useful pantheon.

And there were the politicians, some of whom actually did become statesmen after election. Texas is probably second only to Scotland in the production of provincial pols capable of taking city slickers to the cleaners. But the politician has always remained a dubious hero to Texans; as many writers have pointed out, and Yankee explorer James A. Michener mentioned, Texans like their politicians best when they are doing something else. Houston, a true, tragic Tribal Hero, messed up his image by devoting his later life to politics. Lamar, like Lyndon Johnson, was a complex, enormously gifted person, but people do not dream that their children will grow up to be like him. The fact is, no true Texan has ever completely trusted a politician. Politics is a wonderful spectator sport, but it doesn't fit in with the frontier, land-grabbing, empire-building ethos. Houston, after all, did not politic himself out of that cul-de-sac at Buffalo Bayou; everything was downhill after San Jacinto.

Smart Texans remembered why they had come to Texas in the first place and latched onto property, not political office.

Politicians are also a constant reminder of danger to the Texan dream. In office, they not only want to tell people what to do on their private kingdoms, but, worse, put their hands in property owners' pockets. The King Ranch can handle almost any adversity except a politician purporting to speak for the people. Even politicians' success in snaring Yankee dollars for places like Turkey and Muleshoe is a sour reminder that Texas lost "that" war and now has to fight for its rights with hypocrisy and fast footwork in the Congress.

So the principal theme of Texas history-mythology is this: Texas was created by heroes. We know that speculators and such played key roles, but Stephen F. Austin never made it to the rank of Tribal Hero. Myths, after all, belong to the people, and people are choosy about them. Fortunately, whatever myths Texans attached to heroic deeds were never meant to explain the cosmos, so religious fanaticism could be kept out of any quarrel.

III

We can put most Texas mythology under one big tent: it tells us how "our kind" came to Texas and made it, a very near-run thing in the face of all the human and natural obstacles. It shows us examples of raw—and sometimes utterly belligerent—courage and implies that we wouldn't be here without it. It teaches us that our ancestors had big dreams, and some few of them actually found the end of the rainbow, after disposing of the dragon. And it throws up for us, to use Toynbee's symbology, a "creative minority" who led us in the mimesis or imitation of chasing property. The elite of Texas history-mythology is not an intellectual or philosophical elite (although Mirabeau B. Lamar founded a Philosophical Society, still in business but not noted for philosophy, of which I am a member). The artistry of admired Texas lives was devoted to ceaseless action.

The heroes who survived did not spend too much time being heroic. Heroism is held up to be natural, although an interruption of real business. Great Rangers and cowboys quit young, and the successful ones hired other young men to ride their ranges. Rip Ford, who was present at the creation but never got the hang of it, wasted years on horseback and being mayor and ended up embittered, having to peddle his memoirs for a living. Steamboaters, speculators, merchants, railroaders, and ranchers were heroic when they had to be, but the best ones never got carried away with their own mythology. The pattern is not unique to Texas; Daniel Boone crossed many a mountain before he was done in by lawyers and died broke across the far Missouri.

Texas history-mythology teaches us that the land is ours, and we made it. So what's to worry?

Whatever the sins of the adventurers in the Alamo, or of the poor lads who probably thought as much about Mexican silver and *señoritas* as about Texas liberty on the way to Goliad, they paid for them by sacrificial blood to rinse us all clean. Whatever the crimes of Rangers and cowmen, nobody, not even the U.S. Supreme Court, is going to give the land back to the Indians. As for the Mexicans, the land of the *rinches* has become the Promised Land, though some would prefer it under different management.

The major problem, I think, is that some moderns worry that this history-mythology continues to infuse the tribe with ideals and notions that now seem out of place among newer, emerging mythologies. A relation of a creation that makes sense of the world to Texans does not necessarily make sense to other Americans. To many modern Americans, the winning of the West is a footnote to the real themes of American history, and its mythology is not only outworn but possibly dangerous; and they worry that to the Texan the conquest of the continent *is* American history. One person's mythology can be another's poison.

Much of Texas history-mythology is very confusing to present-day observers. Why did a Travis and a Bowie, but especially a bunch of men who didn't own an inch of Texas, court extinction, even after they had been advised against it? What made a Crockett ride to the Alamo and accept the most dangerous position on the wall as an honor? Why did González's men rush to early unmarked graves and glory? No burning ideology we now recognize, no humanistic religion was involved; there are concepts of courage and honor and cowardice that this age has trouble comprehending.

The Texan advance beyond the timbers cost seventeen white lives per mile. Would anybody today accept that sacrifice?

The interstices of Texas history-mythology are full of disturbing things. We find blood courage, determination, self-reliance, aggressive initiative, honest desire for land and power. But we also may find the notion that a bullet is the shortest distance between two points, or that Mexicans and Indians are varmints, or that black Texans, as property, played about the same role in the creation as longhorns. It doesn't make much difference to some that at least one-third of all nineteenth-century cowboys were black or brown; after all, a significant part of the modern Texas labor force consists of illegal aliens.

Things change daily, and in a day when Indians are winning in court and "Mexicans" are out-voting the old stock in many places handily, old mythologies can have a bad time of it.

But the Texan history-mythology does what all such mythologies are supposed to do: it relates the creation, and makes some sense of it. It offers both inspiration and example while telling us how it all came about, gives even johnny-come-latelies a feeling of shared experience. A common past is important; without it, it's hard to believe in a common destiny. All of us can still stand in spirit at the Alamo, ride armchairs up the Chisholm Trail, face down badmen in pistol-heavy imagination. And just maybe, all this might lead young people to become warriors on the walls, blaze trails, or keep-a-comin' for the right if we need those actions again.

There's the rub.

Texas myths, such as they are, seem to hold up role models that rub some modern sensibilities raw. They are mother's milk to curdle in some mouths. The idea that the person in the right should keep-a-comin' scares people in the nuclear age.

The frontier image and models are mostly male models, holding up "male" values, and these are resented by some females. The Texas frontier never actually denigrated women; it was simply hell on them. The mythology made room for the lady and for the good ol' girl, but nothing else either existed or fit in nineteenth-century Texas. However, there's no getting around one salient fact about the American frontier experience. From first to last it reflects a desire on the part of men, not to dominate women or keep them in certain roles, but simply to get away from them and everything they seemed to stand for. From Huck Finn to the teenagers who had to run away from their mothers to get killed riding with McNelly, American males saw the frontier as one way of shucking preachers and women. It was certainly no accident that en route to fame or apotheosis every Tribal Hero of the first pantheon either deserted a wife and family or else had suffered a cathartic loss of one. The frontier, like war, was a marvelous escape. In some tamer future, the only escape may be homosexuality.

Texas society, as reflected in history-mythology, also grates on some souls. Neither society nor state took much part in the creation; it was the work of individuals to whom "society" was only the nexus of individual relationships, without meaning in itself. Like the "state," it was an abstraction, and those who dwelt on abstractions didn't last long in Indian country. Self-reliance was absolutely necessary, for nineteenth-century Texas did not suffer fools, the weak or disabled, the fearful, or the unlucky. The first Texans turned their hogs loose to forage, looking for them only when they needed bacon—thus the old saying, "Root, hog, or die." People on the frontier faced the same imperative. A generation or two back, fathers sometimes shouted that at children. Today most Texans have never heard it articulated, but it is splendidly reflective of what Texan mythology teaches us about society.

Finally, the mythology is shot through with visions of landed empire, and it holds such visions good. No sensible family ever suffered in Texas except to get land. Opportunity was the lure; Texas was settled by empire builders, not refugees, even if the acquired empire was a few acres and a mule. Texans approached the question of property in Austin's time without hypocrisy; they were prepared to surrender their citizenship for several thousand acres. Texans still approach the question with less hypocrisy than most Americans: some property is good; more is better. The creative minority are those who have raised their station in life in the most logical way, by becoming propertied. Certain foreigners, of course, did come with notions about communes or Commonwealths of Man, but Indians or internal contradictions usually got 'em.

IV

Should this history-mythology—relating the role of heroes, holding up frontier values, denigrating the value of society and the state (seemingly always intent on usurping the creation)—be demythologized? Does the Texas mystique, to put it in another light, bug us? In some cases, yes.

The very Alamo is suspect in some eyes. To be willing to die for one's country, or the prospect of a country, or for some personal concept of honor, strikes many moderns as bizarre. Many who are not happy with the shape of the original creation profess to see the Shrine of Texas Liberty as a Symbol of Anglo-Saxon Superiority.

And the fact is that the sort of self-reliance suffused through the Texas mythos and mystique is anathema to the welfare state.

The code of the old-time Texan, willing to give a meal to any bum who happened by at mealtime but equally determined to see him hanged if he stole a cow, seems to some archaic in a world in which most codes are passé.

The idea that the frontier created few if any role models for women beyond the lady and the good ol' girl annoys modern women. And the idea that nineteenth-century American men (notwithstanding the occasional company of women) willfully escaped female society affronts some modern sensibilities.

The basic tribalness of Anglo-Texan creation, though it involved Poles, Germans, Irish, Czechs, French, Jews, and a little of every nationality, frets twentieth-century immigrants, who still believe there is some importance attached to where they came from. Texans often have no notion of where their ancestors came from; after all, their important history happened on this continent. And the ethnicity of the Texan outrages those who look fondly on every form of ethnicity except the

Old American. That kind of ethnicity does not seem to have a place in a nation-state busily pursuing a flabby cosmopolitanism and turning itself into a multicultured empire.

The image and influence of entrepreneurism in Texas angers more than leftists. The old entrepreneur seized land; the new one invents microchips and such, tearing up everything by the roots and adding insult to injury by making a fortune at it. The entrepreneur, offered lip service everywhere, even in the universities, is really an ogre figure to those who would prefer a social democracy for the masses.

There are a lot of people who instinctively dislike the Texas past and would like to amend Texas history-mythology or, better yet, forget it. Would it make sense to devise a new "history," one teaching us that Americans should have stayed on the far side of the Appalachians (or perhaps in Europe) because this was Indian country? Should we proclaim the defense of the Alamo a form of pathology, hopefully now passé? Shall we come to see the liberation of Texas from a decadent Mexican empire as the rape of the mother country by Teutonic barbarians? Should we point up the thorny independence of the Westerner, the stay-off-my-line attitude of the Texan toward his property, as antisocial bourgeois? Should we, in presenting the panorama of the past to tender minds, water it down to the pablum of a new folk consciousness pleasing to all palates?

I know a few people who are already, one way or another, trying to do all these things.

Truth aside, there are serious problems involved in trying to soften or amend Texan mythology. I think the effort might be applauded by certain elites, but it would never be swallowed whole by the common people. And if we tried it, as Plato warned, the poets would do it in. I think at best any effort to try to make the past palatable to the changing consciousness of the present can only create schism in the soul.

We have already gone too far, I believe, in creating schism in the body cultural. The most splendid aspect of Texas history-mythology is that it is easily comprehended by all classes, the educated and the uneducated. There's mystery but not much sophistication surrounding the fall of the Alamo. Whatever happened at San Jacinto, no one can argue about the result. Whatever the psychic trauma, the Rangers, cowboys, and army did get rid of the Indians. And one does not have to be a doctor of philosophy to understand the men and acts involved— though at times training in psychiatry might help. In Texas, it rained or it went dry, the market rose or it collapsed, people survived all the country could throw at them or they did not. Texas history, fortunately, has few nuances and no Neros.

We need to recall that the great age of Greek culture derived from the use of conventional subject matter, mythology, which the Greeks regarded as their hoary history, preserved by poets. Greek art, theater, literature were all elaborations on these myths. They explained the past and made some sense of the present, with elaboration.

But the Greeks were too smart not to outsmart themselves in time. By the era of Euripides (d. 406 B.C.) the intelligentsia felt it could no longer express itself within the ancient cosmos; it no longer believed in the myths and gods. On the other hand, it could not comfortably repudiate them either. There was nothing to replace them except philosophy, which left the mob cold; further, impiety of any kind made the mob hot, judging from the demise of Socrates at the hands of Athenian democrats.

The writers now began to caricature the old heroes, a slick, conscious sacrilege conceived in mockery. The literati understood what was going on; the others didn't. Here opened up chasms between the citizens and the intellectual elites, and about this time Greek tragedy ceased to be a vehicle for serious ideas or ideals. Historians ever since have made careers out of exploring the subsequent funks of Graeco-Roman philosophy.

Today there is continuing complaint that both writers and official education dwell too much in the last century, elaborating the old themes of the "creation." Historians devote twice as much space, on the average, to the pertinent seventy-five years of the 1800s as to the longer period of this century. We learn more about the Republic than about our current economic empires. I suspect that there is nothing whatever conspiratorial about this and that it does not necessarily imply a lack of modern creativity. The problem is this: the creation still makes sense to us. Most of the modern world does not, unless seen in light of the creation, especially as a continuation of it.

We can still thrill to the cussedness, even the muddleheadedness, of our ancestors, hacking this place out of the wilderness. We can accept Fannin as the protagonist of a Greek tragedy (Texans, out of bitter landed experience, are undoubtedly susceptible to understanding tragedy) and see Houston as a flawed demigod, which prevents us from worshiping him. Our hearts and minds can still identify with the old cattleman in *Hud*.

These things tell us who we are, or who we would like to be. When it comes to the modern scene we are left mostly with satirists, much like the Graeco-Roman civilization during its decline. They can portray what's going down on North Dallas Forty or among the humorous, sometimes murderous, high society that has replaced real ladies and gentlemen. But none of them do much good with it, because basically none of them can understand or make much sense of this.

I suspect we can only continue to make sense of our world through the elaboration of our beginnings. If we lost this thread, we would wander continually in Chaos. Let the Christian and Jewish poets handle the cosmos; let Texans elaborate and update Texan mythology.

Although its tribalism may be distressing, our history still affords us something all successful societies must have: cohesion. We can still work for fusion, just as we did on the nineteenth-century frontier.

The most interesting fact about Texas society today is that it works. It may not be the most equitable or intelligent, the most developed or the most artistic or the kindest, but, like the society of Singapore, for the present it works. Its denizens believe in it; they have confidence in both the past and present. A sense of common past makes it easier to believe in a common future. And as a student of history, I am far more favorably inclined toward a society, and a future, that works than toward one that coruscates and gives off sparks to illuminate its decline. The psychic tension and despair that make for some great art I can live without quite contentedly.

In any case, I suspect that much of the concern with Texas history-mythology, conscious or concealed, is without merit, not because the body of that mythology is perfect, but because we continue to elaborate and adapt it constantly, sometimes without realizing it. People can cherish old myths without having to reimplement them. The Texan pragmatism that quickly adapted ways and means to rainless prairies (and is still painfully adapting to them) as well as Indian-style warfare has had little trouble adapting to newer forms of society. Discount rhetoric. If one explores the nineteenth century extensively, one learns to discount rhetoric easily; after all, Houston and Lamar sometimes orated for hours, and most Texans fulminated on every subject from slavery to natural selection.

Today, while much fulminating and complaining is going on, Texans along with other Americans are building the New Southwestern City. Some of the blocks are old, as in ethic; some are new, as in technology. But the ethos that permitted Texans to adapt and change (and that is part of our mythology), that led Texans to seize upon Colt's revolving pistols and wire and windmills while others hesitated because of cultural conservatism, hasn't changed. That same ethos, and ethic, make new Texans pursue new dreams with new technology.

And I would hope that the same pragmatism and keen good sense that led Ranger captains to discover how to cow Indians, badmen, and Mexicans will lead our modern captains of the ship of state to the discovery of how to coexist peaceably with minorities while finding new ways to cow badmen.

When one places a template of the past upon a template of the present, or even the passage of a few years, the evidence of pragmatic adaptability is startling. As some dreams of empire dry up or halt at dead ends, new ones are there if one can see them. For forty thousand acres in the Panhandle, substitute a high-technology company. There are always new ways to bring in Yankee bucks.

The real strength of Texas in this day and age, one suspects, is the enduring culture and worldviews that have been successfully transported from the ranch and farm and far frontier to the glass towers of the future. Through it all runs a common cord, a common sense of survivorship.

Texans do see themselves as survivors; if the sense is deepest among those still on the land, it still exists everywhere, for even the largest cities are still close to the surrounding land. Those who understand that they are survivors may seem callous or even cruel to those who have not been through the maelstrom. But societies without this sense have no continuity, and thus, no meaning to themselves.

When Texans have lost their mythology—if they ever do—they will have lost their sense not only of belonging, but also of meaning; they will have repudiated not history but themselves.

Compared with the power of old pieties, the foibles and sins of a society are nothing; vide the Romans.

We live in an era in which the dominant classes seem to take their pulse hourly from fear of dying. But I believe beneath all this panic many realize, from the evidence of the past, that cowardice is just as deadly on the new frontiers, in civilian society, as it was in the isolated borderlands. Texas history-mythology teaches us that cowardice is worse than dying, that ennui is unthinkable, that sloth is disgraceful. It is better to do something badly than not to do it at all. These are all mythic values I have heard derided. But I saw them serve Texas and the greater nation well on many a bloody field in this century; I and most Texans know they will be demanded again on future disputed barricades.

There will always be new choices, new Alamos, because the world is never made; there must be new creations.

The empires of the soil and spirit that open up can be seized only by those who are inculcated with imperial vision.

As the first creation fades, I hope the tales of its coming will be related forever, not to mire us in the past, but to connect the realizations of who we are and where we came from with the understanding of where we're going.

JAMES F. VENINGA

Epilogue: Prospects for a
Shared Culture

I

THIS volume tells of the remarkably different traditions, experiences, and worldviews that can be found in Anglo, Mexican, Native American, and Afro-American cultures of nineteenth- and twentieth-century Texas. The concept *worldview* implies a mythology: a structuring of human experience through heroes, legends, and stories that express commonly felt ideals and emotions. Each Texas group, with its various subgroups, brought a different mythology to bear on its experience, and each mythology had its own set of specific symbols and images.

Yet one must acknowledge that some twentieth-century scholars, reflecting on diverse cultures worldwide, have emphasized the "monomyth"—the strikingly similar themes that occur in the myths of different places and times. That is, if one looks beneath the specific outer "trappings" of a myth, one finds a core that is psychologically similar to the core of myths from other cultures. Explanations for this phenomenon of universality differ. Otto Rank stressed the biological and psychological inheritance of humankind. Carl Jung found the common source of mythology in the collective unconscious. Joseph Campbell concentrated on the primary structure of culture and of the human psyche.

It should be possible, therefore, to discover beneath the particular myths discussed in this book elements that express human experience at its most fundamental level. Such a study, however, lies beyond the scope of the present work. Instead, these essays shed light

on two preliminary tasks: the identification and interpretation of the
formative myths of the peoples who settled in Texas, and an investigation of how these myths helped to shape the history of the state. Thus,
they disclose the diversity of Texas myths—the extent to which Anglo-
Texan myth was infused with Western European, Protestant myth; the
Mexican-Texan myth with Spanish Catholicism, with strikingly different expressions of authority, family, devotion, and obligation; the Afro-
American myth with West African culture and religion and with American slave culture; the Native-American myth with unique notions of
land and kinship. The writers have not sought to identify the core of
human experience—the common memory, the primary relationships,
the archetypal experiences that lie beneath these particular expressions of myth—that is a challenge that still lies ahead. As Joseph
Campbell writes in *The Hero with a Thousand Faces*: "Myth is the secret opening through which the inexhaustible energies of the cosmos
pour into human cultural manifestation. Religions, philosophies, arts,
the social forms of primitive and historic man, prime discoveries in science and technology, the very dramas that blister sleep, boil up from
the basic, magic ring of myth."

In this land that came to be known as Texas, they boiled up indeed. Although Indian and Spanish-Mexican culture had long flourished, it was the Anglo culture that emerged as the primary driving
force behind the development of Texas. The Anglo-Texan experience
was, of course, intimately related to the conquest of the New World,
the settlement of European peoples on the Atlantic seaboard, the drive
for political and economic self-determination, the American Revolution, the westward movement, the development of an entire continent.
And Anglo-Texans shared in the formative myths of their European-
American ancestors, including the myth of America as the New Israel,
America as a special place with a special people carrying out a divine
commission expressed politically as Manifest Destiny and individually
as the quest for life, liberty, and happiness.

When Anglo-Texans finally got around to writing their history,
which they regarded as *the* history of the state, the story was told as a
sacred history, sharing elements of the basic American myth and, behind that, the European-Protestant myth. Their history flowed from

the pilgrimage to the promised land to the Alamo and San Jacinto to the Republic to annexation to the Confederacy to Reconstruction and industrialization. It included the conquest of the West, the founding of towns, the work of the Rangers, the growth of the cattle industry, the building of railroads, the discovery of oil—events interpreted by historians within the context of Manifest Destiny.

This traditional Texas history, seen perhaps in its purest form in public school texts, was not a social history; it was the history of a people—a linear, patriarchal history, full of sacred moments and complete with heroes. In short, the story of Texas took on epic proportions. The Anglo-Texan story is, therefore, part of a much bigger story, and its myth is part of a much bigger myth. It was a story fit to be told, a story of legendary dimensions, a story made for Hollywood. The American public, influenced deeply by formative American myths and, behind that, Western European Protestant myth, was enchanted by the mythic representations of its Texas cousins.

And so were Texans. One of this country's foremost scholars of myth, Mircea Eliade, tells us that myth is didactic, creating exemplary heroes embodying particular values for a whole society. Protectors of the sacred history and its heroes have never been in short supply in Texas, where transmitters of the Anglo-Texan myth helped the public know who they are, where they came from, and what they ought to do. The Alamo and San Jacinto became shrines, and museums were built to remind us of the lives and accomplishments of Texas heroes—from cowboys to Rangers to oilmen.

An examination of the cultural landscape of present-day Texas indicates that the traditional Anglo myth is very much with us, and certain characteristics associated with heroic figures of that myth—individualism, courage, risk taking, optimism—are still valued by Texans. One sees this, for instance, in the increasingly prominent role of the developer. The Texas developer has taken on heroic proportions and now stands alongside the cowboy, the cattle baron, the Ranger, and the wildcatter as a formative figure commanding attention and, frequently, admiration. In Texas, nearly everything is fair game for development: timberland, farmland, barren land, improved land, urban centers, villages, lakeshores, seashores and offshores, outer space, small businesses. Development for the sake of development—and the wealth that it brings—is an extension of the older Anglo-American myth that "bigger is better" and "progress is our most important product."

The continuance of the Anglo myth is also reflected in the speed and intensity with which Texas has emerged not only as a high-tech center, but as the next "Silicon Valley" in the three-hundred-mile stretch between Dallas and San Antonio. Is it Texas' manifest destiny to be the place where the fifth-generation computer is created and manufactured?

Finally, the continuing influence of the Anglo myth is found in the lives of ordinary Texans. Texans remain a self-reliant people, assured that anything and everything is possible. This is a place where dreams of accomplishment, power, and wealth come easily. The Anglo influence remains an all-important force, even if the historical origins of the myth are frequently forgotten.

II

But powerful social, political, and literary developments in Texas in the last thirty years have led to increased recognition that the Anglo-Texan tradition is not the only one. Of course, in the lives of many ordinary people, it never was the complete story, or even the most important one. For blacks, Mexican-Americans, Native Americans, and even newly arrived immigrants from Eastern and Southern Europe and elsewhere, other histories, heroes, and myths dominated. Music, folklore, customs, family relationships, language, and religious observances preserved the traditions, values, and myths of Texas' subcultures. Internal and external factors prevented easy assimilation.

Extensive progress has been made in identifying, documenting, and disseminating these traditions. The virtual explosion of studies in Mexican-American, Native American, black, and women's history is seen in the exhibits of the Institute of Texan Cultures, in titles of books published by the state's presses, in hundreds of grants awarded in the past decade by the Texas Committee for the Humanities for public programs focusing on ethnic history and culture, in entirely new departments in our colleges and universities devoted to these pursuits. This interest in minority and ethnic studies occurred simultaneously with dramatic social and political change that brought minorities further into "mainstream" (that is, Anglo) culture and society, change that stemmed from a desegregated and far more open society.

As a result, the Anglo-Texan story and myth are no longer the only public story and myth. The traditional history has been augmented by a growing body of historical and literary works that document, interpret, and bring to light the myths, worldviews, and histories of the diverse cultures that make up Texas. For example, historian Roberto Mario Salmón writes in the *Texas Humanist* (January, 1985),

> Through a cultural osmosis, Mexican Americans in Texas represent the vision that drove Coronado. They are the ethnic, racial, and cultural blending of Indians, Mexicans, and Spaniards. They are the northern frontier of Nuevo Santander, later the Mexican State of Tamaulipas; the turbulent national frontier between the United States and Mexico; the political, social, economic, and cultural frontier of a people who became foreigners in their own land; and the societal frontier of a people battling against powerful forces to make a more profound impact on their own destinies.

The point for us is that minority history and myth have slowly made their way into public consciousness; Mexican vision stands alongside Anglo vision as a publicly acknowledged influence in the lives of millions of Texans.

The emergence of minority history, culture, and myth into public awareness has led to a Texas increasingly perceived as a "cultural mosaic." Mexican, black, and Indian traditions have been reclaimed, and many others as well, such as Polish, Czech, German, and Italian. In the 1960s and 1970s, in particular, we tended to acknowledge our own traditions and the worldviews and myths from which they sprang. Cultural pluralism became an unofficial national policy, and Texas seemed to be a case study in living out that policy. Textbooks, for instance, were rewritten to include minority experience and perspectives, and the extent to which Spanish should be taught in the public schools as both a primary and secondary language became a critical public policy issue.

But, more recently, some scholars have argued that perhaps we have gone too far down the road of cultural pluralism, and that insufficient effort is made to understand and to reclaim the dominant tradition behind the development of Texas. Hence, T. R. Fehrenbach writes in this volume that without the traditional Texas hero—flawed as he might be—Texans will lose whatever cohesion they still have left. A similar point—but in a broader context—is made by historian William McNeill in an essay on myth in *Foreign Affairs*:

> Myth lies at the basis of human society. That is because myths are general statements about the world and its parts, and in particular about nations and other human in-groups, that are believed to be true and then acted on whenever circumstances suggest or require common response. That is mankind's substitute for instinct. It is the unique and characteristic human way of acting together. A people without a full quiver of relevant agreed-upon statements, accepted in advance through education or less formalized acculturation, soon finds itself in deep trouble, for, in the absence of believable myths, coherent public action becomes very difficult to improvise or sustain.

At a gut level, we know that McNeill is right: there must be a shared culture if society is to function. The challenge of the present time is that of forging a shared culture from the multiple, sometimes conflicting, histories and traditions that have flourished in Texas.

The Anglo myth, as we have seen, is alive and well, but, more often than not, that myth is cut off from its social, political, religious, and cultural origins. When that happens, we are left with fragments that are perceived to be the whole myth, or worse still, Hollywood-created images that tell us what it is to be Texan. In the former case, we are left with certain values—intense competition, for instance—that are not balanced by other now-forgotten values of the Anglo myth. Such a situation presents the danger of a society with a strong economy but a weak social fabric, a society bubbling with activity but without a clear sense of aims and purposes, a society of the strong that does not know what to do with the weak.

A symptom of this danger can be seen in the rash of teenage suicides that afflicted the affluent, suburban, high-tech communities of Plano, north of Dallas, and Clear Lake City, south of Houston, in 1984. Within a period of ten months, eleven Plano teenagers took their own lives; within two months, six teenagers in Clear Lake City committed suicide. In both cases, psychologists, ministers, school officials, and parents were baffled, but some clues were offered: extreme competition, overindulgence in material goods, drugs, parental pressure for academic excellence, family instability, and intense peer pressure. As one Clear Lake City student put it, "Popularity is based on what you wear and how much money you have. It's not who you are; it's what you are." We may be losing myths that can tell us *who* we are.

We are in need of remembrance. We must remember the forgotten elements of the Anglo-Texan myth—the spirit of adventure of Stephen F. Austin, the love of liberty of the defenders of the Alamo, the courage and fortitude of the frontier family. If we do not remember the whole myth, if we fail to understand the context and nature of its images, we are left with symbols distorted by time.

But we are also in need of synthesis. In addition to understanding more deeply the Anglo myth, we must open ourselves to the myths of other cultures—to appreciate, understand, and learn from those myths that have sustained generations of Native Americans, blacks, and Mexican-Americans.

I think of the murals of Raúl Valdez. In Dallas, Houston, Del Rio, McAllen, and Austin, Valdez has sought to work through his own "cultural confusion" by painting color collages full of history and myth on expansive concrete walls. A recent Austin mural, *Movimiento*, displays in dramatic form the Chicano heritage. It is not enough to admire Valdez's work. If one is Mexican-American, a tradition may have to be rediscovered. If one is not Mexican-American, a history and myth must be learned. We must incorporate what we can.

The challenge we face is to sustain a society based on enduring myths of various traditions that give meaning and purpose to life. We need myths to live by, myths that support fairness, love, compassion, loyalty, and honor—myths that can give us the kind of grounding we need in a high-tech, competitive, commercial world. We would do well to remember that a vibrant outer life must be balanced by a strong inner life, by myths and symbols that speak of ultimate things, that place human experience in a broader, deeper context.

One important task of teachers and writers in the humanities is that of tending to our myths. If the primary purpose of education in the humanities is to orient the student into his or her cultural background *and* surroundings, myth cannot be overlooked, for it is through myth that we discover our spiritual homeland. Indeed, myth might be the starting point in humanities education: the teaching of legends, tales, and heroic characters.

Thus, humanities teachers bear enormous responsibility in preserving our cultural heritage, in selecting what legends, stories, tales, and heroic lives should be taught. Especially those who write our histories, who must choose among events, personages, processes, and even cultures to tell a story, who must weave many fabrics into a complete and artistic whole, have an awesome responsibility, for they are, in a real sense, the mythmakers, and myth, as we have seen, holds a society together. Out of myth flows life itself.

But the ultimate task of those who tend to our myths may be the discovery and clarification of how disparate and even conflicting myths tell us what it means to be human, to be born of mothers and fathers, to feel love and hate, to aspire and to fail, to dream, to be lonely, to achieve, to mourn, to be reborn, to die. At the deepest level, the task is to determine how all myths depict shared human experience.

Prospects for a shared culture in Texas do not rest simply on increased understanding of one's own myth and on the imaginative leap into other cultures, histories, and myths—although that is surely the starting point. In the end, prospects rest on our collective ability to see that the experience portrayed in a myth—alien as it might at first seem—is also everyone's experience. As we have seen, behind the Anglo-Texan myth lies European-American, primarily Protestant, myth. Behind Afro-American myth lie the culture and religions of West Africa. Behind Mexican-Texan myth lies a mix of Spanish Catholicism, Indian tradition, and Mexican culture. The religious symbolism and myth that undergird these varied traditions stem from archetypal experiences that unite humankind, including the experience of rebirth and wholeness. It may not be *my* tradition, but it is a valid expression of my experience as well.

We must remember the many myths that have flourished in this remarkable place called Texas. We must remember the sad myths (those myths that speak, for instance, of greed and murder) as well as the happy myths, for such behavior is part of our collective experience, and understanding that behavior through myth helps us understand what it means to be human. Given the didactic function of myth, cross-cultural dialogue can help each group define for itself the best, most useful myths in its tradition.

Myths shed light on our individual and collective journeys; myths are the guardians of life. Joseph Campbell says it best in *The Hero with a Thousand Faces*:

> The imagery of myth can never be a direct presentation of the total secret of the human species, but only the function of an attitude, the reflex of a stance, a life pose, a way of playing the game. And where the rules or forms of such play are abandoned, mythology dissolves—and with mythology, life.

Contributors

Dr. Richard Bauman, professor of anthropology and director of the Center for Intercultural Studies in Folklore and Ethnomusicology at the University of Texas at Austin, is editor of *The Journal of American Folklore*. His most recent publication is *Let Your Words Be Few: The Symbolism of Speaking and Silence among the Seventeenth-Century Quakers*.

Dr. Louise Cowan is a founding fellow of the Dallas Institute of Humanities and Culture and a former English professor at the University of Dallas. She has recently edited a collection of essays entitled *The Terrain of Comedy*.

Dr. Gilbert M. Cuthbertson, professor of political science at Rice University, is the author of *Political Myth and Epic*.

Dr. Robin Doughty, associate professor of geography at the University of Texas at Austin and a former research associate at the Smithsonian Institution, has recently published *Wildlife and Man in Texas: Environmental Change and Conservation*.

Dr. Elizabeth York Enstam, an adjunct professor of history at Southern Methodist University, is preparing a history of Dallas women as builders of community.

T. R. Fehrenbach, a historian and fellow of the Texas State Historical Association, has written sixteen books, including *Lone Star: A His-*

tory of Texas and the Texans, and *Comanches: The Destruction of a People*.

Dr. William H. Goetzmann, professor of American Studies at the University of Texas at Austin, won a Pulitzer Prize for his book *Exploration and Empire: The Explorer and the Scientist in the Winning of the American West*. He hosted the public television series "The West of the Imagination."

Nicholas Lemann is a correspondent for *Atlantic Monthly* and writes on contemporary Texas culture for *Texas Monthly*.

Dr. Sandra L. Myres, professor of history at the University of Texas at Arlington, has written *Westering Women and the Frontier Experience, 1800–1915*.

Dr. William W. Newcomb, Jr., professor of anthropology at the University of Texas at Austin, is the author of *The Indians of Texas*, and *The People Called Wichita*.

Dr. Robert F. O'Connor, associate director for special projects for the Texas Committee for the Humanities, works closely with scholars and cultural organizations developing public education programs in Texas history and culture. He was project director for the Texas Sesquicentennial Minutes TV series "The Texas Experience."

Dr. Juan A. Ortega y Medina, professor of history at the Universidad Nacional Autónoma de México, is the author of *Destino manifiesto*.

C. W. Smith, author of the novel *The Vestal Virgin Room*, teaches fiction writing at Southern Methodist University.

Dr. Sterling Stuckey, professor of history at Northwestern University, has written *I Want to Be African: Paul Robeson and the Ends of Nationalist Theory and Practice, 1919–1945*.

Dr. James F. Veninga, executive director of the Texas Committee for the Humanities, is editor of *The Biographer's Gift: Life Histories and Humanism,* and coeditor of *Vietnam in Remission.*

Index